SCRUM UNLOCKED

UNVEILING THE SECRETS OF SCRUM FRAMEWORK AND BUILDING HIGH-PERFORMING SCRUM TEAMS

Ignacio Julian Paz

This page intentionally left blank.

SCRUM UNLOCKED: A STEP-BY-STEP GUIDE TO MASTERING THE SCRUM GUIDE™

By Ignacio Paz

Paperback ISBN: 9798390253519

Hardcover ISBN:

Edition: 1.01a

Copyright © Ignacio Paz. All rights reserved.

Contents

Part 1:	Preface	11
1.1	Disclaimer	11
1.2	About the Author	12
1.3	Who should read this book?	12
Part 2:	**Introduction**	**14**
2.1	How to learn about Scrum?	14
Part 3:	**Scrum**	**17**
3.1	Introduction to Scrum	17
3.2	Scrum Definition	24
3.3	Scrum Theory	26
3.4	Scrum Values	43
Part 4:	**The Scrum Team**	**55**
4.1	Cross-functional team	56
4.2	Self-managing team	57
4.3	Scrum Team size	60
4.4	Scaling the Scrum Team	62
4.5	Ownership, empowerment, and success	63
4.6	Empowerment	64
4.7	Accountability	65
4.8	Membership of the Scrum Team	67
4.9	Feature Teams vs. Component Teams	69
4.10	A Mature, High-performing Scrum Team	72
4.11	Other roles outside the Scrum Team	74
4.12	Anti-patterns of the Scrum Team	75
Part 5:	**Developers**	**75**
5.1	Creating a Plan for the Sprint	77
5.2	Instilling quality by adhering to a Definition of Done	77
5.3	Adapting their plan each day toward the Sprint Goal	78
5.4	Holding each other	79
5.5	Leadership Style of the Developers	79
5.6	Stances of the Developers	80

5.7	Anti-patterns of the Developers	81
Part 6:	**Product Owner**	**82**
6.1	Maximizing the value	82
6.2	What is value?	83
6.3	Example of value	84
6.4	Product Backlog management	85
6.5	Own the product	87
6.6	The decision maker	88
6.7	Collaboration with Stakeholders	88
6.8	Collaboration with Developers	89
6.9	Not responsible for keeping Developers busy	90
6.10	Leadership Style of the Product Owner	91
6.11	The 6 Stances of a Product Owner	92
6.12	Do you have all the skills?	94
6.13	Anti-patterns of the Product Owner	94
Part 7:	**Scrum Master**	**95**
7.1	Scrum as defined in the Scrum Guide	95
7.2	Scrum Team's effectiveness	96
7.3	Servant Leadership	97
7.4	Serving the Scrum Team	99
7.5	Serving the Product Owner	106
7.6	Serving the organization	111
7.7	The 8 Stances of a Scrum Master	115
7.8	Anti-patterns of the Scrum Master	116
Part 8:	**Scrum Events**	**117**
8.1	Opportunities to inspect and adapt	118
8.2	All events are timeboxed	119
8.3	Optimally at the same time and place	121
Part 9:	**The Sprint**	**124**
9.1	The Sprint length	125
9.2	Rules during the Sprint	127
9.3	Predictability	132

9.4	Canceling a Sprint	136
9.5	Anti-patterns of the Sprint	141

Part 10: Sprint Planning 142

10.1	Collaborative planning	142
10.2	The first event of the Sprint	142
10.3	Focus on the Product Goal	143
10.4	Invitees to the Sprint Planning	143
10.5	Three topics: Why, what, and how	144
10.6	Max Timebox: 8 hours	148
10.7	Communicating the Sprint Goal	148
10.8	Anti-patterns of the Sprint Planning	149

Part 11: Daily Scrum 150

11.1	Timebox: 15 minutes	151
11.2	Same time and place	151
11.3	No need to solve the problems during the Daily Scrum	152
11.4	Participation of Scrum Master and Product Owner	152
11.5	Attend vs. participate	152
11.6	The Scrum Master in the Daily Scrum	153
11.7	Developers decide the structure	154
11.8	It is not a report meeting	156
11.9	Daily Scrum eliminates the need for other meetings	156
11.10	Do not skip it	157
11.11	Don't wait until the next Daily	158
11.12	Anti-patterns of the Daily Scrum	159

Part 12: Sprint Review 160

12.1	Collaboration with Stakeholders toward goals	160
12.2	Stakeholders' Feedback Before the Sprint Review	163
12.3	It's not a plan for the next Sprint	163
12.4	It's not a "Demo"	164
12.5	Do not cancel it	165
12.6	Timebox: 4 hours	165
12.7	Antipatterns of the Sprint Review	166

Part 13:	Sprint Retrospective	167
13.1	Individuals, interactions, processes, and tools	168
13.2	The Role of the Scrum Master	169
13.3	Inspecting the Definition of Done	170
13.4	Improvements	171
13.5	Managing the improvements	171
13.6	The end of the Sprint	172
13.7	Timebox: 3 hours	172
13.8	Do not skip the Retrospective	173
13.9	Anti-patterns of the Sprint Retrospective	173

Part 14:	Scrum Artifacts	175
14.1	Artifacts represent works of value	175
14.2	Artifacts maximize transparency	176
14.3	Commitments	177

Part 15:	Product Backlog	178
15.1	It is emergent and ordered	178
15.2	It is the single source of work for all Sprints	179
15.3	Is it a list of User Stories?	180
15.4	Types of Product Backlog items	180
15.5	Non-functional Requirements in PB or DoD	181
15.6	A PBI is a Hypothesis of value	183
15.7	Owned by the Product Owner	184
15.8	Ready items	185
15.9	Product Backlog Refinement	185
15.10	Not "ready" items during Sprint Planning	188
15.11	The Developers estimate	188
15.12	Anti-patterns with the Product Backlog	189

Part 16:	Product Goal: Commitment to the Product Backlog	190
16.1	The Product	190
16.2	One Product Goal at a Time	191
16.3	Why not work on two Product Goals?	192
16.4	Product Goal, Product Vision, and Strategic Vision	195

16.5	Progress towards the Product Goal	196
16.6	Flexibility and variable scope	197
16.7	Anti-patterns with the Product Goal	199

Part 17: Sprint Backlog 199

17.1	Why, what, and how	199
17.2	Owned by Developers	200
17.3	Transparent real-time picture	200
17.4	Developers update it during the Sprint	201
17.5	Anti-patterns with the Sprint Backlog	201

Part 18: Sprint Goal: Commitment of the Sprint Backlog 202

18.1	The objective of the Sprint	202
18.2	Flexible scope	202
18.3	Coherence, focus, and collaboration	203
18.4	Discuss deviations	203
18.5	Bad Sprint Goals	204
18.6	Better Sprint Goals	205
18.7	Anti-patterns with the Sprint Goal	205

Part 19: Increment 206

19.1	A stepping stone toward the Product Goal	206
19.2	Deliver vs. Release	207
19.3	Usable Increment	207
19.4	Release or not, and when	208
19.5	Multiple increments per Sprint	209
19.6	Increment during the Sprint Review	210
19.7	Release before Sprint Review	211
19.8	All increments must be according to the Definition of Done	212
19.9	Anti-patterns of the Increment	213

Part 20: Definition of Done: Commitment of the Increment 214

20.1	Quality measures of the Increment	214
20.2	Determines when an Increment is born	214
20.3	Shared understanding and transparency	215
20.4	Unfinished items by the end of the Sprint	215

20.5	It follows organizational standards	216
20.6	The Scrum Team creates the Definition of Done	217
20.7	Developers work according to the Definition of Done	217
20.8	Multiple Scrum Teams, one Definition of Done	218
20.9	Definition of Done Template	220
20.10	Anti-patterns with the Definition of Done	221

Part 21: Scrum is immutable ... 222

| 21.1 | Scrum But | 223 |

Part 22: Scaling Scrum ... 224

22.1	Scaling frameworks	224
22.2	Scrum team size is a guideline, not a rule	225
22.3	Rules of multiple teams working together on the same product	226
22.4	Dedicated or shared team members	231
22.5	Anti-patterns of scaling Scrum	233

Part 23: Related Topics ... 234

23.1	Velocity	234
23.2	Burn down charts	237
23.3	Mechanical Scrum vs. Professional Scrum	240
23.4	The Cone of uncertainty	240
23.5	Technical Debt	242
23.6	Forming, storming, norming, performing	245

Part 24: Putting concepts together ... 248

24.1	How is Scrum aligned with Agile Manifesto?	248
24.2	Scrum Guide Cheat Sheet	253
24.3	Scrum Guide 2020 vs. Scrum Guide 2017	260
24.4	Scrum concepts challenges	264

Part 25: Scrum in Practice ... 272

25.1	Product Vision	272
25.2	Product Backlog Management	276
25.3	Retrospectives	278
25.4	Best wishes	279

Part 26: Bibliography and references ... 280

26.1	Books	280
26.2	Guides	281
26.3	Articles, papers, blogs, and websites	282
26.4	Index of Figures	284

Part 1: Preface

1.1 Disclaimer

1.1.1 A trademark notice statement

Scrum dot org, Professional Scrum™, Professional Scrum Master™, Professional Product Owner™, PSM II™, and PSPO™ are trademarks of Advanced Development Methods and registered in one or more countries.

1.1.2 A disclaimer statement

The statements made and opinions expressed herein belong exclusively to the author and are not shared by or represent the viewpoint of Scrum.org. This document does not constitute an endorsement of any product, service or point of view. Scrum.org makes no representations, warranties or assurances of any kind, express or implied, as to the s, accuracy, reliability, suitability, availability or currency of the content contained in this presentation or any material related to this presentation. In no event shall Scrum.org, its agents, officers, employees, licensees or affiliates be liable for any damages whatsoever (including, without limitation, damages for loss of profits, business information, or loss of information) arising out of the information or statements contained in the document. Any reliance you place on such content is strictly at your own risk.

This book provides information about the Scrum framework and its application in software development projects. The information provided is based on current best practices and the author's experience in the industry. However, the author and publisher do not guarantee the accuracy, completeness, or suitability of the information contained in this book. The readers are responsible for verifying the applicability and relevance of the content to their specific situations. The author and publisher shall not be liable for any direct, indirect, incidental, or consequential damages arising from using the information presented in this book.

1.1.3 Attribution and use of guides

This course or document may use quotes, interpretations, adaptations, and extracts from the Scrum Guide (TM), Nexus Guide (TM), Kanban Guide for Scrum Teams™, and Evidence-Based Management Guide™ to point the attention of the student to essential concepts, ideas, rules, and practices.

- The Scrum Guide (TM) authors are Ken Schwaber and Jeff Sutherland. https://scrumguides.org/
- The Nexus Guide (TM) is developed and sustained by Ken Schwaber and Scrum dot org. https://www.scrum.org/resources/online-nexus-guide

- Evidence-Based Management (TM) was collaboratively developed by Scrum .org (TM), the Professional Scrum Trainer community, Ken Schwaber, and Christina Schwaber. https://www.scrum.org/resources/evidence-based-management-guide
- The Kanban Guide for Scrum Teams (TM) was developed and sustained by Scrum .org, Daniel Vacanti, and Yuval Yeret. https://www.scrum.org/resources/kanban-guide-scrum-teams

License under the Attribution Share-Alike license of Creative Commons, accessible at https://creativecommons.org/licenses/by-sa/4.0/legalcode and also described in summary form at https://creativecommons.org/licenses/by-sa/4.0/

Please read the original guides.

1.2 About the Author

Hi, my name is Ignacio Paz. https://www.linkedin.com/in/ignaciopaz/

My main goal is to help you with new knowledge that you can apply at work and be a successful and professional leader.

I have created best-selling online courses with more than 100,000 students. I have helped thousands of professionals to get all types of Scum certifications.

I am a Certified Agile Team Coach. I have led, coached, and managed Agile projects and scrum teams since 2005 for customers worldwide.

During my career with intensive learning, I got many advanced Scrum certifications, including Agile Coaching, Certified Scrum Professional Scrum Master, Certified Professional Scrum Product Owner, Certified Agile Leadership, etc.

I worked for 15 years as a Professor of Agile Methodologies and Systems Design and have more than 20 years of experience in Agile software development. I am a very early adopter of Agile and Scrum.

I trained hundreds of students in Agile that became top professionals in the industry.

Teaching what I learned in my 20 years of experience allows the students to gain realistic learning that they can apply at work.

1.3 Who should read this book?

This book will be valuable if you want to adopt the Scrum framework for your team or organization. Whether you're new to Scrum or an experienced practitioner, you'll find answers to common questions and understand how to apply Scrum principles to your work effectively.

This book is unique in its comprehensive approach to covering the Scrum framework. It's based on years of experience working with Scrum teams and helping individuals prepare for Scrum certifications. You'll find a wealth of information about best practices, common challenges, and real-world examples to help you apply Scrum in your work.

By reading this book, you'll learn the following:

- The foundational principles of Scrum and how to apply them to your work.
- Approaches for effective Sprint Planning, Sprint Reviews, and Sprint Retrospectives.
- Approaches to managing different situations in Scrum.
- Ways to measure progress and track team performance using metrics like velocity and burn-down charts.
- Common Scrum anti-patterns and challenges.
- Key knowledge for preparing for the most demanding and advanced Scrum certifications, including the Certified Scrum Master™ (CSM™) and Professional Scrum Master™ (PSM™) exams.

All the book is based on and aligned with the latest Scrum Guide™ 2020.

Whether you're a developer, project manager, Product Owner, or Scrum Master, this book is designed to help you succeed with Scrum. It's an essential resource for anyone who wants to take their Scrum knowledge to the next level and become a more effective and productive Scrum team member.

1.3.1 Why did I write this book?

As an experienced Scrum Master and Agile Coach, I have worked with numerous teams and organizations in various industries. These experiences have made me realize many misconceptions and misunderstandings about the Scrum framework. Therefore, I wrote this book to provide a comprehensive and practical guide to Scrum based on real-world experiences and the most challenging questions I have encountered.

After having fantastic success with my online courses and mock questions to prepare for certification exams, I created a new format to reach and help more people. So, fortunately, you, everyone studying Scrum, and I will bring more savvy Scrum Masters, Product Owners, and Scrum Professionals to the industry.

Scrum is the most successful Agile framework. However, few professionals are in the market, and industry demand for Scrum professionals is rising.

I aim to create the most complete reference guide to answer all your questions about Scrum, whether you are just starting with Agile or already holding Scrum certifications. The Scrum framework can be applied to any project or product development. It is a powerful tool for teams to deliver value faster, better, and with higher quality.

Through this book, I hope to share my knowledge and help teams and organizations embrace the Scrum framework, overcome challenges, and succeed in their Agile journey. I encourage you to read this book and apply the concepts to your work. If you have any questions or comments, please do not hesitate to contact me. And if you find this book helpful, please consider leaving a review on Amazon.

I hope the ones learning from this book will satisfy such demand and help the world by creating new, better, and exciting products that make an impact.

Part 2:Introduction

2.1 How to learn about Scrum?

2.1.1 With this book

Well, the answer is this book!

This book was written to understand Scrum as defined in the Scrum Guide but disclosing revealing, clarify, and answer all the questions, secrets, doubts, and misunderstandings that people usually have when learning Scrum.

However, if you want to become a great Scrum Master, Product Owner, or Developers, your learning desire should never stop. The resources below and in the bibliography are great options to continue and improve your learning journey.

2.1.2 A view of Scrum

The following illustration represents the Scrum Framework. By the end of this book, you will be able to understand every component, how it works, and what to do in your implementation.

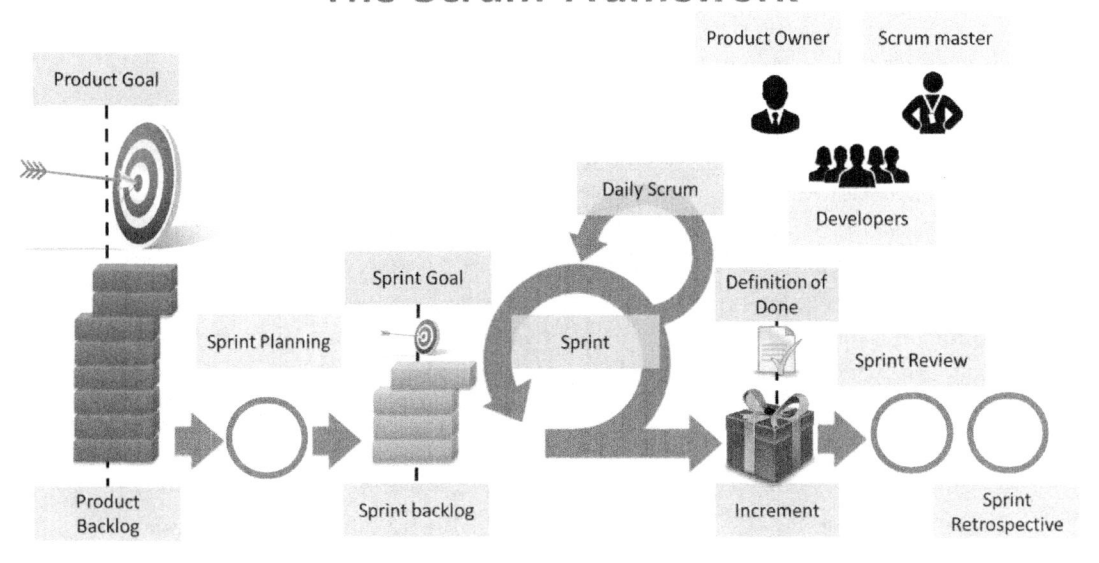

Figure 1 The Scrum Framework.

2.1.3 The Agile Manifesto

Of course, the first source of knowledge you must read and understand is the Agile manifesto. The Agile manifesto was written in 2001 by the most inspiring, influencing, and talented authors of the software industry, including Ken Schwaber and Jeff Sutherland, the authors of Scrum. See more at https://agilemanifesto.org/.

2.1.4 The Scrum Guide

Undeniably, the primary source of knowledge about Scrum and the fundamental way of learning Scrum is by reading the **Scrum Guide** by Ken Schwaber and Jeff Sutherland, the authors of Scrum. The Scrum Guide is free. You can read it online, download it, or print it from https://scrumguides.org/.

The Scrum Guide is the primary source of the bibliography of this book to remain faithful to it.

2.1.5 Glossary, competencies, and resources.

The site Scrum.org provides endless resources and sources of learning. Check the Scrum Glossary (https://www.scrum.org/resources/scrum-glossary), Professional Scrum Competencies (https://www.scrum.org/professional-scrum-competencies), and resources (https://www.scrum.org/resources).

2.1.6 Advanced guides and frameworks

Once you understand the basics of Scrum, learn some advanced topics. The following free guides are essential for many certifications, advanced Scrum Masters, advanced Product Owners, advanced Scrum Team members, and Agile Coaches:

- Evidence-Based Management Guide: Evidence-Based Management (EBM) is an empirical approach that helps businesses enhance customer outcomes, organizational capabilities, and financial results across time, even when the future is unknown. It gives companies a framework for improving their capacity to offer value in an unpredictable world while pursuing strategic goals. EBM helps companies systematically improve their performance over time and adjust their goals based on enhanced knowledge using purposeful experimentation and evidence (measurement). See more at https://www.scrum.org/resources/evidence-based-management-guide.
- Nexus Guide: Product delivery is difficult because integrating product development effort into a helpful product involves coordinating several processes. Nexus is a framework for creating and sustaining large-scale product delivery programs. It extends Scrum to minimize and manage dependencies across different Scrum Teams while supporting empiricism and Scrum Values. See more at https://www.scrum.org/resources/online-nexus-guide.
- Kanban Guide: Kanban is a strategy for optimizing the flow of value across a process. It is almost impossible to discuss Kanban without mentioning flow. Kanban's basic premise is that optimizing process flow is one of the most excellent methods to improve value delivery. In other words, how something is completed can be just as important as the job itself. See more at https://kanbanguides.org/.
- Kanban Guide for Scrum Teams: The Kanban Guide for Scrum Teams is the product of cooperation between Scrum.org community members and Kanban community leaders. They are the co-authors of The Kanban Guide for Scrum Teams. They both believe using Kanban with Scrum may assist professional product development practitioners. See more at https://www.scrum.org/resources/kanban-guide-scrum-teams.
- Less: Scrum is Scrum—Large-Scale Scrum (LeSS) is not a remixed version of Scrum. It is not Scrum as a base or topping placed on top for each team. Instead, it is about figuring out how to implement Scrum's ideas, purpose, and components as efficiently as possible in a large-scale setting. See more at https://less.works/.
- Scrum@Scale Guide: Scrum@Scale was designed to help teams collaborate more effectively in this new ecosystem. It accomplishes this objective by establishing a "minimum viable bureaucracy" through a "scale-free" design. See more at https://www.scrumatscale.com/scrum-at-scale-guide/.
- SAFe: The Scaled Agile Framework® (SAFe®) enables large-scale businesses to reap the benefits of Lean-Agile software and system development at scale. See more at https://www.scaledagileframework.com/.

Part 3: Scrum

We will go through every single sentence from the Scrum Guide and analyze it in the following sections.

Anything that you see with the format below is an extract from the Scrum Guide:

> *We developed Scrum in the early 1990s.*

3.1 Introduction to Scrum

3.1.1 Myths and facts

Here is a list of some common myths and facts about Scrum:

Myth	Fact
Scrum is only for software development.	Scrum was initially developed for software development but can be applied to any complex project or product development effort.
Scrum is only for small teams.	Scrum can be applied to teams of any size, but larger teams may require additional coordination and scaling techniques to ensure effective collaboration.
Scrum is an unstructured approach to project management.	Scrum is a structured framework for project management that provides a clear set of rules, roles, and events to guide the team's work.
Scrum guarantees project success.	Scrum does not guarantee project success, but it provides a framework for continuous improvement and stakeholder engagement that can help increase the likelihood of success. Besides any framework, the main focus is stakeholder happiness.
Scrum is just a series of meetings.	While meetings are an important part of Scrum, the framework is more than just a series of meetings. It is a holistic product development approach emphasizing collaboration, transparency, and continuous improvement. Its main purpose is to deliver value.
Scrum eliminates the need for planning and documentation.	While Scrum does prioritize working software over comprehensive documentation, planning, and documentation are still important components of the framework. The team must plan their work for each

	Sprint, and the Product Owner must maintain a well-groomed Product Backlog.
Scrum is only for teams that work in an Agile environment.	Scrum is an Agile framework, but it can be applied to teams that work in various environments and methodologies.
Scrum doesn't allow for changes to the product during development.	Scrum encourages changes to the product during development to respond to feedback and changing requirements, but these changes must be managed within the framework to avoid disrupting the team's work.
Scrum ensures that all the project resources will be used most efficiently.	While Scrum does promote the team's ability to self-organize and collaborate to achieve the common goal, it does not guarantee the most efficient use of all project resources. Other factors, such as team composition, product complexity, and stakeholder engagement, can also impact project efficiency.
Adding more resources to the Scrum Team will proportionally increase the value delivered.	This is a fallacy. In Scrum, the focus should be on delivering value through effective teamwork rather than simply adding more people to the team. The Scrum Team should have the right mix of skills and expertise to achieve its objectives, and team members should work collaboratively and share responsibility for delivering value. Therefore, adding more resources may lead to communication breakdowns, coordination challenges, and increased complexity, which can decrease the value delivered. Instead, while adding more resources could be necessary, the focus should be on maximizing the efficiency and effectiveness of the existing team members to deliver high-quality products that meet the needs of stakeholders. On the other hand, more resources may bring more features but not more value necessarily. If the value is low, the Product Owner should review their approach to maximize value from the Product Backlog.
When multiple Scrum Teams work on the same Product, some changes must be made	The Scrum Guide does not require any changes to implement Scaled Scrum. Instead, it provides a framework for scaling Scrum that can be adapted to

to the Scrum Guide to implement Scaled Scrum.	meet the organization's specific needs. While various scaling frameworks are available, such as Nexus and LeSS, they are designed to complement Scrum rather than replace it. Therefore, organizations can scale Scrum without deviating from the core principles and values of Scrum outlined in the Scrum Guide.
Scrum provides detailed steps on how to implement complex projects.	Scrum is a framework, not a prescriptive process. Scrum is founded on empirical process control theory or empiricism. While Scrum provides a clear set of accountabilities, events, artifacts, and rules, it does not dictate how to implement complex projects. Instead, it empowers teams to self-organize and make decisions based on their unique context. This means that Scrum can be applied to a wide range of projects, from simple to complex and from software development to marketing and sales. Scrum's strength lies in its flexibility and adaptability, allowing teams to experiment, learn, and continuously improve.
Velocity is a key success metric used by the Product Owner.	Velocity is not related to product success or value. Velocity is a non-mandatory metric typically used by Developers to measure their performance regarding the amount of work completed in a Sprint, whether valuable or not. While it can be useful for the Developers to track their progress and plan future Sprints, it is not a key success metric for the Product Owner. The Product Owner focuses on delivering value to the stakeholders by creating a high-quality product that meets their needs. This involves prioritizing the Product Backlog based on its value and ensuring that the Definition of Done is met for each Product Backlog item. While velocity can provide insight into the team's performance, it should not be used as the sole measure of success. Other factors, such as customer satisfaction, business outcomes, and stakeholder feedback, should also be considered.
Scrum cannot be used in a company where product time, scope, and budget are established in advance.	Scrum is a framework for product development and project management across various industries. While Scrum acknowledges that time and money are finite resources, it aims to maximize the product's value within these constraints. However, in a highly rigid environment where time, scope, and budget are all

	predetermined, the effectiveness of Scrum may be limited, as it hampers the team's ability to respond to changing circumstances. In such cases, it may be more beneficial to establish a fixed goal with a flexible scope, allowing the team to adapt and adjust as necessary.

3.1.2 The Scrum Guide

You can read and download the latest Scrum Guide from https://scrumguides.org/. In addition, the Scrum Guide is available in over 30 languages.

The following chapter is not meant to skip reading or replace the Scrum Guide. On the contrary, I encourage you to read the Scrum Guide.

While reading this book, we will:

- Analyze the Scrum Guide.
- Provide further explanations for concepts that are typically misunderstood.
- Extend the Scrum Guide with knowledge and references from the community, books, articles from agile practitioners, the author's experience, and the Scrum Authors themselves.

3.1.3 History of Scrum

> *We developed Scrum in the early 1990s.*

The original paper on Scrum was "SCRUM Development Process" OOPSLA 1995, written by Ken Schwaber in 1995.

- The paper describes Scrum as a metaphor for Rugby, claiming that Scrum shares many characteristics with the sport of Rugby.
- The paper describes it as a methodology. However, lately, in the Scrum Guide 2009, it was clarified that "Scrum is not a process or a technique for building products; rather, it is a framework within which you can employ various processes and techniques."
- The original paper was inspired by "The New Product Development Game" by Hirotaka Takeuchi and Ikujiro Nonaka and published in Harvard Business Review in 1986 describes a holistic approach called the "Rugby" approach.

Gunther Verheyen provides a nice summary of the Scrum history in his paper "Scrum: A Brief History of a Long-Lived Hype" https://www.scrum.org/resources/blog/scrum-brief-history-long-lived-hype

> *We wrote the first version of the Scrum Guide in 2010 to help people worldwide understand Scrum. We have evolved the Guide since then through small, functional updates.*

- You can review the changes of each Scrum version from https://scrumguides.org/revisions.html
- The site https://www.mitchlacey.com/resources/official-scrum-guide-current-and-past-versions/ contains each version of the Scrum Guide.
- Each version attempts to fix misunderstandings and includes the feedback and learnings of using Scrum by many teams worldwide.

> *Together, we stand behind it.*

Ken Schwaber and Jeff Sutherland wrote the Scrum Guide. They stand behind it. Ken Schwaber and Jeff Sutherland are also two of the well-respected authors of the Agile Manifesto, written in 2001, along with the most remarkable and influencing authors of that time.

3.1.4 Purpose of the Scrum Guide

> *The Scrum Guide contains the definition of Scrum.*

Everything defined in this Guide is part of Scrum. Many practices and approaches are typically related or combined on top of Scrum, but anything not in this Guide is not part of Scrum. However, the Scrum Guide is not enough to understand Scrum. Therefore, consider the following guideline:

- Allowed: anything that is not forbidden in the Scrum Guide is permitted.
- Not allowed: Anything that breaks a rule of Scrum is not allowed.

> *Each element of the framework serves a specific purpose that is essential to the overall value and results realized with Scrum. Changing the core design or ideas of Scrum, leaving out elements, or not following the rules of Scrum, covers up problems and limits the benefits of Scrum, potentially even rendering it useless.*

The elements, rules, events, artifacts, commitments, and accountabilities are mandatory.
- If you implement only part of them, you are not doing Scrum.
- Sometimes an incomplete implementation of Scrum is referred to as ScrumBut, where a team wants to implement Scrum, but there is an excuse to avoid one or more elements of Scrum.
- An incomplete Scrum implementation usually exposes weak values, pillars, and agility.

3.1.5 Uses of Scrum

> *We follow the growing use of Scrum within an ever-growing complex world. We are humbled to see Scrum being adopted in many domains holding essentially complex work, beyond software product development where Scrum has its roots.*

As you can read in the original Scrum paper of 1995, Software development teams were the early adopters of Scrum. Scrum is useful for solving complex problems with products that need adaptability. Software products typically fall in this category because:

- Business uncertainty: Software requirements are unclear and hard to define upfront.
- Technological complexity: Building software is technologically complex.
- Adaptability: Modifying software products is generally easier than changing other product types.

However, business uncertainty and complexity are part of almost every business or product nowadays. Markets are more demanding, and businesses and products must continuously adapt to compete. At the same time, industries developed ways to adjust their product faster. Products and services of any industry show high technological or implementation complexity. This situation makes Scrum an excellent fit for any complex product or industry.

In conclusion, Scrum fits any complex product or service well.

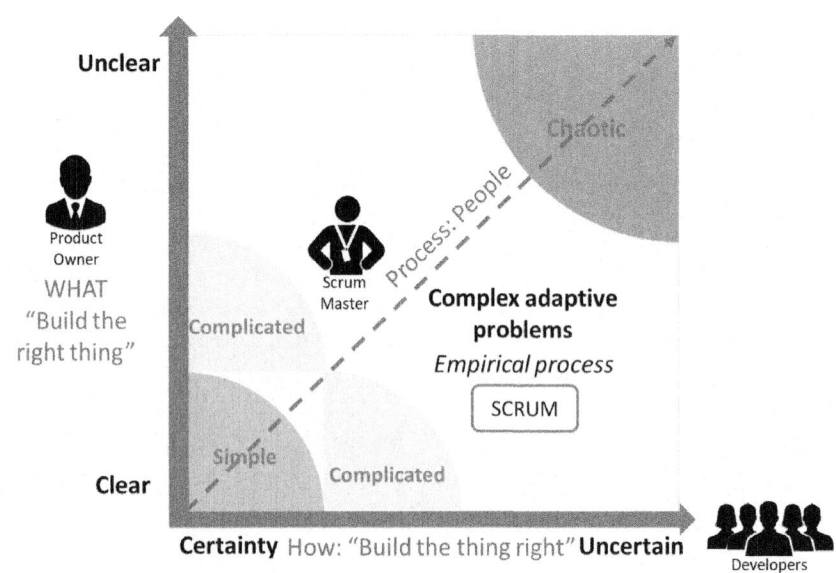

Complex domains represent the "unknown unknowns" where cause and effect can only be deduced retrospectively, and there are no right answers.

- Chaotic problems: The relationship between cause and effect is not clear.
- Complex problems: The relationship between cause and effect is only understandable with experience.

- Simple problems: The relationship between cause and effect is known.
- Complicated problems: The relationship between cause and effect can be understood through some analysis.

To deal with complexity, in Scrum,

- A Product Owner decides what the next most valuable idea to adapt the Product in an uncertain market and satisfy the stakeholders is.
- The Developers decide how to implement these ideas, adapting the Product using complex technology and adopting new technological trends or needs as necessary.
- The Scrum Master leads the process within the Scrum Framework rules and continues improving the Scrum Team's effectiveness.

3.1.6 The term "Developers"

> *As Scrum's use spreads, Developers, researchers, analysts, scientists, and other specialists do the work. We use the word "Developers" in Scrum not to exclude, but to simplify. If you get value from Scrum, consider yourself included.*

The term "Developers" is sometimes misunderstood as "programmers" or "coders." However, Developers include anyone with one or more skills needed to make the product Increment releasable to users. For instance, these skills may consist of design, coding, testing, quality assurance, etc. Although each Developer may have one or more skills and lack some of these skills, we prefer not to call them coders, testers, analysts, etc. Instead, we call them Developers because they must have all the necessary skills needed to build the product Increment. Their combined effort, collaboration, and skills are needed to deliver an Increment in the product.

Scrum uses the term Developers to avoid the idea of specialization, subtitles, or hierarchies between them.

3.1.7 Patterns and processes within Scrum

> *As Scrum is being used, patterns, processes, and insights that fit the Scrum framework as described in this document, may be found, applied and devised. Their description is beyond the purpose of the Scrum Guide because they are context-sensitive and differ widely between Scrum uses. Such tactics for using within the Scrum framework vary widely and are described elsewhere.*

Scrum is a framework and does not promote or suggest any practice, process, tactic, tool, or approach to use with Scrum. It defines the rules of Scrum, but it does not advise how to use it.

Leaving Scrum as a pure framework free of any concrete practice has several advantages:

- It allows the community to think freely of new approaches and practices that can be used with Scrum.
- It allows each Scrum Team to select the practices, processes, and tools that work best in their context and within the rules of Scrum.
- It acknowledges the relative efficacy of any practice or process. A new one can always supersede every practice and process.

3.2 Scrum Definition

> *Scrum is a lightweight framework that helps people, teams and organizations generate value through adaptive solutions for complex problems.*

Let's look at each part of this definition:

- Lightweight: Scrum is lightweight. It defines just a few rules. That makes Scrum easy to understand but hard to master.
- Framework: Scrum is not a methodology! It is not a process, technique, or method. Instead, it is a framework within which a team can utilize diverse processes and techniques.
- People, teams, and organizations: The framework is not magical and will not do anything for you by itself. Implementing Scrum will not succeed unless the people involved work to succeed.
    - People and teams: We need skilled people working as a team within an organization strategy to use the framework and work on challenging problems.
    - Organizations: Organizations can use Scrum in many of their areas.
        - Organizations can benefit from Scrum by focusing on business strategies, mission, and company vision instead of wasting time controlling the teams.
        - Organizations align the company vision with the Scrum Teams, empower them, and provide the environment to decide how to achieve the goals.
        - Organizations can delegate the implementation of Scrum to Scrum Masters.
        - Organizations must empower and trust the Scrum Teams to be self-managed.
        - Organizations must provide the work environment and resources that the Scrum Teams need to succeed as self-managing teams.
- Generate value: The main reason for adopting an agile approach is to generate an outcome and tangible benefit for the users and stakeholders of the product.
    - Utilization: Often, it is misunderstood that the main reason for using Scrum is to maximize team members' utilization and deliver faster. While this can be an observable output of using Scrum, it is not the main reason.

Conversely, when one focuses on maximizing utilization, it generates waste and delays value.
- Adaptive solutions: We will work on products that need adaptation according to unexpected business variables.
- Complex problems: complex problems cannot be defined and described in advance. They include unclear requirements and technological uncertainty. To understand these complex problems, we do short iterations to learn about them, produce small increments, get customer feedback, and adapt and iterate again.

> *In a nutshell, Scrum requires a Scrum Master to foster an environment where:*
>
> - *A Product Owner orders the work for a complex problem into a Product Backlog.*
> - *The Scrum Team turns a selection of the work into an Increment of value during a Sprint.*
> - *The Scrum Team and its stakeholders inspect the results and adjust for the next Sprint.*
> - *Repeat*

Every Sprint requires to create at least one product Increment. There is nothing tangible to learn from and get feedback on if there is no Increment, even a tiny one. So, to start the first Sprint, Scrum requires no more than a Product Owner, a Scrum Master, Developers, and some ideas to work on a product Increment.

The Product Backlog, in itself, will never be a complete list of detailed requirements. The Product Backlog is emergent and constantly evolves. As long as a product exists, so will its backlog. Therefore, an essential Product Backlog can be just composed of basic ideas.

The Stakeholders are necessary to make the product meaningful. We don't build the product for ourselves; we create it to improve someone's life. Without stakeholders, there is no reason for a product to exist.

To start the first Sprint, A Scrum Team only needs a Product Owner with at least a few ideas for the product to experiment with, Developers that can implement such ideas, and a Scrum Master to lead the process within the Scrum Framework.

> *Scrum is simple. Try it as is and determine if its philosophy, theory, and structure help to achieve goals and create value. The Scrum framework is purposefully incomplete, only defining the parts required to implement Scrum theory. Scrum is built upon by the collective intelligence of the people using it. Rather than provide people with detailed instructions, the rules of Scrum guide their relationships and interactions.*

Scrum is simple to understand. However, it is like a mold where its incomplete parts can be filled with many options. Therefore, when team members ask themselves how to implement Scrum, Scrum is perceived as difficult to master. Fortunately, extensive community-sharing techniques and practices can be tried to implement Scrum in many flavors.

An exemplary Scrum implementation does not depend on individuals working alone; it relies on team members collaborating, interacting, and sharing the responsibility of success or failure.

Nevertheless, a Scrum implementation and practices that work great for one team may not work for another. Every team is unique and faces unique problems. The term "try it as is" reminds me of the "start with what you now" Kanban principle and the idea of "avoid wishful thinking." No team will find the perfect implementation from its first Sprint. On the contrary, each team must retrospect often and continuously adapt and improve the process to its specific needs.

> *Various processes, techniques and methods can be employed within the framework. Scrum wraps around existing practices or renders them unnecessary. Scrum makes visible the relative efficacy of current management, environment, and work techniques, so that improvements can be made.*

Again, Scrum is a framework that neither provides nor suggests any practices. On the contrary, it allows any practices, processes, techniques, and methods that the Scrum Team finds useful within the framework's rules.

Practices, approaches, and techniques such as User Stories, Story points, Story Mapping, Burndown charts, Planning Poker, pair programming, continuous integration, continuous delivery, continuous deployment, Test Driven Development, Acceptance Test Driven Development, automated testing, and Design Thinking are typically associated with Scrum or used by Scrum Teams. However, none of them nor any other practice are part of Scrum. Therefore, no Scrum Team is required to use any of them. But because many of them emerged from Agile practitioners and fit well with Scrum, they are good options. In the end, the empirical nature of Scrum will put any approach under inspection and adaption to prove itself useful for the goals of the Scrum Team. Therefore, trying an approach can be considered an experiment by the team members and never a long-term commitment.

3.3 Scrum Theory

3.3.1 Empiricism

> *Scrum is founded on empiricism and lean thinking. Empiricism asserts that knowledge comes from experience and making decisions based on what is observed.*

Scrum is founded on empirical process control theory or empiricism. Let's distinguish between two process control theories.

3.3.1.1 Defined process control

Defined process control is a process with pre-defined steps. It is a static process that expects minimal volatility. For a given input, the process delivers the same output. It is based on repeatability and predictability.

Defined process control is useful when the requirements can be defined upfront; we have certainty that they will not change, and the work may be repetitive.

The defined process has the following characteristics:

- Common and control.
- We plan what we expect to happen.
- The plan is enforced, regardless of the change condition.
- Any change must be controlled and may be expensive.

Defined process control can't deal well with complex problems and adaptive solutions. Therefore, it is not a good fit for Scrum.

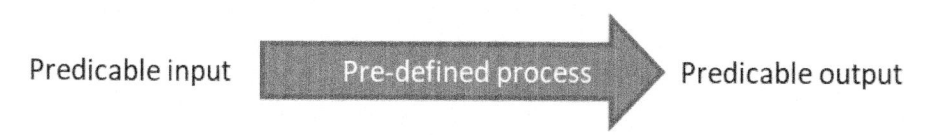

Figure 2 Defined process control.

3.3.1.2 Empirical process control

In empirical process control, we expect the unexpected. Instead of upfront process planning, an empirical process emerges as we progress. The process is constantly inspected and adapted based on facts, evidence, observation, and experimentation.

The relationship between cause and effect is only understandable in complex problems with experience. Empirical process control helps deal with complex problems and adaptive solutions; therefore, Scrum's base is to work.

The Empirical Process Control has the following characteristics:

- We learn how to perform the best work as we progress.
- Instead of denying change, we expect it and embrace it.
- We inspect and adapt the process using short cycles.
- Estimates are indicative only and may not be accurate.

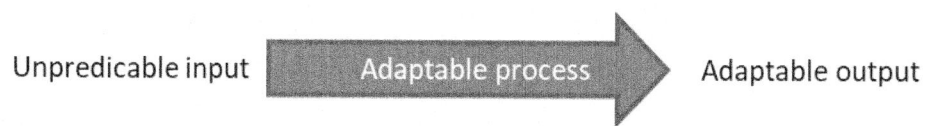

Figure 3 Empirical process control.

3.3.2 Lean Thinking

> *Lean thinking reduces waste and focuses on the essentials.*

Scrum is also founded on Lean thinking. The term Lean thinking describes making business decisions in a Lean way.

In the book Lean Software Development: An Agile Toolkit, Mary Poppendieck, and Tom Poppendieck describe Lean with seven principles. The table below provides a basic definition of the principle and references how Scrum addresses such a principle.

Lean Principle	How is it addressed in Scrum
1. **Eliminate waste**: Any activity that we do and does not add value to a product is waste. Value is only what the customer perceives as valuable.	The Product Owner maximizes the value, orders the Product Backlog, and throws out waste. For instance, sometimes, the value of a Product Backlog item is defined as a hypothesis and validated with the customer outcomes. The Scrum Master enhances effectiveness by helping the Scrum Team remove wasteful activities. The Developers focus on meeting the Sprint Goal.
2. **Amplify learning**: Development requires discovering the process and the product. Therefore, lean teams must provide the infrastructure to retain valuable learning and create knowledge.	The value of openness promotes knowledge sharing. The Scrum events such as the Daily Scrum, Sprint Review, and Sprint Retrospective offer opportunities to learn from the work product and create improvements. Scrum encourages the Scrum Team to collectively share and gather all the skills needed to do the work.
3. **Decide as late as possible**: Keeping design options open is more valuable than committing early in an uncertain context. Instead of committing early with little evidence, we prefer to commit and make decisions before starting the work with the latest information and evidence.	Product Backlog Refinement promotes discussing the details of only the most valuable items just before development. Hence, they have fresh details, and Sprint Planning promotes making product decisions as late as possible.

4.	**Deliver as fast as possible**: Speed ensures customers get what they need now, not in a month when it is late. It also allows them to validate what they really need and decide what they need next. Compressing the value stream as much as possible is a key lean strategy for eliminating waste.	The Sprint is a timebox to deliver something valuable; even with a small thing, we can validate its value and learn a lot.
5.	**Empower the team**: The ones doing the work are the ones that understand the details better to make technical and process decisions.	Scrum Teams are defined as self-managing and cross-functional. Scrum Teams are structured and empowered by the organization to manage their work.
6.	**Build integrity in**: In Lean development, quality is everyone's job, not just that of the quality engineer.	The Definition of Done defines the quality attributes for an Increment to be considered done. The Scrum Team defines it, and every member must adhere to it.
7.	**See the whole**: When a team has many specialists like UX design, DBA, Backend Developer, or Tester, and their specialized contribution is measured, each member tends to optimize on their area of expertise rather than the overall performance, and suboptimization is likely to result. This problem is even more noticeable when two organizations, areas, or teams work together because people naturally want to maximize their own company's performance, and friction may appear. So instead of suboptimization, we look for contributions to the product as a whole.	There are no sub-teams, titles, or hierarchies within a Scrum Team. The Scrum Team is responsible for all product-related activities. A Scrum Team is a cohesive unit of professionals focused on a single Product Goal.

3.3.3 Iterative, incremental, and risk control

Scrum employs an iterative, incremental approach to optimize predictability and to control risk.

3.3.3.1 Iterative

An iterative approach is a method of project development or problem-solving that involves breaking down the work into smaller, more manageable pieces and then repeatedly cycling through the process of planning, executing, and evaluating those pieces until the desired outcome is achieved.

Instead of trying to create a perfect result all at once, the iterative approach focuses on creating a version of the final product or solution that can be tested, evaluated, and improved upon with each cycle. Each iteration, or cycle, typically involves a small set of tasks or objectives that build upon the previous iteration's work to eventually achieve the desired outcome.

This approach allows flexibility and adaptation as new information is learned or as goals and requirements evolve. It also allows for early feedback and validation of the work being done, which can help identify issues and make improvements more quickly.

In software development, for example, an iterative approach might involve creating a minimum viable product (MVP) with basic features, testing and gathering feedback on that product, making adjustments based on that feedback, and then repeating the process until the final product is ready.

In the end, an iterative approach can be a powerful way to achieve a complex goal, as it allows for continual learning, adaptation, and improvement throughout the process.

3.3.3.2 Iterative vs. linear approach

The iterative and linear approaches are two different methods for project development or problem-solving, with distinct characteristics and benefits.

Linear Approach:

- The linear approach involves completing a set of tasks or a feature before sequentially moving on to the next set.
- This approach is more structured and predictable, with each completed piece of work adding to the overall solution linearly.
- The linear approach is often used in projects with well-defined goals and requirements and a clear understanding of the tasks and dependencies involved.

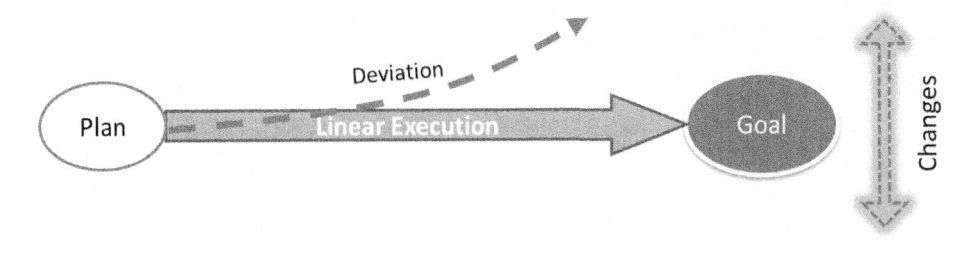

Figure 4 Linear approach.

Iterative Approach:

- The iterative approach involves breaking down the work into smaller, more manageable pieces and then repeatedly cycling through the process of planning, executing, and evaluating those pieces until the desired outcome is achieved.
- Each cycle involves a small set of tasks or objectives that build upon the previous iteration's work to eventually achieve the desired outcome.
- This approach allows flexibility and adaptation as new information is learned or as goals and requirements evolve.
- It also allows for early feedback and validation of the work being done, which can help identify issues and make improvements more quickly.

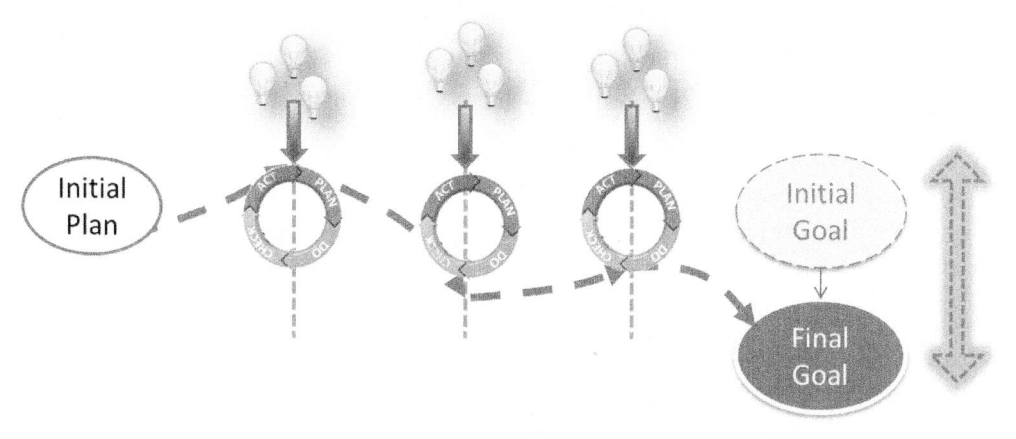

Figure 5 Iterative Approach.

Example of Linear approach:

- Building a bridge using a traditional construction process is an example of a linear approach. The project begins with a design phase, then a planning phase, then a construction phase, and finally, an inspection and testing phase. Each phase must be completed before the next one can begin, and changes made later in the process can be difficult and costly to implement.
- Developing a film using traditional methods is another example of a linear approach. The script is written, actors are cast, sets are built, filming takes place, and post-production work is done sequentially. Changes made later in the process can be expensive and time-consuming.

Example of Iterative approach:

- Developing a software application using an Agile approach is an example of an iterative approach. The development process is broken down into small, iterative cycles or Sprints, each building on the previous one. Each Sprint delivers a working version of the software, which is tested and refined before moving on to the next cycle. Changes can be made easily and quickly based on user feedback and testing results.
- Creating a new product design using an iterative approach is another example. The designer might create several prototypes or versions of the product, each

incorporating feedback and improvements from the previous version. The final product results from an iterative process of refining and improving the design based on user feedback and testing.

One of the main differences between the iterative and linear approaches is their approach to change. The iterative approach is better suited for projects where change is expected, or the end goal is not well-defined. On the other hand, the linear approach is better suited for projects with well-defined goals and requirements, where change is unexpected, and where a more structured and predictable approach is preferred.

In summary, the iterative approach is characterized by flexibility, adaptation, and early feedback, while structure, predictability, and a clear understanding of tasks and dependencies characterize the linear approach.

3.3.3.3 Incremental

An incremental approach is a method of project development or problem-solving that involves breaking down the work into small, distinct pieces and linearly completing each piece, with each completed piece building on the previous one to achieve the desired outcome gradually.

Unlike an iterative approach, where each cycle involves planning, executing, and evaluating a small set of tasks, an incremental approach involves completing an entire set of tasks or a feature before moving on to the next set. This approach is more linear and structured, with each completed piece of work adding to the overall solution sequentially.

For example, an incremental approach in software development might involve developing a feature-rich product in stages, where each stage includes additional functionality or enhancements. Each stage builds on the previous one and may require additional testing and quality assurance before moving on to the next stage.

The incremental approach allows for a more structured and predictable development process. Each stage is clearly defined and provides a clear understanding of the progress toward the final product or solution. It is also useful in scenarios where the outcome is well-defined and the requirements are clearly understood from the beginning.

To summarize, the incremental approach can be a useful project management method when the end goal is well-defined, and the steps to achieve that goal can be broken down into distinct stages or phases.

3.3.3.4 Modular vs. incremental approach

Modular and incremental approaches are both project development strategies that can be used in different contexts. Here are the key differences between the two:

Modular approach:

- This approach involves dividing a project into smaller, independent modules or components that can be developed and tested separately.
- Each module is designed and developed to meet specific requirements and can be assembled with other modules to create the final product.

- This approach allows for greater flexibility and scalability, as individual modules can be added or modified without affecting the entire system.
- However, this approach may require more planning and coordination to ensure that the modules are properly integrated and work together effectively.

Incremental approach:

- This approach involves developing a project in small, incremental stages or iterations, with each stage building on the previous one.
- Each iteration involves adding new features or functionality to the product to deliver a working product at the end of each iteration.
- This approach allows for more frequent feedback and testing, which can help to identify and address issues earlier in the development process.
- However, this approach may require more time and resources to develop and test each iteration and may not be suitable for projects with strict timelines or budgets.

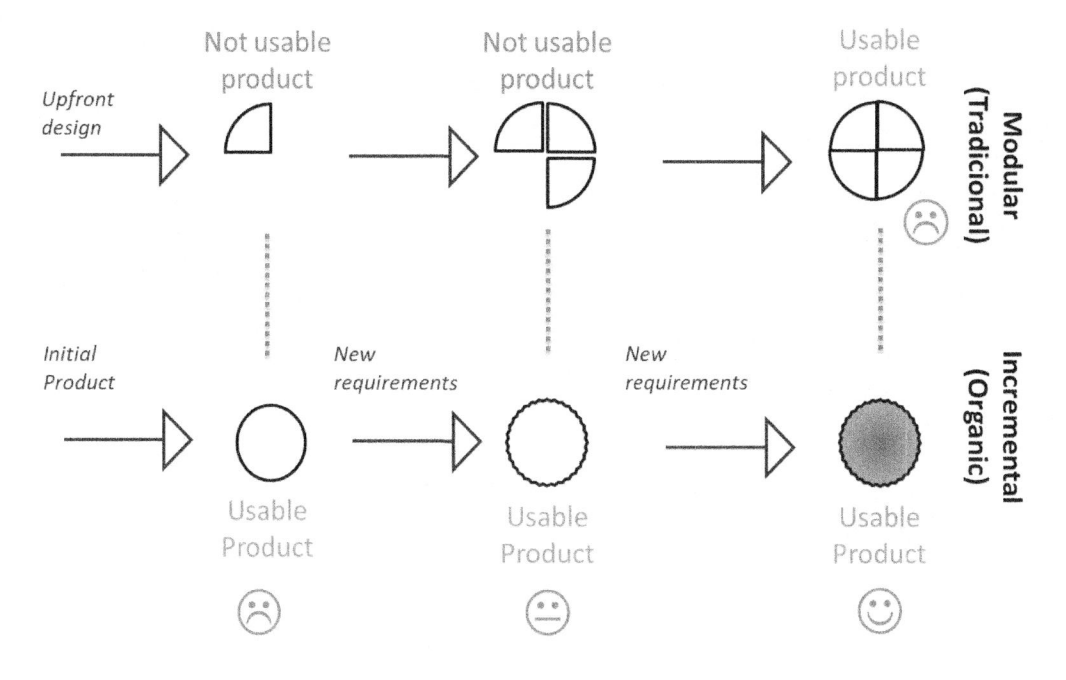

Figure 6 Modular vs. Incremental approach.

Example of Modular approach:

- A software company developing a complex application might use a modular approach to break down the application into smaller, independent modules that can be developed and tested separately. For example, they might develop separate modules for the user interface, database management, and networking components, which can be assembled to create the final product.

- An automotive company might use a modular approach to develop cars with interchangeable parts. For example, they might design and manufacture a range of engines, transmissions, and suspension systems that can be mixed and matched to create different car models with varying features and performance.

Example of Incremental approach:

- A software company might use an incremental approach to develop a new version of an existing product. They might release the new version in stages, with each stage adding new features or improvements to the product. This allows them to get user feedback and adjust before releasing the final version.
- A construction company might use an incremental approach to build a new housing development. They might build a few houses at a time, with each set of houses adding new features or designs based on feedback from buyers. This allows them to adjust their plans and designs based on market demand and buyer preferences.

To summarize, both modular and incremental approaches can be effective for project development, depending on the project requirements and constraints.

3.3.3.5 Iterative and Incremental

The iterative and incremental approach combines elements of both the iterative and incremental approaches to project development or problem-solving. This approach involves breaking down the work into small, manageable pieces and then repeatedly cycling through a series of iterations, each of which builds on the previous iteration, with each iteration completed incrementally.

In an iterative and incremental approach, each cycle involves a small set of tasks or objectives that build upon the previous iteration's work to achieve the desired outcome eventually. However, unlike the incremental approach, the iterative and incremental approach emphasizes flexibility and adaptation as new information is learned and goals and requirements evolve.

The iterative and incremental approach enables Scrum Teams to learn and adapt quickly by allowing them to iterate on specific features or functionality, which are completed incrementally. Each iteration may involve planning, executing, and evaluating a small set of tasks or features to improve the previous iteration's work.

For example, in software development, an iterative and incremental approach may involve creating a minimum viable product (MVP) with basic features, testing and gathering feedback on that product, making adjustments based on that feedback, and then repeating the process until the final product is ready.

The iterative and incremental approach allows flexibility and structure, with each iteration building on the previous one and adding to the overall solution. It also enables Scrum Teams to respond to changing requirements and customer feedback more quickly, leading to better outcomes and more successful projects.

3.3.3.6 Traditional risk management

Traditional risk management involves identifying, analyzing, and managing risks structured and systematically. This approach involves standardized processes and procedures often used in finance, construction, and healthcare industries.

In traditional risk management, the focus is on identifying potential risks, assessing the likelihood and impact of those risks, and developing strategies to mitigate or manage them. This approach typically involves several steps, including:

- Risk Identification: This involves identifying potential risks and hazards that could affect a project, business, or organization. This may be done through various methods, such as brainstorming, checklists, and expert opinions.
- Risk Analysis: This involves analyzing identified risks' likelihood and potential impact. This is usually done by evaluating the probability and severity of the risk and estimating its potential impact on the project, business, or organization.
- Risk Mitigation: It involves developing strategies to eliminate or reduce risks. This may include implementing safety measures, establishing contingency plans, and transferring risks to third parties.
- Risk Monitoring and Review: This involves ongoing monitoring and review of the identified risks and the effectiveness of the risk management strategies.

Traditional risk management is a formal and structured approach to managing risks. It helps organizations identify potential risks, assess the likelihood and impact of those risks, and develop strategies to mitigate or manage them effectively.

Here is an example of a risk matrix for an online grocery shop:

Risk Description	Likelihood	Impact	Severity	Mitigation Plan
Payment processing failure	High	High	9	Regularly test payment processing system, establish backup payment methods
Cyber attack or data breach	Medium	High	8	Regularly update security measures, perform regular security audits, and train employees on data protection
Supplier delay or cancellation	Medium	Medium	6	Maintain good relationships with suppliers, develop alternative suppliers, and regularly communicate with suppliers to anticipate and address issues

Delivery delay or failure	Low	High	6	Work with reliable delivery partners, provide accurate delivery estimates, and establish a customer service process to manage any delivery issues
Technical failure of website or app	Low	Medium	4	Regularly test the website and app for performance issues, establish backup systems, and implement effective maintenance and support
Customer complaints or negative reviews	Low	Low	1	Implement a customer feedback process, respond promptly to complaints, and take corrective action to address any issues

The severity column is calculated by multiplying the likelihood by the impact. In this example, the risks are sorted by severity, with the highest severity risk at the top. This helps the online grocery shop prioritize the risks and focus its risk mitigation efforts on the most critical areas.

It is important to note that the risk matrix should be regularly reviewed and updated as the business environment and risks change. By monitoring and addressing risks proactively, the online grocery shop can minimize the impact of potential risks and maintain a high level of service for their customers.

3.3.3.7 Risk management in Scrum

In Scrum, risk management occurs more naturally. A Scrum Team usually doesn't need to go into a thorough risk analysis, although they can. Every Sprint provides an opportunity to identify risks and manage them. Because the Scrum Team is empowered and has all the skills to create an increment, they should have the power to control the risks as soon as they are identified, generally without depending on anyone else outside the team.

Scrum mitigates risk by frequently inspecting and adapting its processes and product increment creation during each Sprint. This approach allows the team to be agile and responsive to change, addressing risks as they arise.

Scrum Teams are cross-functional; they are open to asking for and receiving. Scrum's iterative and incremental nature also applies to team skills and technical excellence. Each iteration provides an opportunity to detect the lack of skills, increase the team's cross-functionality, and amplify learning.

The Scrum framework also incorporates several events that help to detect and manage risks throughout the project. For example, the Sprint Retrospective event allows the team to reflect on the previous Sprint and identify areas for improvement. They can identify risks that occurred during the previous Sprint and develop strategies to mitigate those risks in the upcoming Sprints.

In general, Scrum provides a flexible and adaptive approach to risk management. By proactively detecting and managing risks throughout the project, the Scrum team can maintain a high level of agility and deliver a high-quality product that meets the needs of stakeholders.

3.3.3.8 Collective intelligence and skill learning

> *Scrum engages groups of people who collectively have all the skills and expertise to do the work and share or acquire such skills as needed.*

In Scrum, we look to enable the collective intelligence of a group of people instead of individual skills. We acknowledge and respect that individuals have different backgrounds and skills. Still, we look to combine their skills into a mastermind and all the combined skills necessary to deliver a working product without external dependencies.

Scrum is a team-based framework emphasizing collaboration and self-organization to deliver high-quality products. One of the core principles of Scrum is that it engages groups of people who collectively have all the skills and expertise required to complete the work.

This means the Scrum team includes individuals with various skills, including development, testing, design, and project management. The team works together to plan, execute, and deliver the project, sharing their knowledge and expertise to ensure that the product meets the customer's needs.

In addition, the Scrum framework encourages team members to acquire new skills as needed. This means that team members may take on new roles or responsibilities or seek out training or mentorship to enhance their skills and expertise. This helps to create a culture of continuous learning and improvement within the team, which can lead to higher quality work and better outcomes for the customer.

By engaging groups of people with diverse skills and expertise, Scrum enables the team to work collaboratively and adaptively to complete the work. This approach can result in a more efficient and effective development process, with a higher likelihood of meeting the project goals and delivering a high-quality product.

3.3.4 Scrum Pillars

> *Scrum combines four formal events for inspection and adaptation within a containing event, the Sprint. These events work because they implement the empirical Scrum pillars of transparency, inspection, and adaptation.*

Scrum is a framework for product development that uses a set of formal events to manage the development process. These events are organized within a containing event called the Sprint, which is a time-boxed period during which the Scrum team works to complete a set of planned work items.

The five formal events in Scrum are Sprint, Sprint Planning, Daily Scrum, Sprint Review, and Sprint Retrospective. Each of these events has a specific purpose and structure, and they are designed to support the empirical Scrum pillars of transparency, inspection, and adaptation.

- Transparency: The Scrum events promote transparency by making the work and progress of the team visible to all stakeholders. The team shares their work plans, progress, and issues and makes decisions based on this information.
- Inspection: The Scrum events allow the team to inspect their work and progress. They review their work, evaluate their progress toward the Sprint goal, and identify any issues or obstacles that may impact their ability to meet their commitments.
- Adaptation: The Scrum events facilitate adaptation by providing opportunities for the team to adjust their plans and approach based on new information. They can change their work plan, adjust their priorities, and implement new strategies to overcome obstacles.

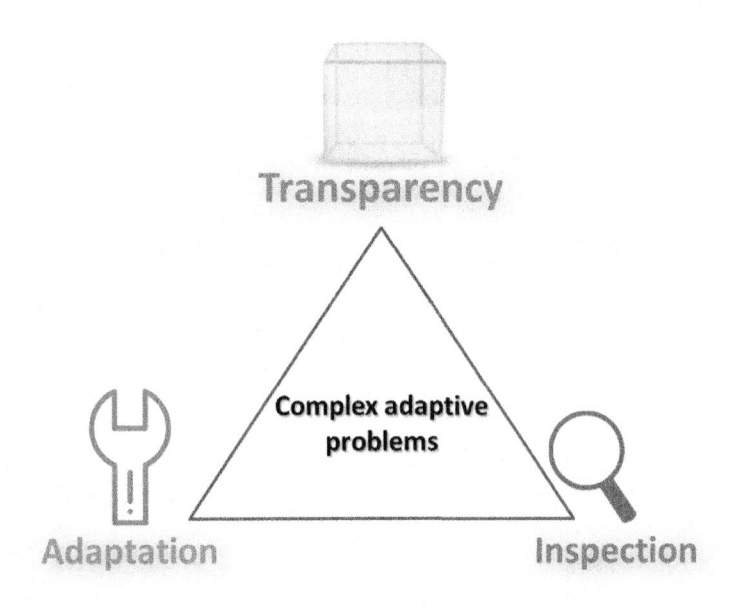

Figure 7 Scrum pillars.

By using these formal events within the Sprint, Scrum enables the team to work collaboratively, transparently, and adaptively toward achieving their goals. The Scrum events provide a structured and predictable framework for the team to manage their work and make decisions based on empirical evidence, which can lead to higher quality work and better outcomes for the customer.

3.3.4.1 Transparency

> *The emergent process and work must be visible to those performing the work as well as those receiving the work. With Scrum, important decisions are based on the perceived state of its three formal artifacts. Artifacts that have low transparency can lead to decisions that diminish value and increase risk.*

Transparency is a core principle of Scrum that emphasizes the importance of making the process and work visible to everyone involved in the project. This includes the people performing the work (i.e., the Scrum team) and those receiving the work (i.e., stakeholders).

In Scrum, the three formal artifacts are the Product Backlog, Sprint Backlog, and Increment. These artifacts represent the team's work planning, executing, and delivering. Maintaining transparency in these artifacts is essential because they provide the basis for important decisions made by the team and stakeholders.

If the artifacts have low transparency, it can lead to decisions that diminish value and increase risk. For example, if the Product Backlog is not transparent, the team may not clearly understand what work needs to be done, leading to misaligned priorities, wasted effort, and missed deadlines. Similarly, if the Increment is not transparent, the stakeholders may not clearly understand the progress being made, leading to a lack of trust and engagement.

By maintaining transparency in the artifacts, Scrum enables the team to make informed decisions based on empirical evidence. The team can assess their progress, identify any issues or obstacles, and adapt their approach accordingly. This leads to a more collaborative and effective development process, with a higher likelihood of delivering a high-quality product that meets the customer's needs.

> *Transparency enables inspection. Inspection without transparency is misleading and wasteful.*

In Scrum, transparency is a core principle that emphasizes the importance of making the process and work visible to everyone involved in the project. In addition, transparency enables inspection, which evaluates the work and progress to identify issues, improve quality, and adapt the approach as needed.

Without transparency, the inspection cannot occur effectively. In addition, evaluating and understanding the progress is difficult if the work and process are not visible. This can lead to misleading information, incorrect assumptions, and poor decision-making. For example, suppose a team is not transparent about their work. In that case, they may not identify issues until it's too late to resolve them, resulting in delays and a lower-quality product.

On the other hand, when transparency is present, the inspection can occur more effectively. By making the process and work visible, the team and stakeholders can evaluate progress, identify issues and obstacles, and take corrective action as needed. This leads to a more collaborative and effective development process, with a higher likelihood of delivering a high-quality product that meets the customer's needs.

In summary, transparency is essential in Scrum because it enables effective inspection. Without transparency, the inspection can be misleading and wasteful. In contrast, transparency helps ensure that the team and stakeholders clearly understand the work and progress being made, leading to better decision-making and more successful outcomes.

3.3.4.1.1 Examples of a Scrum Team being transparent

Here are some examples of how a Scrum Team can be transparent:

- Using a common language: Scrum teams use a common language to refer to the process, including key terms and concepts such as accountabilities, events, artifacts, and values. This promotes clarity and understanding among all team members and stakeholders, regardless of their background or expertise.
- Sharing a common Definition of Done: In a Scrum Team, all team members share a common Definition of Done, which defines the quality criteria the increment must meet to be considered complete. This helps ensure that everyone involved in the process clearly understands what is expected and what constitutes a successful outcome.
- Providing regular updates and feedback: Scrum teams provide regular updates and feedback to each other and stakeholders throughout the process, including progress toward Sprint goals, obstacles or challenges encountered, and potential areas for improvement. This promotes transparency and collaboration and helps ensure everyone is on the same page regarding product development.
- Using Scrum events for inspection and adapt: Scrum Teams use a set of regular events, including Sprint Planning, Daily Scrum, Sprint Review, and Sprint Retrospective, to inspect and adapt their processes and progress. These events promote transparency by providing opportunities for all team members to share updates, feedback, and insights on their work and the product development process. By regularly inspecting and adapting their approach, Scrum Teams can identify areas for improvement and optimize their performance and productivity over time.

3.3.4.2 Inspection

> *The Scrum artifacts and the progress toward agreed goals must be inspected frequently and diligently to detect potentially undesirable variances or problems. To help with inspection, Scrum provides cadence in the form of its five events.*

In Scrum, the artifacts and progress toward the agreed goals must be inspected frequently and diligently to detect potential problems or variances. The three formal

Scrum artifacts are the Product Backlog, Sprint Backlog, and Increment, and they represent the work being planned, executed, and delivered.

To facilitate the inspection of these artifacts and progress, Scrum provides a structured cadence of five events that occur during each Sprint: Sprint Planning, Daily Scrum, Sprint Review, Sprint Retrospective, and Sprint itself.

The Sprint Planning event sets the goals for the upcoming Sprint, and the Sprint Review evaluates the progress and results achieved during the Sprint. The Daily Scrum is a brief meeting every day to ensure everyone is aligned and focused on the Sprint goal. Finally, the Sprint Retrospective is a meeting after the Sprint Review, where the team has all the information to reflect on the previous Sprint and identifies areas for improvement.

By providing this regular cadence of events, Scrum enables teams to inspect their work frequently and diligently. This helps identify potential problems or variances early, allowing the team to adapt their approach and minimize negative impacts.

Frequently and diligently inspecting the Scrum artifacts and progress is an essential aspect of the Scrum framework. By continuously monitoring progress and outcomes, Scrum teams can make informed decisions based on empirical evidence, leading to better outcomes and higher-quality products.

> *Inspection enables adaptation. Inspection without adaptation is considered pointless. Scrum events are designed to provoke change.*

In Scrum, inspection and adaptation are fundamental principles that help teams to improve and deliver high-quality products continuously. The inspection involves evaluating the work and progress against the agreed goals and identifying potential problems or variances. Adaptation involves changing the approach based on the insights gained from inspection.

Inspection enables adaptation by providing feedback to make informed decisions about necessary changes. Without inspection, teams would work blindly, without understanding whether they were on track.

However, inspection without adaptation is considered pointless because it fails to address the issues identified through inspection. For example, if a team identifies potential problems or variances during inspection but does not change its approach, the inspection becomes futile.

This is where Scrum events come into play. Scrum events, such as Sprint Planning, Daily Scrum, Sprint Review, and Sprint Retrospective, are designed to provoke change by providing opportunities for inspection and adaptation. By regularly reviewing progress and identifying areas for improvement, teams can adapt their approach and make changes to their work plan to ensure that they remain on track to achieve their goals.

Taking everything into account, inspection, and adaptation are critical aspects of Scrum that help teams to improve and deliver high-quality products continuously. Scrum events are designed to facilitate these principles and help teams respond more to changing needs and requirements.

3.3.4.3 Adaptation

> *If any aspects of a process deviate outside acceptable limits or if the resulting product is unacceptable, the process being applied or the materials being produced must be adjusted. The adjustment must be made as soon as possible to minimize further deviation.*

In process improvement, continuous improvement is a key principle of many methodologies or frameworks, including Scrum. One of the key aspects of this principle is that any deviations or issues in the process must be addressed as soon as possible to minimize the impact on the overall product.

If any aspect of a process deviates outside acceptable limits, it can impact the quality of the resulting product. This could be due to various factors, such as a change in requirements, a defect in the product, or an issue with the process itself. Regardless of the cause, it is essential to identify and address the deviation as soon as possible to minimize its impact on the final product.

The process or the materials being applied may need to be adjusted to address the deviation. This could involve modifying the process steps, using different materials or resources, or changing the product design. The key is to identify the root cause of the deviation and implement appropriate corrective actions to bring the process back to acceptable limits.

By addressing deviations as soon as possible, teams can minimize the impact on the overall project and ensure that the final product meets the desired quality standards. This requires a proactive and collaborative approach to problem-solving, where team members work together to identify and resolve issues as they arise. This approach can help create a culture of continuous improvement, where teams constantly seek ways to optimize their processes and deliver better outcomes for the customer.

> *Adaptation becomes more difficult when the people involved are not empowered or self-managing. A Scrum Team is expected to adapt the moment it learns anything new through inspection.*

In Scrum, adaptation is a core principle that enables teams to respond quickly and effectively to changing needs and requirements. Adaptation involves changing the approach based on the insights gained from inspection. However, adaptation becomes more difficult when the people involved are not empowered or self-managing.

When team members are not empowered or self-managing, they may not have the autonomy or authority to make the changes necessary to adapt to new information. This can lead to delays or missed opportunities, as teams must seek approval or direction from external stakeholders before taking action.

In Scrum, the Scrum Team is expected to adapt the moment it learns anything new through inspection. This means that team members should be empowered to change the process or product without unnecessary delays or approvals.

To achieve this level of empowerment and self-management, the Scrum Team must clearly understand their roles and responsibilities within the framework. In addition, they should be trained in Scrum principles and practices and have the necessary skills and expertise to make informed decisions.

The Scrum Team must also collaborate transparently, sharing information and knowledge to facilitate continuous improvement. This includes regular inspection and adaptation of the process and product, focusing on identifying areas for improvement and taking proactive steps to address them.

By empowering the Scrum Team and promoting self-management, Scrum enables teams to be more responsive and adaptable to changing needs and requirements. This can lead to faster and more effective problem-solving, higher-quality work, and better outcomes for the customer.

Figure 8 Transparency enables inspection; inspection enables adaptation.

3.4 Scrum Values

> *Successful use of Scrum depends on people becoming more proficient in living five values: Commitment, Focus, Openness, Respect, and Courage*

Scrum is a framework for Product development that emphasizes collaboration, transparency, and continuous improvement. One of the key factors contributing to Scrum's success is the ability of individuals and teams to embrace and embody the five core values: Commitment, Focus, Openness, Respect, and Courage.

- Commitment: Commitment means that team members are dedicated to achieving the product's goals and are willing to make the necessary effort to accomplish them. It also involves being accountable for their work and taking ownership of their responsibilities.
- Focus: Focus means that team members can concentrate on the product's goals and avoid distractions that could hinder their progress. It also involves prioritizing tasks and being mindful of the overall objectives.
- Openness: Openness means that team members are willing to share information and ideas within the team and with external stakeholders. It also

involves asking for help, being receptive to feedback, and being willing to learn from others.
- Respect: Respect means that team members value each other's contributions and perspectives, even if they differ from their own. It also involves treating others with kindness and empathy and avoiding disrespectful or aggressive behavior.
- Courage: Courage means that team members are willing to take risks, challenge the status quo, and try new things, even if they are outside their comfort zone. It also involves speaking up and challenging the status quo when necessary.

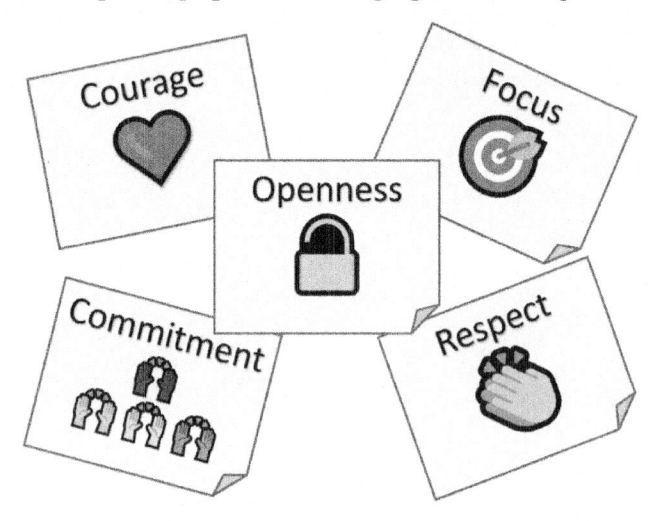

Figure 9 Scrum values.

Successful use of Scrum depends on people becoming more proficient in living these five values. When team members embrace these values, they can work more effectively, communicate more openly and transparently, and be more responsive and adaptable to changing needs and requirements. This can lead to a more collaborative and efficient development process, with a higher likelihood of delivering a high-quality product that meets the customer's needs.

3.4.1 Commitment

> *The Scrum Team commits to achieving its goals and to supporting each other.*

In Scrum, commitment is a core value that emphasizes the importance of the Scrum Team working together to achieve the product's goal. This involves a shared understanding of the Sprint goal and a willingness to make the necessary effort to accomplish it. The Scrum Team commits to achieving its goals and supporting each other in achieving those goals. By embodying this value, the Scrum Team can create a positive and collaborative work environment that promotes effective communication, teamwork, and accountability and helps ensure the project's success.

The Scrum Team commits to the following:

- Meeting the Sprint Goal
- Meeting the Product Goal
- Complete work according to the Definition of Done.
- Uphold transparency.
- Seek Stakeholder feedback and collaboration about the Increment and next steps.
- Check daily the progress to the Sprint Goal and support each other.

3.4.2 Focus

> *Their primary focus is on the work of the Sprint to make the best possible progress toward these goals.*

In Scrum, the primary focus of the Scrum Team is on the work of the Sprint, which is a time-boxed period during which the team works to complete a set of planned work items. The Scrum Team's goal during the Sprint is to make the best possible progress towards achieving their Sprint Goal. This involves a collaborative and iterative approach, where the team works together to identify and prioritize tasks and adapt and adjust their approach based on the insights gained from inspection. By embodying this value and focusing on the work of the Sprint, the Scrum Team can work efficiently and effectively towards achieving their goals and deliver high-quality products that meet the customer's needs.

3.4.2.1 Limit the WIP

The Scrum value of focus emphasizes the importance of dedicating the Scrum Team's efforts towards achieving one goal at a time, the Sprint Goal. One common way to achieve this is by limiting the work in progress and adhering to the principle of "stop starting, start finishing."

Limiting the work in progress means that the Scrum Team should only work on a limited number of Product Backlog items at any given time to complete each item before moving on to the next. This helps to avoid distractions and maintain focus on achieving the Sprint Goal.

This approach can reduce the lead time or time to market because the team can complete work more quickly and deliver smaller pieces of value to stakeholders sooner, even before the end of the Sprint if necessary.

Similarly, the "stop starting, start finishing" principle encourages the Scrum Team to complete their work before moving on to new work. Again, this helps to ensure that the Scrum Team remains focused on completing the Sprint Goal rather than getting sidetracked by new work.

By limiting the work in progress and following the principle of "stop starting, start finishing," the Scrum Team can remain focused on the Sprint Goal and increase their chances of success.

3.4.2.2 Context switching affects the focus

The Scrum value of "focus" is maintaining concentration and minimizing distractions to achieve the Sprint Goal. However, in software development, context switching can be a significant disruption to focus.

Context switching occurs when a developer has to stop working on one task and switch to another. This can happen when a developer is pulled away from their current work to deal with an urgent issue or while working on multiple projects simultaneously. Typically, because there is no WIP limit and the Developers are working on multiple things simultaneously.

Context switching can be detrimental to productivity, as it takes time and effort to get back into the flow of the original task. This can lead to delays, lower-quality work, and an increased risk of errors and mistakes.

By limiting work in progress and adopting a "stop starting, start finishing" approach, the Scrum Team can reduce the number of context switches that occur, allowing team members to maintain focus on the current Sprint Goal. This can lead to shorter lead times, as work is completed more efficiently and with fewer distractions.

3.4.3 Openness

> *The Scrum Team and its stakeholders are open about the work and the challenges.*

In Scrum, openness is a core value that emphasizes the importance of transparent communication and collaboration among the Scrum Team and its stakeholders, focusing on sharing information about the work being done and any challenges that arise. This helps to build trust and transparency, which can improve the development process's effectiveness and increase the likelihood of delivering a high-quality product that meets the customer's needs.

Openness impacts collaboration, product quality, employee satisfaction, time to market, and stakeholder trust.

3.4.3.1 Psychological safety

The Scrum value of openness emphasizes the importance of transparency, honesty, and respect within the Scrum Team. One of the ways to achieve this is by creating a culture of psychological safety, where team members feel comfortable sharing their thoughts, ideas, and concerns without fear of retribution or negative consequences. When team members feel psychologically safe, they are more likely to share information, collaborate, and innovate, which can lead to better outcomes.

For example, during a Sprint Retrospective, team members are typically encouraged to share their feedback on what went well, what didn't, and what they want to improve. However, without psychological safety, team members may not feel comfortable sharing their honest opinions or may withhold important information, leading to a lack of transparency and missed opportunities for improvement.

In contrast, when psychological safety is present, team members can openly discuss their ideas, ask for help, and admit mistakes, leading to a more productive and collaborative team dynamic. This can ultimately lead to higher-quality products, better decision-making, and increased job satisfaction for team members.

3.4.4 Respect

> *Scrum Team members respect each other to be capable, independent people, and are respected as such by the people with whom they work.*

In Scrum, respect is a core value that emphasizes recognizing and valuing all Scrum Team members' skills, expertise, and independence and respecting the contributions of stakeholders and external partners. This involves treating each other with kindness and empathy, avoiding disrespectful or aggressive behavior, and promoting a culture of mutual respect and collaboration. By embodying this value, the Scrum Team can create a positive and supportive work environment that promotes effective collaboration and communication and fosters a sense of ownership and responsibility for the product's success.

3.4.5 Courage

> *The Scrum Team members have the courage to do the right thing, to work on tough problems.*

In Scrum, courage is a core value that emphasizes the importance of being willing to take risks, try new things, and confront difficult challenges to achieve the product's goal. This involves having the confidence to speak up, challenge the status quo when necessary, and tackle tough problems head-on, even if it requires extra effort or discomfort. By embodying this value, the Scrum Team can create a culture of innovation and continuous improvement and be more responsive and adaptable to changing needs and requirements.

Challenging the status quo means questioning and challenging the existing or conventional ways of thinking, behaving, or doing things.

Courage and challenging the status quo often go hand in hand. It takes courage to question established beliefs and practices and to propose new, unconventional ideas. Challenging the status quo can be risky, as it may lead to pushback or resistance from those who benefit from the current state of affairs. However, it is through challenging the status quo that progress can be made and new solutions can be found.

Courage is also essential in facing opposition or adversity when challenging the status quo. It takes courage to persevere in the face of resistance and advocate for change.

3.4.6 Embodying Scrum Values

Values are not a list of nice things you put on a wall and expect people to follow. Values must be embodied every day as part of working the culture.

Because the values cannot be mandated, it is highly recommended that Scrum Team members embody these values in their work and interactions with others.

All team members must embrace and embody the Scrum values for the Scrum Team to be effective. They must collaborate, communicate openly and honestly, and respect each other's opinions and ideas. They must also have the courage to address issues and make difficult decisions and the focus to stay committed to achieving their goals.

While Scrum Team members need to embrace these values, it is also the responsibility of the Scrum Master and other leaders to help foster a culture that supports these values. This can include training, coaching, and other resources to help team members develop their skills and understand the importance of the Scrum values.

Ultimately, the success of the Scrum process depends on the entire team working together collaboratively and respectfully, and embodying the Scrum values is a key part of achieving this. While these values cannot be mandated, they are a vital part of the Scrum framework and can help teams achieve high productivity levels and deliver high-quality products.

> *These values give direction to the Scrum Team with regard to their work, actions, and behavior. The decisions that are made, the steps taken, and the way Scrum is used should reinforce these values, not diminish or undermine them.*

The Scrum Team must embody these values and use them as a guide in making decisions, taking steps, and using Scrum as a framework. The values should not be compromised or undermined in any way, as they are fundamental to the success of Scrum. By adhering to these values, the Scrum Team can create a positive and supportive work environment that promotes effective communication, collaboration, and continuous improvement and helps to ensure the product's success.

> *The Scrum Team members learn and explore the values as they work with the Scrum events and artifacts.*

As the Scrum Team members work together and engage in Scrum events, they learn and explore these values through their interactions with each other, stakeholders, and the Scrum artifacts.

For example, during Sprint Planning, the Scrum Team members work collaboratively to define the Sprint goal and plan the work needed to achieve it. This requires commitment, focus, openness, and respect to ensure the team is aligned and working towards a shared goal.

During the Daily Scrum, the Scrum Team members engage in open and transparent communication about their progress towards the Sprint goal, which promotes trust and transparency among the team members.

During the Sprint Review, the Scrum Team members demonstrate the completed work to stakeholders, which requires courage to showcase their work and openness to receive feedback and critique.

By engaging in these Scrum events and working with the artifacts, the Scrum Team members learn and explore the values, reinforcing these values as a core part of the Scrum framework.

3.4.7 Psychological safety to embrace values

Psychological safety is an important concept in the context of the Scrum values, as it is closely related to the values of openness and respect.

Psychological safety refers to a team's shared belief that it is safe to take interpersonal risks, such as speaking up, making mistakes, and asking for help without fear of negative consequences. When team members feel psychologically safe, they are more likely to be open and honest with each other, leading to better communication, collaboration, and problem-solving.

In the context of Scrum, psychological safety is essential for effective team functioning. The Scrum values of openness and respect require team members to be willing to share their thoughts and ideas and to listen to and respect the opinions of others. If team members do not feel psychologically safe, they may hesitate to speak up or share their ideas, leading to misunderstandings, conflicts, and a lack of cohesion.

To promote psychological safety within a Scrum team, team members must be supportive and respectful of one another, encourage open communication and feedback, and be willing to admit mistakes and learn from them. Scrum Masters can also foster psychological safety by setting clear expectations, providing feedback and coaching, and promoting a culture of openness and collaboration.

On the whole, psychological safety is an important component of the Scrum values and is essential for effective team functioning and achieving the goals of the Scrum framework.

3.4.8 Building trust

In the book "The Five Dysfunctions of a Team" by Patrick Lencioni, trust is the foundation of a strong and effective team. Conversely, according to the author, lacking trust is the first and most fundamental dysfunction that can derail a team's success.

Lencioni defines trust as the willingness of team members to be vulnerable with one another, to admit mistakes and weaknesses, and to ask for help when needed. This type of trust allows team members to be honest and open with each other, leading to better communication, collaboration, and problem-solving.

```
        Inattention to  / RESULTS  \   → Focus on outcomes
       ─────────────────────────────────────────────────────
         Avoidance of  / ACCOUNTABILITY \  → Confront difficult issues
       ─────────────────────────────────────────────────────
              Lack of / COMMITMENT       \  → Focus on clarity and closure
       ─────────────────────────────────────────────────────
              Fear of / CONFLICT           \  → Demand on debate
       ─────────────────────────────────────────────────────
         Absence of  /  TRUST                \  → Be human
```

The five dysfunctions of a team
(Patrick M. Lencioni)

Figure 10 The five dysfunctions of a team (Patrick M. Lencioni).

When trust is lacking within a team, team members may be hesitant to share their thoughts and ideas, leading to misunderstandings, conflicts, and a lack of cohesion. In addition, in the absence of trust, team members may also engage in behavior such as gossiping, backstabbing, or withholding information, which can further erode trust and undermine the team's effectiveness.

To build trust within a team, Lencioni suggests that team members must be willing to be vulnerable with one another, share their thoughts and ideas openly, and take risks to build stronger relationships. He also suggests that leaders can build trust by modeling vulnerability, setting clear expectations, and holding team members accountable for their behavior.

We want	Definition	Example in Scrum
Results	The focus is on achieving results as a team rather than individual performance.	Scrum teams work together towards a common goal, with each individual's contribution essential to the team's success. The product goal is a shared understanding among everyone involved in the project.
Accountability	Taking responsibility for one's actions and commitments.	The Product Owner is accountable for maximizing the product's value, and the Scrum Team is accountable for creating a high-quality product increment every Sprint. The Scrum Master is accountable for facilitating Scrum events and coaching the team.
Commitment	The dedication to achieving the Sprint	The Scrum Team is committed to achieving the Sprint Goal by delivering a valuable

		Goal and delivering a high-quality product increment.	increment every Sprint. Likewise, the Product Owner is committed to maximizing the product's value.
Conflict		Conflict can be positive. The ability to handle disagreements and resolve conflicts constructively.	Scrum encourages transparency and open communication, addressing conflicts promptly and constructively. The Scrum Master is responsible for facilitating discussions and helping the team resolve conflicts.
Trust		The belief in the competence, reliability, and integrity of others.	Scrum is based on trust between team members and stakeholders. The Scrum Team trusts that each team member is capable of completing their tasks and contributing to the success of the Sprint. Likewise, the stakeholders trust that the Scrum Team will deliver a high-quality product increment every Sprint. The Scrum Master helps to build and maintain trust within the team and with stakeholders. The organization empowers the Scrum Team to manage its own work.

On the whole, trust is a key ingredient in building strong and effective teams and is essential to the success of any collaborative effort. By fostering a culture of trust within their teams, leaders can create an environment that encourages openness, honesty, and mutual support, leading to greater success and fulfillment for everyone involved.

When these values are embodied by the Scrum Team and the people they work with, the empirical Scrum pillars of transparency, inspection, and adaptation come to life building trust.

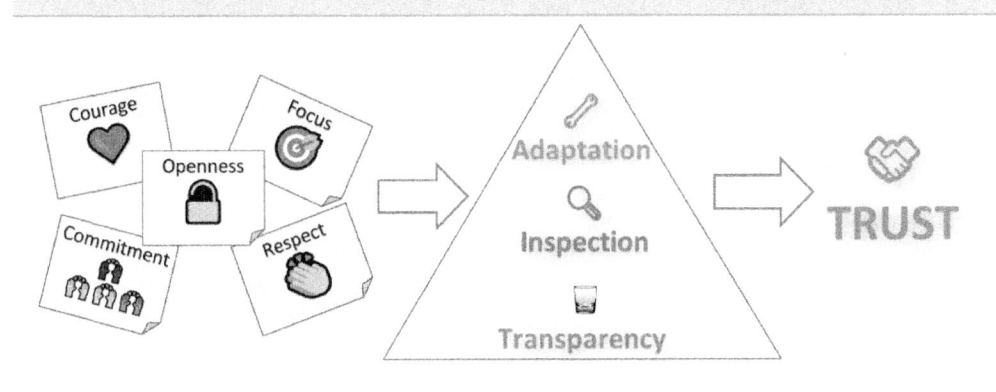

Figure 11 When the Scrum Team embodies the Scrum values, the pillars come to life and build trust.

In Scrum, when the values of commitment, focus, openness, respect, and courage are embodied by the Scrum Team and the people they work with, they reinforce the empirical Scrum pillars of transparency, inspection, and adaptation.

Transparency is promoted through open communication and collaboration, which builds trust and ensures that everyone has a clear understanding of the work being done and the progress being made toward the Sprint goal.

Regular Scrum events, such as the Daily Scrum and Sprint Review, facilitate inspection, which provides opportunities to review and assess the work completed and adjust the approach as needed to ensure the Sprint goal is achieved.

Adaptation is fostered by the courage and willingness of the Scrum Team to take risks and try new things, as well as the respect and openness that allows them to receive feedback and learn from their experiences.

Knowing each other and understanding each other talents, skills, and work history helps with values and trust.

When these values and empirical pillars are embraced and embodied by the Scrum Team and the people they work with, trust is built among the team members and stakeholders. This trust allows for more effective collaboration, communication, and problem-solving, leading to a more efficient and effective development process, with a higher likelihood of delivering a high-quality product that meets the customer's needs.

3.4.9 Examples of not following the Scrum Values

Here are some examples of how each Scrum value can be broken:

1. Lack of Focus:
    - Jumping between multiple tasks frequently leads to incomplete work and reduced productivity.
    - Losing sight of the Sprint goal and working on unrelated or low-priority items.
2. Lack of Courage:
    - Avoiding difficult conversations or conflicts with team members or stakeholders, leading to unresolved issues and a lack of progress.
    - Prioritizing personal interests or preferences over the needs of the team or the product.
3. Lack of Commitment:
    - Failing to meet Sprint commitments or not taking them seriously leading to missed deadlines and poor-quality work.
    - Not holding oneself accountable for their work leads to decreased team morale and trust.
4. Lack of Respect:
    - Disregarding the opinions or contributions of team members leads to a lack of collaboration and trust within the team.

- Ignoring or dismissing the needs or feedback of stakeholders leads to a misaligned product and unsatisfied customers.
- Heated personal arguments.
- Blaming someone directly.
- Asking the Developers to make progress according to the estimates.
- Managing the Developers' progress during the Sprint.
- Expecting the Developers to commit to the forecast.
- A Product Owner or Scrum Master preparing or managing the Sprint Backlog for the Developers.

5. Lack of Openness:
    - Withholding information or feedback from team members or stakeholders leads to a lack of transparency and trust.
    - Being resistant to change or new ideas leads to stagnation and missed opportunities for improvement.
    - Not raising issues or asking for clarification during the Sprint.
    - Being afraid of notifying the rest of the team of mistakes or errors.
    - Breaking any Scrum values can lead to significant problems within a team or organization, including reduced productivity, misaligned priorities, and damaged relationships. Therefore, upholding and reinforcing these values is crucial to promote a positive and effective Scrum environment.

When the Scrum values fail to be embraced by the Scrum team, the Scrum Master can play a crucial role in coaching and advising the team. Here are some ways in which the Scrum Master can help:

1. Facilitating discussions: The Scrum Master can facilitate discussions with the team to understand why they may struggle to embrace the Scrum values. By creating a safe and open space for the team to discuss their challenges and concerns, the Scrum Master can help identify root causes and potential solutions.
2. Providing feedback: The Scrum Master can provide constructive feedback to the team on their behaviors and actions, helping them see how their actions impact their ability to embrace the Scrum values. This can be done in a way that is supportive and non-judgmental, focusing on opportunities for improvement rather than criticism.
3. Encouraging experimentation: The Scrum Master can encourage the team to experiment with different approaches to see what works best in embracing the Scrum values. This can involve trying new techniques or tools or even changing team dynamics to see how that affects their ability to embrace the Scrum values.
4. Leading by example: The Scrum Master can lead by example, demonstrating the Scrum values in their behaviors and actions. By modeling the behavior they want to see in the team, the Scrum Master can help the team to see the value in embracing the Scrum values.
5. Resources and training: The Scrum Master can provide resources and training to the team to help them better understand and embrace the Scrum values. This

can include workshops, training sessions, or even access to external experts who can help the team to learn new techniques and approaches.

The Scrum Master is critical in helping the team embrace the Scrum values. By providing guidance, feedback, encouragement, and resources, the Scrum Master can help the team to overcome any obstacles or challenges they may be facing and to work together more effectively to deliver high-quality products.

3.4.10 Examples of embracing the Scrum Values

Here are some examples of how each Scrum value can be embraced:

1. Focus:
    - Prioritize work based on the Sprint goal and commit to completing it within the timeline.
    - Minimizing distractions and dedicating time and effort to a specific task or objective.
2. Courage:
    - Addressing and resolving conflicts or difficult conversations with team members or stakeholders promptly and respectfully.
    - Experimenting with new ideas or approaches and taking calculated risks to improve the product or process.
    - Saying no to building features with low business value.
    - Developers answer Stakeholders to talk to the Product when they ask for a critical feature during the Sprint.
    - Saying no or postponing stakeholders' requests for changing scope during the Sprint and committing to the current Sprint Goal.
3. Commitment:
    - Holding oneself and team members accountable for meeting Sprint goals and deadlines.
    - Continuously striving to improve and deliver high-quality work to meet stakeholder needs.
4. Respect:
    - Valuing and respecting team members' and stakeholders' opinions, skills, and contributions.
    - Building trust and collaboration through active listening, feedback, and empathy.
    - Respect the expectations of the stakeholders when refining the Product Backlog items.
    - Developers respect the autonomy of the Product Owner in managing the Product Backlog while still providing input and feedback as needed.
    - Respect and trust in the accountabilities within the Scrum Team
    - Members respect people, diversity, experience, and differing points of view.
    - When there are problems in the process or conflicts between the team members, the Scrum Master coaches the team members, teaches, asks

powerful questions, facilitates discussions, promotes or facilities self-managing, and encourages them to bring the topic to the Sprint Retrospective.
5. Openness:
    o Providing transparent and timely feedback and communication to team members and stakeholders.
    o Being open and flexible to change and new ideas, embracing the opportunity for continuous improvement.
    o When there are problems in the process or conflicts between the team members, they bring the topic to the Sprint Retrospective.

Embracing these Scrum values promotes a positive and effective Scrum environment, resulting in increased productivity, aligned priorities, and stronger relationships within the team and with stakeholders. Therefore, it is essential to consistently uphold and reinforce these values to foster a culture of continuous improvement and success.

Part 4: The Scrum Team

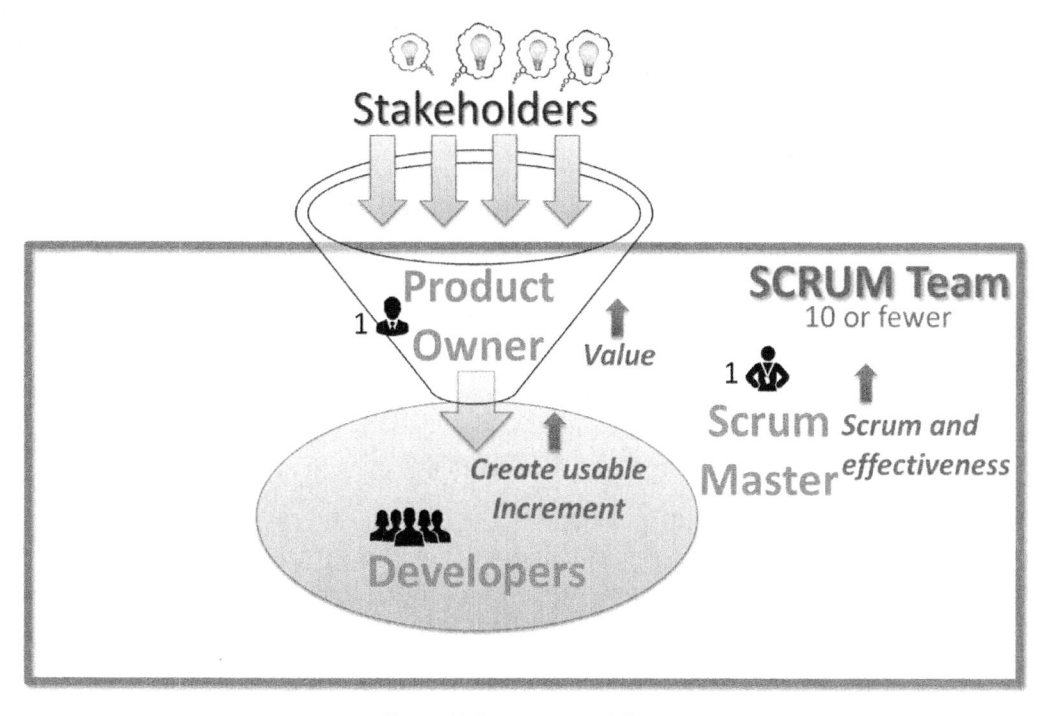

Figure 12 Scrum accountabilities.

The fundamental unit of Scrum is a small team of people, a Scrum Team. The Scrum Team consists of one Scrum Master, one Product Owner, and Developers. Within a Scrum Team, there are no sub-teams or hierarchies. It is a cohesive unit of professionals focused on one objective at a time, the Product Goal.

In Scrum, the fundamental unit is the Scrum Team, a small, self-organizing group of people working together to achieve a shared objective, the Product Goal. The Scrum Team consists of three accountabilities: the Scrum Master, the Product Owner, and the Developers.

The Scrum Master ensures that the Scrum framework is understood and implemented effectively. At the same time, the Product Owner is responsible for maximizing the product's value and maintaining the Product Backlog. Finally, the Developers deliver a potentially releasable product increment at the end of each Sprint.

Importantly, there are no sub-teams or hierarchies within a Scrum Team. Instead, all team members work collaboratively to achieve the shared objective and are responsible for their work and for supporting the work of others.

This approach creates a cohesive and focused unit of professionals who work together to achieve a shared goal and are empowered to take ownership of their work and make decisions that benefit the project. By working this way, the Scrum Team can promote collaboration, communication, and accountability and deliver high-quality products that meet customer needs.

4.1 Cross-functional team

> *Scrum Teams are cross-functional, meaning the members have all the skills necessary to create value each Sprint.*

In Scrum, Scrum Teams are designed to be cross-functional, which means they are composed of individuals with all the necessary skills and expertise to create value each Sprint. This approach reduces the team's dependency on others outside the team. As a result, it minimizes the risk of delays or errors that can occur when work is passed between different teams or individuals. In addition, cross-functional teams have the skills to work on all the architectural layers of the Product and deliver features every Sprint like usable slices of a complete product that is not yet built.

The cross-functional approach also enables the Scrum Team to be more self-sufficient. They have all the skills necessary to create a product increment without relying on external resources. This can lead to faster delivery times and more efficient workflows, as the team is less dependent on others outside of the team.

However, there may be instances when the Scrum Team does not have all the skills necessary to complete a particular task or achieve a specific goal. In these cases, the team can seek support or assistance from others outside the team, such as subject matter experts or other specialists.

Additionally, the Scrum Team can take steps to acquire new skills or knowledge as needed. For example, they may seek training or mentorship opportunities or engage in self-directed learning to build new skills.

Cross-functional does not mean that everybody knows everything, but that the composite of skills within the is enough to deliver an Increment with minimal or no external dependencies.

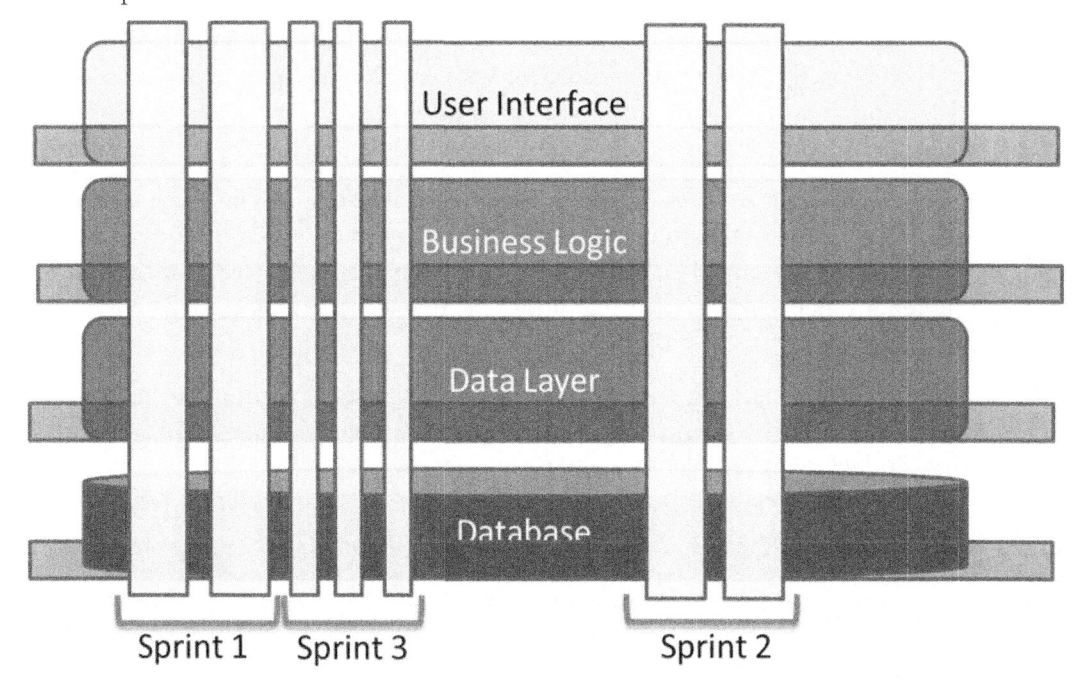

Figure 13 Cross-functional teams have the skills to work on all architectural layers and deliver features every Sprint.

Although having everyone with all the skills is impossible, Scrum Teams prefer Generalizing Specialists as members rather than specialists.

To review, the cross-functional nature of Scrum Teams helps to ensure that the team is self-sufficient and has the necessary skills and expertise to create value for each Sprint. While there may be instances where additional support or learning is needed, the team can generally work independently and deliver high-quality products that meet the customer's needs.

4.2 Self-managing team

They are also self-managing, meaning they internally decide who does what, when, and how.

In Scrum, Scrum Teams are designed to be self-managing, which means team members are empowered to decide how to organize their work and achieve their Sprint goals.

This approach gives the Scrum Team greater autonomy and responsibility for their work and allows them to work more efficiently and effectively. The team members can collaborate more easily and share knowledge and expertise to solve problems and address challenges.

Specifically, the Scrum Team is responsible for deciding who does what, when, and how within the context of each Sprint. This includes tasks related to designing, developing, testing, and other activities necessary to create the product increment.

The team members can make these decisions through self-organization, which involves making decisions based on the team's collective knowledge, skills, and experience. This can include organizing their work based on their strengths and preferences, setting their own goals and deadlines, and prioritizing their work to maximize efficiency and effectiveness.

By being self-managing, Scrum Teams can be highly effective and efficient. They can collaborate effectively and take ownership of their work, leading to high motivation, engagement, and productivity. This approach can also enable teams to be more responsive to changing requirements and market conditions, as they can adapt and adjust their approach in real-time.

In summary, the self-managing nature of Scrum Teams helps ensure that the team is empowered to make decisions and take ownership of their work, leading to higher quality products, faster delivery times, and more satisfied customers.

4.2.1 Self-managing vs. Self-organizing

According to Jeff Sutherland, JJ Sutherland, Avi Schneier, and the Scrum Inc. Team in their blog, they say:

> *Previous Scrum Guides referred to Development Teams as self-organizing, meaning they chose who performed the work and how. With more of a focus on the Scrum Team, the 2020 version emphasizes a self-managing Scrum Team, which chooses what to work on, who is going to do it, and how it will get done.*

Also, a principle of the Agile Manifesto says:

> *The best architectures, requirements, and designs emerge from self-organizing teams.*

Self-managing and self-organizing are two related but distinct concepts in Scrum.

Self-managing refers to the ability of the Scrum Team to manage themselves and their work. The Scrum Team is responsible for organizing their work, making decisions, and ensuring that the work is delivered to a high standard. They are empowered to decide how to accomplish their work best and are accountable for the results.

Self-organizing, on the other hand, refers to the ability of the Scrum Team as a whole to organize and adapt to changing circumstances. The Scrum Team organizes its work, adapts to changing requirements, and ensures that the product meets customer needs. They are empowered to decide how to organize themselves best to achieve the Sprint Goal and are accountable for the results.

While self-managing and self-organizing are related concepts, there are some key differences. First, self-managing refers primarily to the Scrum Team's ability to manage themselves and their work. In contrast, self-organizing refers to the Scrum Team's ability to adapt to changing circumstances and organize themselves to achieve the Sprint Goal. In other words, self-managing is focused on the micro-level of individual tasks and work assignments. In contrast, self-organizing is focused on the macro-level of overall team organization and adaptation.

In other words, the Scrum Teams don't need to be managed; they self-organize to manage themselves.

Self-managing and self-organizing are important concepts in Scrum, as they empower the Scrum Team to work effectively and efficiently to deliver a high-quality product. In addition, by providing the team with the autonomy and responsibility to manage and organize themselves, Scrum helps to foster a culture of collaboration, innovation, and continuous improvement.

4.2.2 Examples of self-managing Scrum team

Here are some examples of how a Scrum team is self-managing:

- Resolving internal conflicts between members: In a self-managing Scrum team, team members are empowered to resolve conflicts and disagreements respectfully and collaboratively. This can involve having open and honest conversations, seeking input from all team members, and finding solutions that align with the team's goals and values.
- Deciding who does what, when, and how: A self-managing Scrum team can decide how to organize and divide work among its members. This can involve collaborating to assign tasks and responsibilities based on individual strengths and skills and prioritizing work according to the Sprint goals and priorities.
- Establishing their own Sprint Backlog: In a self-managing Scrum team, the Developers are responsible for establishing their own Sprint Backlog, which includes any work that falls within the Definition of Done. This involves collaborating to prioritize and estimate work and adjusting their plan as needed throughout the Sprint based on their progress and feedback.
- Re-plan work during the Sprint: During the Sprint, Developers collaborate to select and re-plan the work every day to meet the Sprint Goal.
- The Scrum Team explores different possibilities and fosters creativity in its approach.

A self-managing Scrum team has the flexibility and autonomy to make decisions and resolve issues independently while still collaborating and aligning with the team's overall goals and values. This promotes a culture of trust, transparency, and accountability and helps teams maximize their productivity and effectiveness.

4.3 Scrum Team size

> *The Scrum Team is small enough to remain nimble and large enough to complete significant work within a Sprint, typically 10 or fewer people.*

In Scrum, the Scrum Team is typically composed of 10 or fewer people, which allows the team to remain nimble while still being able to complete significant work within a Sprint.

Having 10 or fewer people on a Scrum Team is a guideline rather than a strict rule. The key consideration is ensuring the team can collaborate effectively and efficiently, communicate clearly, and achieve their Sprint goals. Therefore, the team size should be determined based on these factors rather than adhering strictly to a specific number.

In a team with 4 members, each member has 3 others to collaborate. So in total, there are 6 channels of collaboration:

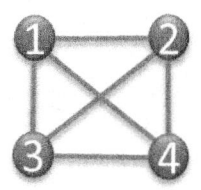

Figure 14 Communication between a team with 4 members.

All team members can likely communicate face-to-face and collaborate.

Notice how the communication between members becomes more complex for a team with 8 members:

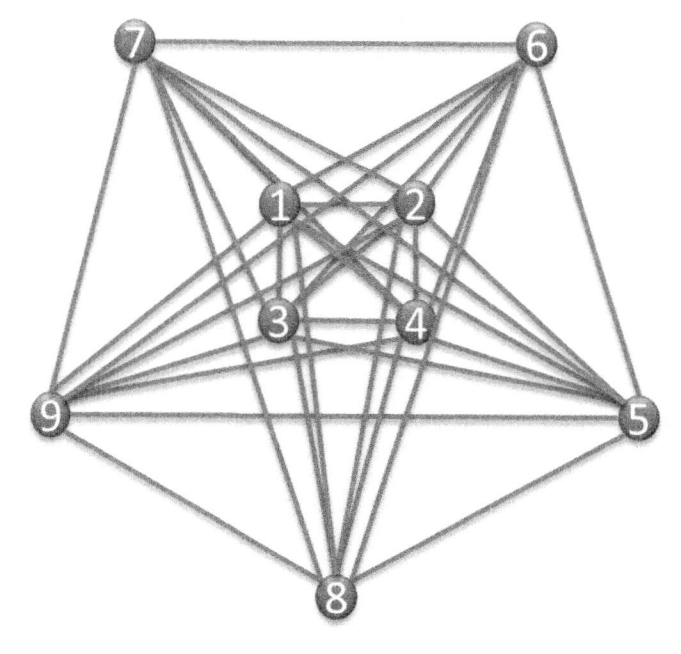

Figure 15 Communication between a team with 8 members

Each member now has 7 other members to communicate with. There are 36 channels of communication in total. Face-to-face communication and collaboration are still possible, but it is becoming more challenging with more team members.

> *In general, we have found that smaller teams communicate better and are more productive.*

In Scrum, team communication is critical for the product's success. By working in small, cross-functional teams, Scrum promotes effective communication, collaboration, and knowledge sharing among team members.

Research has shown that smaller teams communicate better and are more productive than larger teams. This is because smaller teams can better establish clear lines of communication, share information, and make decisions quickly. They also tend to have a greater sense of accountability and ownership among team members, leading to higher engagement and productivity.

In Scrum, having smaller teams can help promote more effective communication and collaboration, leading to higher-quality products and faster delivery times. This is because smaller teams can better respond to changing requirements and market conditions, as they can adapt and adjust their approach more easily.

Additionally, smaller team sizes can help promote greater accountability and ownership among team members. With fewer people involved, each team member significantly impacts the team's overall performance, which can lead to a greater sense of responsibility and engagement.

However, it's important to note that the ideal team size can vary depending on the work's nature and the project's requirements. In some cases, a larger team may be necessary to achieve the desired outcomes, while in other cases, a smaller team may be more appropriate.

When the team size is too large, communication can become more challenging, as it can be difficult to ensure that everyone is on the same page and has the same level of understanding. This can lead to delays, misunderstandings, and errors impacting the team's performance.

Conversely, when the team size is too small, the team may struggle to complete the necessary work within a Sprint or may lack the necessary skills or expertise to achieve their goals. In these cases, bringing in additional team members or seeking support from others outside the team may be necessary.

If the team size is large, instead of telling the Scrum Team to split, the Scrum Master can raise the increased team size as a potential impediment and help the Developers decide what to do.

In summary, Scrum promotes the use of smaller teams as a way to enable effective communication and collaboration, which is critical for the product's success. By working in smaller, cross-functional teams, Scrum Teams can deliver high-quality products that meet the customer's needs promptly and efficiently.

4.4 Scaling the Scrum Team

> *If Scrum Teams become too large, they should consider reorganizing into multiple cohesive Scrum Teams, each focused on the same product. Therefore, they should share the same Product Goal, Product Backlog, and Product Owner.*

In Scrum, the Scrum Team is designed to be a small, cross-functional team focused on achieving a specific product goal. However, if a Scrum Team becomes too large, it can be challenging to maintain effective communication and collaboration among team members.

To address this issue, the Scrum Guide suggests that if a Scrum Team becomes too large, they should consider reorganizing into multiple cohesive Scrum Teams, each focused on the same product. This approach enables the teams to work independently while still sharing a common goal and product vision.

To ensure that the teams are aligned and working toward the same product goal, they should share the same Product Goal, Product Backlog, and Product Owner. The Product Goal provides a shared understanding of the overall objective that the teams are working toward. The Product Backlog represents the work needed to achieve the Product Goal and is managed by the Product Owner. The Product Owner is responsible for ensuring the Product Backlog is prioritized and aligned with the overall Product Goal.

By sharing these common elements, the multiple cohesive Scrum Teams can work more efficiently and effectively toward the same Product Goal while still maintaining their independence and ability to work autonomously. In addition, this approach can help improve communication and collaboration among team members, enabling the teams to work more efficiently and effectively.

4.5 Ownership, empowerment, and success

> *The Scrum Team is responsible for all product-related activities from stakeholder collaboration, verification, maintenance, operation, experimentation, research and development, and anything else that might be required.*

This sentence is usually misunderstood as, "Now anyone can do anything, and the Scrum Team must decide everything together," but that is not the point. There are still accountabilities within the Scrum Team.

This sentence intends to reinforce that the Scrum Team is responsible for the success or failure of the result of such activities by managing itself with no one outside the team managing the team or telling it how to do it. However, each team member will contribute to this team's responsibility within their accountabilities and respect each other's accountabilities. For instance:

The Scrum Team is accountable for creating and releasing an Increment:

- The Product Owner decides everything that affects the value for the users. They identify the most valuable items that the upcoming Increment should include and the best time to release it to make it valuable.
- The Developers build an Increment that meets the Sprint Goal according to the Definition of Done.
- The Scrum Master helps to make the process and artifacts transparent. In addition, they help or facilitate ways to identify and remove impediments and encourage the Scrum Team to improve its effectiveness.

However, they are all still responsible for the final output and outcome. Therefore,

- If a team member is struggling or stuck with their accountabilities, it is the team's problem.
- If one fails, everybody fails.
- No one can be left behind; the team members must support and hold each other to fulfill their accountabilities and become better at them.
- No one should work isolated or in silos. Each one contributes to a greater purpose than their individuality.

The Scrum Team ensures that the product meets the customer's needs and is delivered promptly and efficiently. In addition, the Scrum Team works collaboratively with stakeholders to identify and prioritize requirements and ensure that the product meets their needs and expectations.

The Scrum Team is also responsible for verifying the product, which involves testing and validating that it meets the acceptance criteria and is of high quality. In addition, they are responsible for maintaining the product, ensuring it remains functional and up-to-date.

Additionally, the Scrum Team is responsible for experimentation, research, and development, which involves exploring new technologies, ideas, and approaches to improve the product and enhance the customer experience.

In summary, the Scrum Team is responsible for all aspects of the product, from ideation to delivery. It is accountable for ensuring that it meets the customer's needs and delivers value to the organization.

4.6 Empowerment

> *They are structured and empowered by the organization to manage their own work.*

In Scrum, the Scrum Team is structured and empowered by the organization to manage its own work. This means that the organization trusts the Scrum Team to make decisions, determine how best to achieve the Sprint Goal, and manage their own work. The organization empowers the Product Owner to make the decisions to make the product successful and valuable.

The Scrum Team has three accountabilities: the Scrum Master, the Product Owner, and the Developers. Each one has a specific set of responsibilities, but they work collaboratively and are collectively responsible for achieving the Sprint Goal.

The organization promotes self-organization and self-management by structuring the team in this way and empowering them to manage their own work. This approach allows the Scrum Team to make decisions and take ownership of their work, leading to higher engagement, creativity, and innovation.

Additionally, this approach allows the Scrum Team to work more efficiently and effectively. The organization can improve productivity and quality by eliminating unnecessary bureaucracy and enabling the team to make decisions quickly.

In summary, empowering the Scrum Team to manage their own work is a fundamental aspect of Scrum. This approach promotes self-organization, collaboration, and efficiency and can help organizations achieve their goals more effectively.

> *Working in Sprints at a sustainable pace improves the Scrum Team's focus and consistency.*

The Scrum Team works in Sprints, which are time-boxed periods (usually 2-4 weeks) during which a potentially releasable product increment is created.

Working in Sprints at a sustainable pace is important for improving the Scrum Team's focus and consistency. This approach helps the team to manage their workload effectively, avoid burnout, and maintain a healthy work-life balance.

By working in Sprints, the Scrum Team is able to set achievable goals and focus on completing a specific set of tasks during each Sprint. This approach helps break down larger projects into smaller, more manageable pieces, improving productivity and reducing stress.

In addition, by setting a sustainable pace, the Scrum Team is able to maintain consistency in their work. This approach allows the team to deliver a predictable output level during each Sprint, which can help build trust with stakeholders and improve overall project outcomes.

In summary, working in Sprints at a sustainable pace is a key aspect of Scrum. This approach helps improve the Scrum Team's focus and consistency, which can lead to higher productivity, quality, and satisfaction.

4.7 Accountability

The entire Scrum Team is accountable for creating a valuable, useful Increment every Sprint.

In Scrum, the entire Scrum Team is responsible for creating a valuable and useful Increment every Sprint. This means that every team member shares accountability for delivering a potentially releasable product increment at the end of each Sprint.

The purpose of each Sprint is to deliver a potentially shippable product increment that adds value to the overall product being developed. This means that the Scrum Team must work together to create a high-quality product that meets the needs of its stakeholders.

By sharing accountability for the product increment, the Scrum Team is motivated to work collaboratively and take ownership of their work. This approach promotes a sense of shared responsibility and can lead to higher engagement, creativity, and innovation levels.

Additionally, by delivering a valuable and useful Increment every Sprint, the Scrum Team can demonstrate progress and build trust with stakeholders. Finally, this approach allows the team to respond quickly to changing market conditions or customer needs, which can help the organization stay competitive.

The entire Scrum Team is accountable for creating a valuable and useful Increment every Sprint. This approach promotes collaboration, ownership, and accountability and can help organizations achieve their goals more effectively.

Scrum defines three specific accountabilities within the Scrum Team: the Developers, the Product Owner, and the Scrum Master.

Although the entire Scrum Team is accountable for creating a valuable and useful Increment every Sprint, Scrum defines three specific accountabilities within the Scrum Team: Developers, the Product Owner, and the Scrum Master.

These accountabilities are designed to help the Scrum Team work more effectively and ensure that everyone understands their responsibilities clearly. Each of the accountabilities has a specific role to play in the Scrum process:

- Developers: The Developers are responsible for creating the product increment during each Sprint. They are cross-functional and self-organizing, meaning they have all the skills necessary to create the product and are empowered to manage their own work.
- Product Owner: The Product Owner is responsible for maximizing the product's value by prioritizing the Product Backlog and the Scrum Team delivering the highest possible value each Sprint.
- Scrum Master: The Scrum Master is responsible for ensuring that the Scrum Team is adhering to the Scrum framework, removing impediments preventing the team from achieving its goals, and facilitating communication and collaboration between the team and its stakeholders.

While all members of the Scrum Team are responsible for creating a valuable and useful Increment every Sprint, each of the accountabilities has a specific focus and set of responsibilities that help to ensure the success of the Scrum process. By working collaboratively and taking ownership of their respective accountabilities, the Scrum Team can achieve high productivity levels and deliver high-quality products.

4.7.1 Accountability vs. roles

The previous Scrum Guide used the term "roles," which was changed to "accountabilities." In the Scrum Guide 2020. According to Jeff Sutherland, JJ Sutherland, Avi Schneier, and the Scrum Inc. Team in their blog, they say:

> *The word 'roles' was being misunderstood in some situations. Scrum has never been about creating a taxonomy of titles. Roles were never intended to be a title. What matters is clearly defining who is accountable for what.*
>
> *This change puts the emphasis where it belongs, on specific accountabilities. You can still refer to them as 'roles' if you like. We are. But we too will emphasize these are roles with defined accountabilities.*

Therefore, Product Owner, Developers, and Scrum Master are not meant to be titles or positions. Instead, they are accountabilities for which someone in the Scrum Team will be accountable. It is also not a crime to refer to accountabilities informally as roles.

Typically, we see companies having these accountabilities as roles or titles in the organization, and they hire people to fulfill the title.

It seems that the authors of Scrum intend that the members of the Scrum Team should fulfill these accountabilities as a self-managing team. However, there is no explicit rule about this.

4.8 Membership of the Scrum Team

In Scrum, it is allowed to add or remove members of the Scrum Team, although it is generally recommended to avoid making changes during a Sprint. Here's how adding or removing team members can affect the short-term performance or velocity of the Scrum Team, as well as coordination, onboarding, and productivity:

- Short-term performance or velocity: Adding or removing team members can affect the short-term performance or velocity of the Scrum Team. When a new member is added, there may be a temporary decrease in velocity as the team adjusts to the new member's skills and working style. Similarly, when a member is removed, there may be a temporary decrease in velocity as the team adjusts to losing that member's skills and contributions.
- Coordination: Adding or removing team members can also affect coordination within the team. When a new member is added, it may take time for the team to establish effective communication and collaboration processes. Similarly, when a member is removed, it may disrupt the existing communication and collaboration processes and require the team to adapt to new ways of working.
- Onboarding: When a new member is added to the team, there is a period of onboarding required to get them up to speed with the team's processes, tools, and practices. This can take some time and may require the team to slow down temporarily as the new member is brought up to speed.
- Productivity: Adding or removing team members can also affect productivity in the short term. When a new member is added, it may take some time for them to become fully productive and for the team to adjust to their working style. Similarly, when a member is removed, it may affect the productivity of the remaining team members as they adjust to the loss of that member's contributions.

Changes in teams and membership always affect productivity. Gradually feature teams will become more productive as people from the different layers and components will get used to delivering unified functionality together as one Scrum Team. The Business Value is also likely to increase over the team. The Scrum Master should not re-organize people but let them decide how to re-arrange teams to cover all the skills of self-managing teams.

In summary, changing the members of the Scrum Team is allowed as needed, but a short-term reduction in performance or velocity might be considered. Adding or removing members will require coordination and onboarding so that productivity will drop.

Generally, adding or removing members of the Scrum Team can have short-term impacts on performance, coordination, onboarding, and productivity. However, if the team can effectively manage the change, these impacts can be minimized, and the team can continue to deliver value to the customer. Therefore, it's important for the Scrum Master and Product Owner to consider the potential impacts of adding or removing team members and to work with the team to manage the transition effectively.

4.8.1 Adding new team(s) to work with existing teams

Adding new Scrum Teams to work on the same product with existing teams will have similar effects to changing the membership. In addition, the velocity of the original teams will drop because of the need for coordination with new teams. However, over time, we expect the overall velocity of the group of teams and the product's value to increase, assuming good work from the Product Owner to maximize the value.

4.8.2 How to decide the membership of Scrum Teams?

When changing the membership of the Scrum Team, adding members, splitting into multiple Scrum Teams, or adding a new Scrum Team to work on the same product as self-managing teams, the Scrum Team members decide how to re-organize the team members. Typically, the Scrum Master can facilitate the discussion to agree.

4.8.3 Multiple accountabilities

Can a Product Owner also work as a Developer in a Scrum Team? Can Scrum Master work as a Developer too in a Scrum Team?

The Scrum Guide does not forbid a Product Owner or Scrum Master to work also as Developer. However, product Owner, Developers, and Scrum Master are not meant to be titles or positions. Instead, they are accountabilities for which someone in the Scrum Team will be accountable.

However, in general, this is not considered a good practice as it will likely affect the focus and increase the context switching of that member.

It is recommended that one member can focus on one accountability and one Product at a time. This is easier in a big team, but it could be challenging in a very small team.

Let's say that John, Monica, and Daniel are three Developers working for a company, but they have a great idea for a VR game. They start working on the project using Scrum during their free time. They don't have any budget and will not hire anyone else. The three of them want to write code to make progress on the working software. However, John is very good at creating a vision and talking to stakeholders, and Monica always liked processes and facilitating. Daniel has the most knowledge of the technology, and he can lead the technical development. Therefore, John will take the Product Owner accountability, Monica will take the Scrum Master accountability, and Daniel will only take the Developer accountability. However, John and Monica will also take Developer accountabilities. As long as this works well for the team and can satisfy their accountabilities, the Scrum Team should be fine. If the team encounters problems with accountabilities, it should reflect in the retrospective and find alternatives.

4.8.4 Being a member of more than one team

The Scrum Guide does not forbid a Product Owner, Developer or Scrum Master to work for multiple Scrum Teams.

It is allowed that one Product Owner, Scrum Master, or Developers work for two or more teams. It is also allowed a Product Owner to work with more than one Product.

However, this is not considered a good practice as it will likely affect the focus and increase the context switching of that member.

On the other hand, if a team becomes too large, it may be split into several teams working for one Product, one Product Backlog, one Product Goal, and with one Product Owner. In that case, one Product Owner will work with many Scrum Teams for one Product. This situation can be very challenging for one Product Owner.

Scrum does not address the problem, but frameworks like Scrum@scale include a structure to scale the Product Owner accountability.

4.9 Feature Teams vs. Component Teams

These two approaches differ in how the Developers organize and assign work.

4.9.1.1 Feature Teams

Feature Teams are cross-functional teams that are organized around features or user stories. Each Feature Team is responsible for delivering a complete feature, including all the development work required to implement the feature, such as design, coding, testing, and documentation. Feature Teams are highly collaborative and work together to ensure the feature is delivered to a high standard.

For example, the Developers deliver a web page to select and compare products. For that, Developers build the User interface, business logic, and data queries and modify the necessary database schema. That scenario is aligned with the idea of cross-functional teams described and preferred by Scrum, as the team has all the skills to deliver value.

Cross-functional teams are preferred because they can deliver front-to-back working and valuable products. Delivering valuable functional products requires several layers/components to deliver a single feature.

Feature teams don't depend on third parties to deliver and have all the skills necessary to create value for each Sprint.

When Multiple Scrum Teams work together on the same product, all Scrum Teams must be cross-functional. Also, when multiple Feature Teams work together for the same product, they can provide value independently while collaborating effectively on the shared vision.

4.9.1.2 Component Teams

Component Teams are organized around specific components or technical areas of the product. Each Component Team is responsible for a specific part of the product, such as the user interface or the database layer. Component Teams are often made up of specialists with deep technical expertise in a specific area. Work is assigned to Component Teams based on the technical requirements of the product.

An example of two Component Teams working for the same product in Scrum could be a team responsible for the database layer and a team responsible for the user interface. Both teams would be working on different technical components of the product but would need to ensure that their work is properly integrated with the other and the rest of the product. While each team may feel they can focus on the technical aspects better, their focus may be too technical, and they may struggle to provide meaningful value to the end users.

One challenge for these Component Teams could be a lack of visibility into each other's work, leading to integration issues and delays in delivering value to the end user. For example, the UI team may have a feature that requires changes to the database schema but may not fully understand the implications of those changes on the database team's work. Similarly, the database team may change the schema that impacts the UI team's work but may not fully understand the implications of those changes on the UI. Therefore, multiple component teams working for the same product will struggle to provide value independently.

This challenge can be related to the type of cohesion called Sequential Cohesion. Sequential Cohesion is a type of cohesion where individuals work together sequentially, where the output of one individual or team is the input of another individual or team. In the case of the UI and database Component Teams, their work is sequential, and they need to work closely together to ensure that their work is properly integrated and aligned with the rest of the product.

4.9.1.3 Advantages and disadvantages

Feature teams create increments with vertical slices of the functionality of the product. They work in all the layers of the Product.

Component teams create modules of horizontal slices of a technical layer of the product.

A feature team can create an increment of value, while a component team typically needs to integrate its work with other modules to create value.

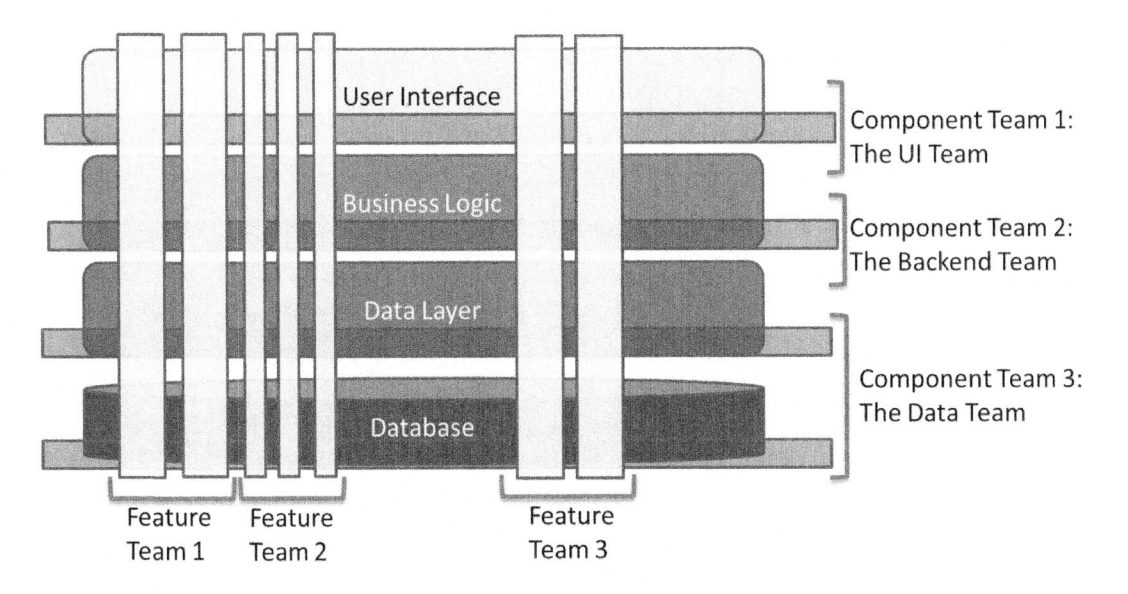

Figure 16 Feature teams vs. Component Teams.

There are advantages and disadvantages to both approaches:

Advantages of Feature Teams:

- Cross-functional teams are highly collaborative and can deliver features quickly and efficiently.
- Feature Teams can provide a better customer focus, focusing on delivering complete features that meet customer needs.
- Feature Teams encourage product ownership, as each team is responsible for delivering a complete feature.

Disadvantages of Feature Teams:

- Feature Teams require high coordination and communication to ensure that work is properly integrated and dependencies are managed.
- Feature Teams can be more difficult to manage, as they require high trust and collaboration between team members.

Advantages of Component Teams:

- Component Teams can be more efficient for highly technical products, as work can be assigned based on technical requirements.
- Component Teams can provide a deeper level of technical expertise as team members specialize in specific areas.
- Component Teams can be easier to manage, as work is assigned based on specific components or technical areas.

Disadvantages of Component Teams:

- Component Teams can lead to silos, as team members focus on their specific area rather than the overall product.

- Component Teams can lead to integration issues, as work from different teams may not be properly integrated and tested.
- Component Teams can be less customer-focused, as work is assigned based on technical requirements rather than customer needs.

4.9.1.4 Moving from a Component team to a feature team

When moving from component teams to feature teams, changes in teams and membership always affect productivity. Gradually feature teams will become more productive as people from the different layers and components will get used to delivering unified functionality together as one Scrum Team. The Business Value is also likely to increase gradually. The Scrum Master should not re-organize people but let them decide how to re-arrange teams to cover all the skills of self-managing teams.

4.10 A Mature, High-performing Scrum Team

A mature Scrum team or a team in the performing stage of group development has developed high efficiency, effectiveness, and cohesion in executing the Scrum framework.

Notice that the qualitative signs and quantitative metrics are a reference and great opportunities to celebrate. However, it might be difficult for a team to outperform in all these areas at the same time.

4.10.1 Qualitative signs

Qualitative signs that a Scrum team is mature include:

1. Customer Focus: The team has a strong customer focus, understanding the needs and requirements of the customer and delivering a product that meets or exceeds their expectations.
2. Self-Managing: The team has developed the ability to self-organize and determine how to best accomplish their goals without needing external guidance or direction.
3. Collaborative: The team has developed a culture of collaboration and trust where team members openly share ideas, concerns, and feedback. The team embodies and lives the Scrum Values.
4. Continuous Improvement: The team actively seeks to identify areas for improvement and makes incremental changes to its processes and practices to increase efficiency and effectiveness.
5. Autonomy: The team makes decisions and takes ownership of their work without needing micromanagement or oversight.
6. High Productivity: The team consistently delivers high-quality products that meet customer needs and business goals within the agreed-upon timeframes.
7. Adaptable: The team has the ability to adapt quickly to changing requirements or circumstances and can pivot their approach to ensure they are delivering the

most value. The team is focused on meeting goals and can adapt the scope as necessary to meet them on time.
8. Clear Accountabilities and Responsibilities: The team members clearly understand their roles and responsibilities within the team and can work together seamlessly to achieve their goals.
9. Empowered: The team feels empowered to make decisions and take actions that will contribute to the product's success and the organization as a whole.
10. Continuous Learning: The team is committed to ongoing learning and development and regularly seeks new knowledge and skills to improve performance.

4.10.2 *Quantitative metrics*

Several quantitative metrics can indicate that a Scrum Team has matured:

1. Consistent Velocity: The team consistently delivers a predictable amount of work each Sprint, indicating a high level of understanding and ability to estimate accurately.
2. Reduced Cycle Time: The time it takes to complete a user story or feature decreases over time, indicating that the team is becoming more efficient and effective at their work. The Lead time is decreasing. The mean time to repair and Time to Restore Service are decreasing.
3. Increase commitment to improvements: The number of improvements selected from the Retrospective vs. the improvements implemented per Sprint is increasing. As a result, the time to remove Impediments decreases.
4. Increased Throughput: The number of Product Backlog items or features completed per Sprint increases over time, indicating that the team can handle more work and is becoming more productive.
5. Improved Quality: The number of bugs or defects found after a Sprint decreases over time, indicating that the team is becoming more skilled at producing high-quality work. The team regularly adapts the Definition of Done to increase the quality standards. The production incident count is decreasing. Technical Debt decreases. Change Failure Rate decreases.
6. High Team Morale: Team members are happy, motivated, and engaged in their work, indicating a positive team culture and high levels of collaboration and communication. Low turnover rate, Positive feedback, Low absenteeism, etc.
7. High rate of meeting the Sprint Goal: Increase the number of times the Scrum Team meets the Sprint Goal. This can be measured by tracking the percentage of Sprints where the Sprint Goal was met or exceeded.
8. Release frequency increases Increments per Sprint: The percentage or number of Sprints that the Scrum Team delivers at least one Increment with one or more valuable features to the users every Sprint increased. The Scrum Team can release an increment at any time, or the release or deployment frequency increases. Active product code branches are decreasing. Time spent switching

contexts is decreasing. The innovation rate is increasing. Build and Integration Frequency increases.
9. Rise in customer satisfaction: The Customer Satisfaction metrics are increasing. These metrics will indicate if they are providing value through the product. The Customer satisfaction gap is decreasing. The Customer usage index is increasing. The Desired customer experience gap is decreasing.

It's important to note that these metrics should be used with qualitative assessments of the team's performance and should not be the sole measure of a team's maturity.

4.11 Other roles outside the Scrum Team

The Scrum Team consists of the Product Owner, Developers, and the Scrum Master. However, several other roles outside of the Scrum Team interact with it and play a vital role in the product's success. Some of these roles include:

1. Stakeholders: These are individuals or groups interested in the project and its outcomes. They can include customers, users, managers, executives, investors, and regulatory bodies. The Scrum Team must engage with stakeholders to understand and incorporate their needs and expectations into the product development process.
2. Customers and Users: These individuals will ultimately use the product being developed. The Scrum Team must engage with customers and users to understand their needs, preferences, and pain points. This helps to ensure that the product delivers value to its intended audience.
3. Organization: The Scrum Team operates within the larger organizational context, which includes policies, procedures, and culture. The organization must support the Scrum Team by providing the necessary resources, removing obstacles, and facilitating collaboration across teams and departments.
4. Managers and Executives: These individuals are responsible for setting the organization's strategic direction and overseeing its operations. They play a critical role in providing the necessary environment, support, and resources for the Scrum Team to deliver value to the organization. They should also fully empower the Scrum Team to achieve the goals.
5. CEO: The CEO is the highest-ranking executive in the organization and is responsible for setting the overall vision and direction. The CEO plays a critical role in creating a culture that supports Scrum and empowering the Scrum Team to deliver value to the organization.

In summary, the success of a Scrum Team depends on the collaboration and engagement of all stakeholders, both within and outside the Scrum Team. Therefore, the Scrum Team must work closely with stakeholders to understand their needs and expectations and incorporate them into the product development process. In addition, the organization, managers, and executives must provide the necessary support and resources to enable the Scrum Team to deliver value to the organization.

4.12 Anti-patterns of the Scrum Team

Here are some common Scrum team antipatterns:

1. Lack of collaboration: When team members work in silos, fail to communicate effectively, or don't share knowledge and skills, it can lead to reduced productivity, duplication of effort, and suboptimal outcomes.
2. Micromanagement: When the Product Owner or Scrum Master dictates how the team should work or what they should focus on, it can lead to resentment, reduced motivation, and lack of ownership and accountability among team members.
3. Lack of focus: When team members take on too many tasks or work on items not aligned with the Sprint goal, it can reduce productivity, missed deadlines, and result in poor quality outcomes.
4. Lack of trust: When team members do not trust each other or are not trusted by the Product Owner or Scrum Master, it can lead to a lack of collaboration, reduced transparency, and suboptimal outcomes.
5. Lack of engagement: When team members are not actively engaged in the Sprint events, fail to attend or participate, or are not committed to the Sprint goal, it can lead to reduced productivity, missed deadlines, and poor quality outcomes.
6. Lack of alignment: When team members have different priorities or goals, it can lead to conflicts, duplication of effort, and suboptimal outcomes.
7. Lack of continuous improvement: When the team does not regularly reflect on its practices, identify areas for improvement, and take action to implement changes, it can lead to stagnation, reduced productivity, and missed opportunities for improvement.

These antipatterns can significantly impact the Scrum team's effectiveness and can lead to suboptimal outcomes. Therefore, the Scrum Team should be aware of these antipatterns and take action to address them to optimize their performance and achieve their goals.

Part 5: Developers

Developers are the people in the Scrum Team that are committed to creating any aspect of a usable Increment each Sprint. The specific skills needed by the Developers are often broad and will vary with the domain of work.

In Scrum, the Developers are the Scrum Team members responsible for creating a usable product increment during each Sprint. They are the ones making changes in the Product as Increments. The Developers work together to design, build, and test the product increment, using their collective skills and expertise to deliver high-quality work.

The Developers are committed to delivering a usable increment of product each Sprint, which means they focus on creating working software that can be tested, demonstrated, and potentially released to customers. In addition, they are responsible for implementing the Product Backlog items identified by the Product Owner and ensuring that they meet the Definition of Done, a set of criteria defining what it means for a Product Backlog item to be "done."

The Developers in a Scrum team are cross-functional and self-organizing, meaning they have a wide range of skills and are responsible for managing their own work. They collaborate closely with other Scrum Team members, such as the Product Owner and the Scrum Master, to ensure that the product increment meets the customer's needs and aligns with the overall product vision.

> *However, the Developers are always accountable for:*
>
> - *Creating a plan for the Sprint, the Sprint Backlog;*
> - *Instilling quality by adhering to a Definition of Done;*
> - *Adapting their plan each day toward the Sprint Goal; and,*
> - *Holding each other accountable as professionals.*

In Scrum, Developers are accountable for several key responsibilities throughout the Sprint. These responsibilities include:

- Creating a plan for the Sprint: The Developers work with the Product Owner and other stakeholders to create a plan for the Sprint that identifies the Product Backlog items to be delivered and the tasks required to complete them. Next, they create a Sprint Backlog, which is a prioritized list of items that they will work on during the Sprint.
- Instilling quality by adhering to a Definition of Done: The Developers are responsible for ensuring that the Product Backlog items they deliver meet the Definition of Done, a set of criteria defining what it means for an item to be considered "done." In addition, they are accountable for delivering high-quality work that meets these criteria, such as completing testing, documentation, and other requirements.
- Adapting their plan each day toward the Sprint Goal: The Developers hold the Daily Scrum event to discuss progress toward the Sprint goal and to adapt their plan based on feedback and changes in circumstances. They are accountable for adjusting their work plan as needed to ensure that they are making progress toward the Sprint goal.
- Holding each other accountable as professionals: The Developers are accountable for holding each other accountable to the commitments they make during the Sprint. They work collaboratively to ensure everyone does their part

to deliver the Product Backlog items and meet the Sprint goal. They also take ownership of their work and strive to improve their professional skills and abilities.

In summary, the Developers in a Scrum team are accountable for a wide range of responsibilities that are critical to the success of the Sprint. By working together and holding each other accountable, they can deliver high-quality work that meets the customer's needs and contributes to the overall product's success.

5.1 Creating a Plan for the Sprint

Developers are responsible for creating a Sprint plan, including creating the Sprint Backlog.

The Sprint Backlog is a list of items the Developers plan to deliver during the Sprint. It is created based on the Product Backlog items selected for the Sprint and is updated as needed throughout the Sprint. In addition, the Sprint Backlog includes a set of tasks required to complete each Product Backlog item.

The Developers work with the Product Owner and other stakeholders to create the Sprint Backlog. They also consider the capacity of the team and the Sprint length to forecast that the Sprint Backlog is achievable within the given time frame.

Once the Sprint Backlog is created, the Developers are accountable for delivering the items on the list and ensuring they meet the Definition of Done. In addition, they are responsible for managing their own work and collaborating to ensure that the Sprint Backlog is completed on time and to the satisfaction of the Product Owner.

Generally, the Developers are accountable for creating a plan for the Sprint and the Sprint Backlog, which is essential to the product's success. By working collaboratively to create a realistic plan, they can ensure that they are progressing toward the Sprint goal and delivering value to the customer.

5.2 Instilling quality by adhering to a Definition of Done

Developers are accountable for instilling quality in the product by adhering to a Definition of Done (DoD).

The DoD is a shared understanding among the Scrum team of what it means for a Product Backlog item to be considered "done." The DoD typically includes a set of criteria that the Developers must meet to ensure that a Product Backlog item is complete and meets the team's standards for quality.

The DoD may include requirements such as completing all necessary testing, ensuring that the code is well-documented, adhering to coding standards, and ensuring that the Product Backlog item meets the acceptance criteria agreed upon with the Scrum Team.

The Developers are responsible for ensuring they meet the DoD for each Product Backlog item they deliver. This means they must perform the necessary testing, documentation, and other quality assurance activities to ensure the Product Backlog item is complete and meets the team's standards.

By adhering to the DoD, the Developers ensure that the product they deliver is high quality and meets the customer's needs. They are accountable for delivering high-quality work that meets the team's standards for excellence.

The Developers are accountable for instilling quality in the product by adhering to the DoD. This is essential to the product's success and ensures that the product delivered is of the highest quality possible.

5.3 Adapting their plan each day toward the Sprint Goal

Developers are accountable for adapting their plan each day toward the Sprint goal. This is an essential part of the Scrum framework, which emphasizes adaptability and flexibility in response to changing circumstances.

The Developers hold Daily Scrum, also known informally as daily standup meetings, to discuss progress and plan their work for the day. During these meetings, they discuss what they accomplished the previous day, what they plan to accomplish today, and any obstacles or impediments they face that may impact their progress.

These meetings aim to ensure that the team is working together effectively and progressing toward the Sprint goal. The Developers are accountable for adapting their plan daily based on the feedback and information they receive during the Daily Scrum.

For example, suppose a developer has difficulty completing a task or encounters an unexpected issue. In that case, they may need to adjust their plan for the day to address the issue and ensure they are progressing toward the Sprint goal. In addition, they may need to collaborate with other team members or seek assistance from the Scrum Master or Product Owner to overcome the obstacle.

By adapting their plan each day, the Developers ensure that they are progressing toward the Sprint goal and delivering value to the customer. They are accountable for managing their own work and collaborating with others to ensure the Sprint succeeds.

In summary, the Developers are accountable for adapting their plan each day toward the Sprint goal, which is essential to the product's success. By remaining flexible and adaptable, they can overcome obstacles and ensure that they are making progress toward delivering a high-quality product.

5.4 Holding each other

In Scrum, Developers are accountable for holding each other accountable as professionals. This means they are responsible for ensuring that all team members perform their duties to the best of their ability and follow the Scrum framework.

Holding each other accountable as professionals involves several key responsibilities. First, the Developers are responsible for ensuring they are all working collaboratively and communicating effectively. This means they must be open and honest with each other, providing constructive feedback and support when necessary.

Second, the Developers are responsible for ensuring that all team members adhere to the Scrum framework and follow the established processes and procedures. This means they must hold each other accountable for meeting the framework's requirements, such as attending the Daily Scrum meetings, delivering on commitments, and adhering to the Definition of Done.

Third, the Developers are responsible for ensuring that everyone on the team performs their duties to the best of their ability. This means they must hold each other accountable for producing high-quality work, meeting deadlines, and contributing to the overall product's success.

By holding each other accountable as professionals, the Developers ensure that the team works collaboratively and effectively and that everyone meets their obligations and contributes to the product's success. This accountability helps to ensure that the team can deliver high-quality products that meet the customer's needs and that the project is completed on time and within budget.

Overall, the Developers are accountable for holding each other accountable as professionals, which is essential to the success of the Scrum framework. By working collaboratively and holding each other accountable, they can ensure they progress toward the Sprint Goal and deliver value to the customer.

5.5 Leadership Style of the Developers

In Scrum, the Developers are self-organizing and cross-functional, meaning there is no designated leader within them. However, this does not mean there is no leadership among the Developers.

Leadership within Scrum Developers is shared among team members, and it is based on expertise, influence, and collaboration. Each Developer brings their skills, knowledge, and experience to the team, and they take on leadership roles depending on the situation.

For example, a team member with expertise in a particular area may lead the team in that area of work. Or a team member with strong communication skills may take on a leadership role in facilitating meetings or communicating with stakeholders. This shared leadership approach allows the team to take ownership of the product and to work collaboratively towards achieving the team's goals.

In summary, the leadership of the Developers is based on shared ownership, collaboration, and expertise. Team members take on leadership roles based on their strengths and the team's needs, and they work together to achieve the team's goals.

5.6 Stances of the Developers

We cannot generalize the leadership style of Developers of a Scrum Team, as it can vary depending on their personalities, skills, and responsibilities within the team. However, in Scrum, the focus is on collaboration, self-organization, and shared ownership of the product, which can influence the leadership style of Developers. Therefore, certain characteristics or traits can help Developers to be effective in the team. Some of these traits or stances include:

1. Collaborative: Developers in a Scrum team work collaboratively with each other, the Product Owner, and other stakeholders to ensure that the team is aligned and working towards the same goals. They participate in Sprint Planning, daily stand-ups, Sprint Reviews, and retrospectives to ensure everyone is on the same page and working towards the same goals.
2. Self-Organizing: In Scrum, the Developers are responsible for organizing their work and deciding how to achieve their goals best. Developers are encouraged to take ownership of their work and to work together to achieve the team's goals. Developers manage their own tasks.
3. Servant Leadership: Developers in a Scrum team can exhibit servant leadership by focusing on the needs of the team and the product. They can coach or mentor other team members, providing guidance and support where needed.
4. Agile: Developers in a Scrum Team should be agile and able to adapt to changing market conditions, customer needs, and technical constraints. They should be able to pivot the product direction if necessary and be flexible in their approach to product development.
5. Technical Expertise: Developers should have technical expertise in their area of work and be able to share their knowledge with the team. They should be able to provide technical guidance to other team members and ensure that the product is developed with high quality.
6. Continuous Improvement: Developers should be committed to continuous improvement, seeking feedback and finding ways to improve the product, the team's processes, and their skills.
7. Solution-Focused: Developers should be solution-focused, working collaboratively to find solutions to challenges during product development. They should be able to identify and resolve issues and make necessary changes to the product to ensure that it meets the customer's needs.

In summary, the leadership style of Developers in a Scrum team should be focused on collaboration, self-organization, and shared ownership of the product. They should work together to achieve the team's goals and deliver customer value.

5.7 Anti-patterns of the Developers

Here are some common Developers' antipatterns in Scrum:

1. Overcommitting: When Developers commit to more work than they can realistically complete within a Sprint, it can lead to missed deadlines, poor quality outcomes, and reduced trust and credibility with stakeholders.
2. Lack of collaboration: When Developers work in silos, fail to communicate effectively, or don't share knowledge and skills, it can lead to reduced productivity, duplication of effort, and suboptimal outcomes.
3. Lack of ownership: When Developers do not take ownership of their work, fail to follow through on commitments, or lack accountability for their actions, it can lead to missed deadlines, poor quality outcomes, and reduced trust and credibility with stakeholders.
4. Lack of skills or knowledge: When Developers lack the necessary skills or knowledge to complete their work effectively, it can lead to poor quality outcomes, missed deadlines, and reduced productivity.
5. Resistance to change: When Developers resist changing their processes or ways of working, it can lead to stagnation, missed opportunities for improvement, and reduced effectiveness.
6. Lack of engagement: When Developers are not actively engaged in the Sprint events, fail to attend or participate, or are not committed to the Sprint goal, it can lead to reduced productivity, missed deadlines, and poor quality outcomes.
7. Lack of focus: When Developers take on too many tasks or work on items not aligned with the Sprint goal, it can lead to reduced productivity, missed deadlines, and poor quality outcomes.
8. Monopolizing ownership: When one or a few Developers take ownership of all the work items, it can lead to reduced collaboration, duplication of effort, and bottlenecks in Sprint. This can also result in a lack of diversity in perspectives and skills, leading to suboptimal outcomes. All Developers need to share ownership of the work items and collaborate effectively to achieve the Sprint goal.

These antipatterns can significantly impact the effectiveness of the Developers and the Scrum team as a whole. The Developers need to be aware of these antipatterns and take action to address them to optimize their performance and achieve their goals.

Part 6: Product Owner

6.1 Maximizing the value

> *The Product Owner is accountable for maximizing the value of the product resulting from the work of the Scrum Team.*

The Product Owner is accountable for maximizing the value of the product resulting from the work of the Scrum Team. This means that the Product Owner is responsible for ensuring that the product being developed by the Scrum Team meets the customer's needs and provides the greatest possible value.

Maximizing the value of the product involves several key responsibilities. First, the Product Owner is responsible for creating and maintaining the Product Backlog, which is a prioritized list of features and requirements for the product. The Product Owner must work collaboratively with the Scrum Team and other stakeholders to ensure that the Product Backlog is aligned with the overall product vision and strategy.

Second, the Product Owner is responsible for prioritizing the items in the Product Backlog based on their value to the customer. This involves considering factors such as customer needs, market trends, and business goals to determine which items will provide the greatest value to the customer.

Third, the Product Owner is responsible for ensuring that the Scrum Team understands the Product Backlog items and their priorities. This involves communicating effectively with the Scrum Team and providing guidance and support to ensure the team delivers high-quality work that meets the customer's needs.

> *How this is done may vary widely across organizations, Scrum Teams, and individuals.*

The specific strategies and techniques used to maximize the product's value may vary widely across organizations, Scrum Teams, and individuals. Some Product Owners may use data-driven approaches to prioritize the Product Backlog, while others may rely more on intuition and experience. There is no mandatory technique or approach. Regardless of the approach, the Product Owner is accountable for ensuring that the product being developed by the Scrum Team delivers the greatest possible value to the customer.

Overall, the Product Owner plays a critical role in the Scrum framework, and their accountability for maximizing the product's value is essential to the product's success. By working collaboratively with the Scrum Team and other stakeholders, the Product Owner can ensure that the product being developed is meeting the customer's needs and providing the greatest possible value.

6.2 What is value?

In the context of Scrum, value refers to the benefit or worth that a product or service provides to its users or customers. A product or service's value justifies its existence and determines its success.

Many models or frameworks define value. As a reference, we can mention the Evidence-Based Management™ (EBM) Framework.

According to Evidence-Based Management by scrum.org, there are three levels of measurement in the value framework: activities, output, and outcome.

1. Activities:
    a. Activities are the actions that are taken to deliver a product or service.
    b. They are the things that people do, such as coding, testing, designing, or writing documentation.
    c. Examples of activities in software development might include coding a new feature, writing test cases, or creating a user interface design.
2. Outputs:
    a. Outputs are the tangible things created as a result of the activities.
    b. They are the produced artifacts, such as code, documentation, or designs.
    c. Examples of outputs in software development might include a working piece of software, a user manual, or a design specification.
3. Outcomes:
    a. Outcomes are the results that are achieved as a result of the outputs.
    b. They are the behavior, attitudes, or performance changes that occur because of the product or service.
    c. Examples of outcomes in software development might include increased user satisfaction, improved productivity, or reduced support costs.

It is important to note that outcomes are the most important value aspect, as they represent the ultimate impact of the product or service. Activities and outputs are necessary to achieve outcomes, but they are not valuable in and of themselves. The focus should be on delivering outcomes that meet the customer's needs and stakeholders.

According to Evidence-Based Management™ (EBM), there are four types of value that organizations should focus on when delivering products and services:

1. Current Value (CV): This refers to the value a product or service currently provides its customers. It is measured by analyzing customer satisfaction, sales revenue, and other relevant metrics. Example: A software application with high customer satisfaction scores and significant revenue.
2. Unrealized Value (UV): This refers to the potential value that a product or service could provide in the future. It is measured by analyzing customer needs, market trends, and other relevant data. Example: A software application with

untapped potential to attract new customers and increase revenue by adding new features.
3. Time to Market (T2M): This refers to the speed at which a product or service value can be delivered to customers. It is measured by analyzing the time it takes from idea to release. Example: A company that can quickly develop and release new products or services, gaining a competitive advantage by being the first to market.
4. Ability to Innovate (A2I): This refers to an organization's capacity to innovate and improve its products and services continuously. It is measured by analyzing employee engagement, experimentation, and learning factors. We can see it as the amount of value in a given timeframe or goal. Example: A company encouraging employees to experiment with new ideas and continuously improve their products or services.

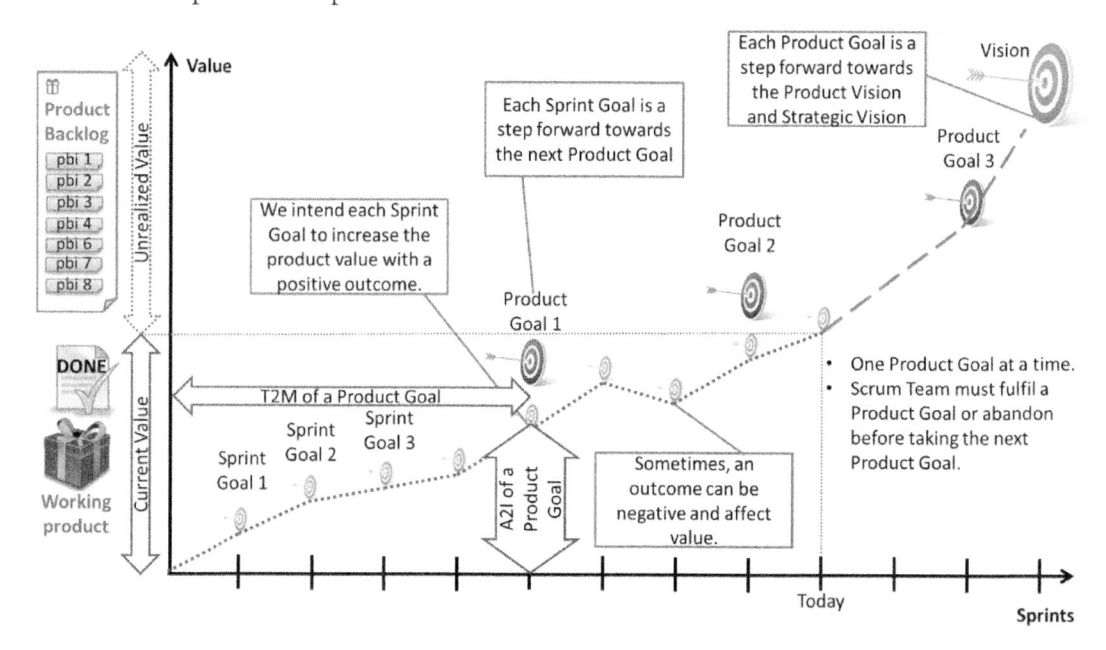

Figure 17 Creating value through Sprints.

6.3 Example of value

The features "Mobile app redesign" and "Add new payment options" are at the top of the Product Backlog of an e-commerce platform. The CEO is pushing to start a "Mobile app redesign" to improve the user experience and potentially attract more customers. Conversely, if "Add new payment options" is not implemented, the product will lose many customers who prefer to use those options. Implementing this feature requires four weeks and collaboration with the finance department to integrate the new payment options. "Mobile app redesign" is a change to improve the user interface and add new features to the mobile app. The main stakeholders are aware of it and request it to improve user engagement. Implementing this feature requires eight weeks of collaboration with external designers, other teams, and user groups.

The best value choice for the Product Owner depends on various factors, such as business objectives, user needs, and technical feasibility. In the example above, the Product Owner should prioritize "Add new payment options" over "Mobile app redesign" because it addresses a critical customer need and directly impacts the product's revenue.

Product Backlog:

- Add new payment options
- Mobile app redesign

By implementing new payment options, the product can retain customers who prefer those options and attract new customers who were previously hesitant to use the product. This will lead to increased revenue and customer satisfaction.

On the other hand, while "Mobile app redesign" can improve the user experience and engagement, it may not immediately impact revenue or customer retention. However, the Product Owner should still consider the long-term benefits of this feature and ensure that it is prioritized appropriately in the future.

In summary, the best value choice for the Product Owner is to balance the short-term and long-term objectives of the product and prioritize features that deliver the most value to the customers and the business.

6.4 Product Backlog management

The Product Owner is also accountable for effective Product Backlog management, which includes:

- *Developing and explicitly communicating the Product Goal;*
- *Creating and clearly communicating Product Backlog items;*
- *Ordering Product Backlog items; and,*
- *Ensuring that the Product Backlog is transparent, visible and understood.*

The Product Backlog is a living document constantly refined and updated as the project progresses.

The Product Owner is accountable for effective Product Backlog management, which includes several key responsibilities. First, the Product Owner must work with stakeholders and the Scrum team to develop a clear product vision and goals. The product vision and Product Goal should provide a shared understanding of what the product is and why it is being developed. The goals should provide a set of clear, measurable objectives that the team can work towards.

Second, the Product Owner creates and maintains the Product Backlog. This involves breaking down the product vision into smaller, manageable items that the Developers can work on. Ideally, each Product Backlog item should be independent, negotiable, valuable, estimable, small, and testable. The Product Owner should also ensure that the Product Backlog is prioritized. For instance, the Product Owner may prioritize based on business value, with the most valuable user stories at the top of the list.

Third, the Product Owner must collaborate closely with the Developers to ensure the Product Backlog is understood and refined as needed. This involves regularly reviewing and updating the Product Backlog and working with the Developers to clarify requirements, resolve issues, and identify dependencies.

Finally, the Product Owner is responsible for ensuring the Product Backlog is transparent and visible to the Scrum team. This involves ensuring that the Product Backlog is easily accessible and understandable by everyone on the team and that any changes or updates to the backlog are communicated effectively.

On the whole, effective Product Backlog management is critical to the success of Scrum, and the Product Owner plays a key role in ensuring that the backlog is effectively managed, refined, and prioritized throughout the product lifecycle.

> *The Product Owner may do the above work or may delegate the responsibility to others. Regardless, the Product Owner remains accountable.*

The Product Owner is responsible for managing the Product Backlog, which includes developing and communicating the product vision, creating and prioritizing Product Backlog items, and collaborating with the Developers to refine and update the backlog.

However, it is not necessary that the Product Owner personally carry out all these tasks. The Product Owner may delegate some or all of the Product Backlog management responsibilities to others, such as the Scrum Master or Developers.

Regardless of whether the Product Owner personally manages the Product Backlog or delegates the responsibility to others, the Product Owner remains accountable for the overall management and success of the Product Backlog. This means that even if the Product Owner allows others to change the Product Backlog, the Product Owner is ultimately responsible for ensuring that the Product Backlog is aligned with the product vision, reflects the priorities of the stakeholders, and is clearly understood by the Developers.

Furthermore, the Product Owner is responsible for ensuring the Developers have the information and resources they need to deliver the product increments during each Sprint successfully. This includes making sure that Product Backlog items are well-defined, dependencies are clearly understood, and the Developers have access to any necessary resources or subject matter experts.

In summary, the Product Owner may delegate some or all of the Product Backlog management responsibilities to others. However, they are still accountable for the product's success and ensuring that it supports the Product Goal and stakeholder priorities. The Product Owner is also responsible for providing the Developers with the information and resources they need to deliver the product increments during each Sprint successfully.

6.5 Own the product

> *For Product Owners to succeed, the entire organization must respect their decisions.*

For the Product Owner to be successful in their role, the entire organization must respect their decisions. This means that the Product Owner's decisions about the product and priorities must be trusted and supported by everyone in the organization, including senior management, stakeholders, and Developers.

When the Product Owner's decisions are respected, they can make the necessary trade-offs and decisions about what work should be done and when based on the priorities and needs of the business. This allows the Product Owner to focus on delivering value to customers and stakeholders and to ensure that the product meets the market's needs.

However, if the organization does not respect the Product Owner's decisions, it can lead to confusion and conflict within the team, ultimately undermining the product's success. When the Product Owner's decisions are not respected, it can lead to delays, misaligned priorities, and a lack of trust between the Product Owner and other stakeholders.

Therefore, it is important for organizations to recognize the critical role that the Product Owner plays in the product's success and to ensure that they are supported and respected in their role. This includes providing the necessary resources and support to enable the Product Owner to make informed decisions and fostering a culture of trust and collaboration across the organization.

> *These decisions are visible in the content and ordering of the Product Backlog, and through the inspectable Increment at the Sprint Review.*

The Product Owner's Product decisions are visible in the content and ordering of the Product Backlog. The content of the Product Backlog reflects the priorities and needs of the business, as well as the Product Owner's decisions about what features or functionality should be included in the product. The Product Owner decides which Product Backlog items should be included in the Product Backlog based on factors such as the overall product vision, customer needs, market trends, and other relevant factors.

In addition to the content of the Product Backlog, the Product Owner's decisions are also reflected in the ordering of the Product Backlog. The Product Owner is responsible for prioritizing the Product Backlog normally based on business value, with the most valuable user stories at the top of the list. This prioritization reflects the Product Owner's decisions about which features or functionality are most important to the business and which should be developed first.

The Product Owner's decisions are also visible through the inspectable Increment at the Sprint Review. The Sprint Review is an event held at the end of each Sprint, where the Scrum Team presents the Increment of the product completed during the Sprint. The Increment is the sum of all the completed user stories and reflects the Product Owner's decisions about what work should be completed during the Sprint.

During the Sprint Review, the Scrum Team and stakeholders inspect the Increment and provide feedback on whether it meets the business's expectations and needs. The Product Owner's decisions are reflected in the feedback they provide and any changes or updates they request for the Product Backlog.

6.6 The decision maker

> *The Product Owner is one person, not a committee. The Product Owner may represent the needs of many stakeholders in the Product Backlog. Those wanting to change the Product Backlog can do so by trying to convince the Product Owner.*

The Product Owner is the one who ultimately makes decisions about what work should be done and when based on the priorities and needs of the business.

It is important to note that the Product Owner is one person, not a committee. This means the Product Owner is the sole decision-maker regarding the Product Backlog and the product's direction. While the Product Owner may represent the needs of many stakeholders in the Product Backlog, they are ultimately responsible for making decisions that best serve the business and the product vision.

If multiple people make decisions about the product, it can lead to disagreements about what work should be done and how it should be prioritized. This can lead to delays in the project and a lack of clarity and direction for the team.

If someone wants to change the Product Backlog, they must convince the Product Owner. This means that anyone who wants to add, remove, or change a feature or functionality in the product must work with the Product Owner to make their case. This may involve providing data or research to support the change or demonstrating how the change aligns with the overall product vision and goals.

However, the Product Owner has the final say in all decisions related to the Product Backlog. While they may take input and feedback from stakeholders, the Product Owner is the one who ultimately decides what work should be done and when.

6.7 Collaboration with Stakeholders

> *The Product Owner may represent the needs of many stakeholders in the Product Backlog.*

The Product Owner is responsible for collaborating with stakeholders to ensure that the Product Backlog reflects the needs and priorities of the business. The Product Owner works with stakeholders throughout the project to gather feedback, clarify requirements, and ensure that the product meets the market's needs.

There are several ways in which the Product Owner can collaborate with stakeholders:

- Gathering feedback: The Product Owner works with stakeholders to gather feedback on the Product Backlog, including new feature requests, changes in business requirements, and feedback on existing features.
- Prioritizing requirements: The Product Owner works with stakeholders to prioritize requirements based on business value, with the most valuable requirements at the top of the Product Backlog.
- Providing updates: The Product Owner provides regular updates to stakeholders on the progress of the project, including updates on the Product Backlog, the Developers' progress, and any issues or risks that have been identified.
- Demonstrating progress: The Product Owner works with the Scrum Team to demonstrate progress on the product during each Sprint, providing stakeholders with a preview of the product and an opportunity to provide feedback.
- Facilitating communication: The Product Owner facilitates communication between the Developers and stakeholders, ensuring that everyone has a clear understanding of the product vision, requirements, and priorities.

The Product Owner can collaborate with stakeholders outside of Scrum events. In fact, it is important for the Product Owner to work with stakeholders throughout Sprint to gather feedback, clarify requirements, and ensure that the product meets the market's needs.

In summary, the Product Owner should collaborate with stakeholders throughout the project, both during Scrum events and outside of them, to ensure that the Product Backlog reflects the needs and priorities of the business and that the product is meeting the needs of the market.

6.8 Collaboration with Developers

Collaboration between the Product Owner and Developers during the Sprint is critical to ensure that the team is working towards a common goal and avoiding surprises at the Sprint's end.

For instance, if during the Sprint Review, the implementation done by the Developers is not what the Product Owner expected, it is a sign that the Product Owner and Developers are not collaborating enough.

Here are some ways in which the Product Owner can collaborate with Developers during the Sprint:

- Attend Sprint events: The Product Owner should attend all relevant Sprint events, such as Sprint Planning, Sprint Review, and Sprint Retrospective, to ensure that they are aware of the team's progress and any issues or challenges they may be facing. The Product Owner can attend the Daily Scrum as a listener to serve the Developers and clarify details as needed but without affecting the event and responsibility of the Developers to self-organize to achieve the Sprint Goal.
- Provide clear priorities: The Product Owner should provide clear priorities for the team at the beginning of the Sprint and be available to answer any questions or clarify any requirements as needed throughout the Sprint.
- Work with the team to refine the Product Backlog: The Product Owner should work with the team to regularly refine the Product Backlog, ensuring that it is up to date and that the team clearly understands the requirements for each backlog item.
- Collaborate with the team during Sprint Execution: The Product Owner should collaborate with the team during Sprint Execution, answering any questions or concerns that arise and providing feedback on completed work as needed.

By collaborating with Developers during the Sprint in these ways, the Product Owner can help ensure that the team is working effectively and efficiently toward the Sprint goal and that there are no surprises or unexpected roadblocks at the end of the Sprint. This can ultimately lead to higher-quality products, greater stakeholder satisfaction, and improved organizational business outcomes.

6.9 Not responsible for keeping Developers busy

The Product Owner is not responsible for maximizing the utilization of the Developers. The Product Owner's main concern is maximizing the Product's value. Higher utilization does not mean higher value.

For example, a company is developing a new e-commerce platform. The most valuable item in the Product Backlog is the integration with a payment gateway that a third-party provider is developing. The development of this payment gateway is delayed, and the Developers cannot work on this item until the integration is complete. As a result, the Developers request the Product Owner to reorder the Product Backlog to work on other low-priority features that do not require the payment gateway integration.

In this situation, it is important to remember that the Product Owner's primary responsibility is to maximize the value delivered to the stakeholders. The Product Owner is not responsible for keeping the Developers busy but for finding ways to deliver the most valuable items first. The Product Owner can work with the third-party provider to expedite the development of the payment gateway or identify other items in the Product Backlog that can be worked on in the meantime. It is crucial to maintain flexibility in the Product Backlog and adapt to changing circumstances to ensure that the most valuable items are delivered in a timely manner.

6.9.1 Impact of adding low-value items to a Sprint

Suppose there are no high-value items to work on. In that case, Developers can use this time to improve the quality of the product, refactor code, address technical debt, automate tests, or work on any other improvements that could benefit the product in the long run. They can also use this time for personal or professional development, such as learning new skills or attending training sessions. It's important to note that the Scrum framework encourages self-organizing teams, so it's up to the Developers to decide how best to use their time when no high-value items are available to work on.

Adding low-value items to the Product can have several negative impacts on the project, including:

- Waste of time and resources: If the team spends time and resources working on non-valuable items, it can waste effort and budget that could have been utilized for valuable items.
- Delay in delivering valuable items: Prioritizing non-valuable items can cause delays in delivering valuable items, impacting the project timeline and business objectives.
- Decrease in team motivation: Working on non-valuable items can decrease team motivation, as team members may feel that their efforts are not contributing to the product's success.
- Increased technical debt: Working on non-valuable items may lead to shortcuts and compromises in the development process, resulting in an increase in technical debt that can negatively impact product quality.
- Higher complexity: Adding non-valuable items can increase the complexity of the product, making it more difficult to use and maintain.
- Confused users: Users may become confused or frustrated by non-valuable or useless features, leading to decreased satisfaction and slower product adoption. In addition, the product may become harder to use unnecessarily.

Adding non-valuable items to the Product Backlog can harm the product's success. The Product Owner ensures that only the most valuable items are added to the backlog.

6.10 Leadership Style of the Product Owner

The Product Owner can be both a designated and emergent leader.

In some organizations, the Product Owner is a designated leader who is assigned to a position and given the authority to make decisions about the product. They may have formal training in product management and a clear set of responsibilities.

However, in other organizations, the role of the Product Owner can be emergent. This means that the Product Owner may be someone who emerges as a leader on the team, taking on responsibilities for the product and working closely with the Scrum Team to ensure its success. They may not have formal training in product management or a clearly defined set of responsibilities. Still, they have the skills and knowledge necessary to lead the team toward achieving the product vision.

Regardless of whether the Product Owner is a designated or emergent leader, they should have a strong vision for the product, be able to communicate that vision effectively and be able to make tough decisions about the product direction. They should also be collaborative, agile, and able to balance the needs of the business with the needs of the team and the customer.

The leadership style of a Product Owner can vary depending on their personality, the type of product they are managing, and the team they are working with. However, there are some general leadership qualities and styles that are typically associated with effective Product Owners:

- Visionary: A good Product Owner should have a clear and compelling vision for the product and be able to communicate that vision to the team. They should inspire and motivate the team to work towards the vision and ensure everyone is aligned with the overall product direction.
- Servant Leader: A Product Owner should act as a servant leader, putting the needs of the team and the product above their own. They should empower the team to make decisions and provide guidance and support where needed.
- Collaborative: Product Owners should work collaboratively with their teams, stakeholders, and customers to ensure that everyone is aligned and working towards the same goals. They should foster a culture of collaboration and communication and encourage open dialogue and feedback.
- Decisive: A Product Owner should be decisive, making tough decisions about the product and setting priorities. They should be able to make trade-offs between different features and aspects of the product and ensure that the team stays on track to meet deadlines and goals.
- Agile: An effective Product Owner should be agile and able to adapt to changing market conditions, customer needs, and technical constraints. They should be able to pivot the product direction if necessary and be flexible in their approach to product management.

In the end, the leadership style of a Product Owner should be focused on empowering the team, delivering value to the customer, and achieving the overall product vision. They should be able to balance the needs of the business with the needs of the team and the customer and create a culture of innovation and excellence.

6.11 The 6 Stances of a Product Owner

In Scrum, the Product Owner has six key stances to adopt to be effective in their role. Robbin Schuurman first introduced these stances in his blog post titled "The Six Stances of the Product Owner."

The six stances of the Product Owner are:

1. The Visionary: As the Visionary, the Product Owner has a clear and compelling vision for the product. They understand the market and target audience and can communicate the product vision to the team. They set the direction for the product and ensure that everyone is aligned with the overall vision. They inspire stakeholders and the Scrum Team to pursue the vision.
2. The Customer Representative: The Customer Representative stance involves representing the voice of the customer. The Product Owner understands the needs, desires, and pain points of the target audience and advocates for them within the Developers. They gather and analyze customer feedback, conduct market research, and ensure that the product meets the needs of its target audience. It also involves negotiating between multiple interests and points of view.
3. The Experimenter: As an Experimenter, the Product Owner takes a data-driven approach to product development. They use experimentation and testing to validate hypotheses and make informed decisions about the product. They analyze data, measure the impact of changes, and continuously improve the product.
4. The Decision Maker: The Decision Maker's stance involves making tough decisions about the product. The Product Owner sets priorities, makes trade-offs between different features and aspects of the product, and ensures that the team stays on track to meet deadlines and goals.
5. The Influencer: The Influencer stance involves working closely with stakeholders and team members to ensure everyone is aligned with the product vision and goals. The Product Owner influences and persuades others to support the product and its development. They collaborate with stakeholders, build relationships, and negotiate with other departments to ensure the product's success.
6. The Collaborator: As a Collaborator, the Product Owner works closely with the Developers to ensure that the product is delivered on time and meets quality standards. They collaborate with Stakeholders to sponsor the product decisions and vision. They provide guidance and support and remove obstacles that may hinder progress. They foster a culture of collaboration, communication, and trust within the team.

It's important to note that these stances are not mutually exclusive, and a Product Owner may need to switch between them depending on the situation.

These six stances represent the diverse skills and abilities required of the Product Owner to successfully manage the Product Backlog and drive the product's direction. By adopting these stances, the Product Owner can ensure that the product meets the business and market needs while empowering the Scrum Team to deliver value to customers and stakeholders.

6.12 Do you have all the skills?

It is rare for a Product Owner to excel at all six stances equally. However, a good Product Owner should be competent in most of them and strive to improve in areas where they may be lacking.

To cover gaps in their abilities, Product Owners can take several steps, including:

1. Seek feedback: Product Owners can seek feedback from their team, stakeholders, and customers to identify areas where they may need improvement. They can use this feedback to develop a plan to address any gaps in their abilities.
2. Learn from others: Product Owners can learn from other Product Owners who excel in areas where they may be lacking. This could involve attending industry events, participating in online forums, or seeking out mentors.
3. Continuous learning: Product Owners should strive to learn and improve their skills continuously. They can read books, attend workshops, and take online courses to develop new skills and stay up-to-date on industry trends.
4. Practice: Practice makes perfect, and Product Owners can practice their skills by taking on new challenges, working on side projects, or collaborating with other departments within their organization.

By taking these steps, Product Owners can improve their abilities in areas where they may be lacking and become more effective at managing products and leading their teams.

6.13 Anti-patterns of the Product Owner

Here are some common Product Owner antipatterns in Scrum:

1. Lack of vision or strategy: When the Product Owner lacks a clear vision or strategy for the product, it can lead to unclear goals, poorly defined requirements, and suboptimal outcomes.
2. Micromanaging: When the Product Owner micromanages the work of the Developers, it can lead to reduced autonomy and creativity, missed opportunities for improvement, and reduced productivity.
3. Lack of collaboration: When the Product Owner works in silos, fails to communicate effectively, or doesn't collaborate with stakeholders, it can lead to reduced productivity, duplication of effort, and suboptimal outcomes.
4. Inadequate prioritization: When the Product Owner fails to prioritize the Product Backlog effectively, it can lead to missed deadlines, poor quality outcomes, and reduced trust and credibility with stakeholders.
5. Lack of engagement: When the Product Owner is not actively engaged in the Sprint events, fails to attend or participate, or is not committed to the Sprint goal, it can lead to reduced productivity, missed deadlines, and poor quality outcomes.

6. Changing requirements mid-Sprint: When the Product Owner changes requirements mid-Sprint without proper consultation or collaboration with the Developers, it can lead to missed deadlines, poor quality outcomes, and reduced morale and trust within the Scrum team.
7. Lack of transparency: When the Product Owner fails to provide transparency into the product vision, goals, and priorities, it can lead to confusion, misalignment, and reduced engagement and productivity within the Scrum team.
8. Acting as a business analyst: When the Product Owner acts solely as a representative of the stakeholders, rather than taking ownership of the product and making decisions based on their expertise and knowledge, it can lead to suboptimal outcomes, a lack of innovation, and reduced trust and credibility with the Scrum team.

These antipatterns can significantly impact the effectiveness of the Product Owner and the Scrum team as a whole. The Product Owner needs to be aware of these antipatterns and take action to address them to optimize their performance and achieve their goals.

Part 7: Scrum Master

7.1 Scrum as defined in the Scrum Guide

> *The Scrum Master is accountable for establishing Scrum as defined in the Scrum Guide. They do this by helping everyone understand Scrum theory and practice, both within the Scrum Team and the organization.*

The Scrum Master is one person accountable for establishing Scrum as defined in the Scrum Guide, which is the official document that defines the Scrum framework. This accountability is based on the principle of servant-leadership, where the Scrum Master serves the needs of the Scrum Team and the organization by ensuring that Scrum is implemented effectively and consistently.

To establish Scrum as defined in the Scrum Guide, the Scrum Master may take on a range of responsibilities as needed, including:

1. Educating the Scrum Team: The Scrum Master helps the Scrum Team to understand the theory, values, principles, and practices of Scrum. In addition, they facilitate workshops, training sessions, and other activities to ensure that everyone has a solid understanding of Scrum.
2. Coaching the Scrum Team: The Scrum Master coaches the Scrum Team to apply Scrum in their work, helping them to improve and optimize their performance continuously. They provide guidance, feedback, and support, helping the team to overcome obstacles and achieve their goals.

3. Ensuring Compliance with the Scrum Framework: The Scrum Master ensures that the Scrum Team follows the Scrum framework, including the roles, events, artifacts, and rules of Scrum. In addition, they help the team to understand and apply the framework effectively and to improve their practices within the framework continuously.
4. Facilitating Scrum Events: The Scrum Master facilitates Scrum events, such as Sprint Planning, Daily Scrum, Sprint Review, and Sprint Retrospective. They ensure that these events are effective and efficient and provide value to the Scrum Team and the organization.
5. Promoting Scrum: The Scrum Master promotes Scrum across the organization, helping stakeholders to understand the benefits of Scrum and how it can be applied to different areas of the business. They work closely with other Scrum Masters, Agile Coaches, and leaders in the organization to ensure that Scrum is adopted and implemented effectively.

Overall, the Scrum Master is responsible for establishing Scrum as defined in the Scrum Guide, ensuring that it is implemented effectively and consistently across the Scrum Team and the organization. Therefore, the Scrum Master's accountability for establishing Scrum is essential for the success of the Scrum Team and the organization as a whole.

7.2 Scrum Team's effectiveness

The Scrum Master is accountable for the Scrum Team's effectiveness. They do this by enabling the Scrum Team to improve its practices, within the Scrum framework.

The Scrum Master is accountable for the Scrum Team's effectiveness, meaning they are responsible for ensuring that the team can improve and deliver value to the customer and the organization. This accountability is based on the principle of servant-leadership, where the Scrum Master serves the needs of the Scrum Team to enable them to achieve their goals.

To ensure the Scrum Team's effectiveness, the Scrum Master takes on a range of responsibilities, including:

1. Ensuring that the Scrum framework is understood and applied: The Scrum Master is responsible for ensuring that the Scrum framework is understood and applied consistently across the team. They help the team understand the principles and practices of Scrum and ensure that the team follows the Scrum framework.
2. Facilitating Scrum events: The Scrum Master is responsible for facilitating Scrum events such as Sprint Planning, Daily Scrum, Sprint Review, and Sprint Retrospective. They ensure that these events are effective and provide value to the Scrum Team and the organization.
3. Coaching and Mentoring the Scrum Team: The Scrum Master coaches and mentors the Scrum Team, helping team members to improve their skills and to

work effectively within the Scrum framework. They provide guidance, feedback, and support to team members and help them to overcome obstacles that may hinder their effectiveness.
4. Removing impediments: The Scrum Master is responsible for identifying and removing impediments that may prevent the team from achieving its goals. They work closely with the Product Owner and the Developers to ensure that any impediments are addressed and resolved promptly.
5. Promoting Self-Organization: The Scrum Master promotes self-organization within the Scrum Team, empowering the team to make decisions and take ownership of their work. They help the team to develop their skills and expertise and to work collaboratively towards achieving their goals.
6. Promoting continuous improvement: The Scrum Master promotes continuous improvement within the Scrum Team, encouraging experimentation and learning. In addition, they facilitate retrospectives, which provide opportunities for the team to reflect on their work and identify areas for improvement.

In summary, the Scrum Master plays a critical role in ensuring the effectiveness of the Scrum Team. They are responsible for creating a supportive and collaborative work environment, removing obstacles, and promoting continuous improvement. The Scrum Master's accountability for the Scrum Team's effectiveness is essential for the success of the team and the organization.

7.3 Servant Leadership

7.3.1 A True Leader who serves

> *Scrum Masters are true leaders who serve the Scrum Team and the larger organization.*

One thing to mention is that Scrum Guide 2017 used the term "Servant Leader," but in Scrum Guide 2020, it was updated to "Leader who serves."

According to Jeff Sutherland, JJ Sutherland, Avi Schneier, and the Scrum Inc. Team, in the blog post, "2020 Scrum Guide Changes and Updates Explained", they say:

> *"This change will undoubtedly catch many by surprise. But don't be fooled, the reordering of these words better captures the purpose and accountabilities the Scrum Master has always had."*

> *"Understanding this expanded role of the Scrum Master is key to understanding why we replaced 'servant leader' with the term 'leader who serves.*

> *"By going from 'servant leader' to 'leaders who serve,' we've emphasized the leadership aspects of a Scrum Master. We have no intention of creating a hierarchy inside the Scrum Team. Nor are we saying the Scrum Master is now a manager."*

> *"What we are saying is that effective Scrum Masters do more than just facilitate Scrum Events and surface*

> *impediments. They are active, not passive. Great Scrum Masters do what must be done to help the Scrum Team and organization achieve great results."*

> *"Why This Update Was Made: It was time to clarify a misunderstanding. One that led many organizations to question why a Scrum Master was needed at all."*

> *"Some have misinterpreted the term servant leader in a way that has led us away from real leadership. So we changed the term to 'leaders who serve.'"*

This change was intended to avoid some people misunderstanding the term "Servant leader" as a weak leader. However, it doesn't mean "servant leader" is no longer valid. According to Wikipedia, "Servant leadership is a philosophy in which the leader's goal is to serve."

7.3.2 Servant leader

The leadership style of the Scrum Master can be described as servant-leadership. Scrum Masters are true leaders who serve the Scrum Team and the larger organization by facilitating the adoption and implementation of Scrum. They are servant-leaders who put the needs of the Scrum Team and the organization above their own and work tirelessly to ensure that Scrum is applied effectively and consistently.

A servant leader puts the needs of others first and works to serve them rather than prioritizing their own needs or interests. The concept of servant leadership is often associated with Robert K. Greenleaf, who first introduced the idea in his 1970 essay, "The Servant as Leader."

A servant leader focuses on empowering others, helping them to develop their skills and achieve their goals. They prioritize the well-being of their team members and work to create a supportive and collaborative work environment. They listen to feedback and concerns from their team members and use this information to make informed decisions that benefit the team and the organization as a whole.

In the context of Scrum, the Scrum Master is a servant leader who works to serve the needs of the Scrum Team and the organization. They coach and mentor the team, helping them understand and apply Scrum's principles and practices. They facilitate collaboration, promote continuous improvement, and remove obstacles hindering the team's progress. They focus on creating a supportive and empowering work environment and prioritize the team's needs over their own needs or interests.

In general, a servant leader leads with empathy, compassion, and a deep commitment to the needs of others. They work to empower their team members, promote collaboration, and create a work environment that is supportive and empowering. In Scrum, the Scrum Master embodies these qualities, serving the needs of the Scrum Team and the organization as a whole.

The Scrum Master serves the Scrum Team, Product Owner, and the organization.

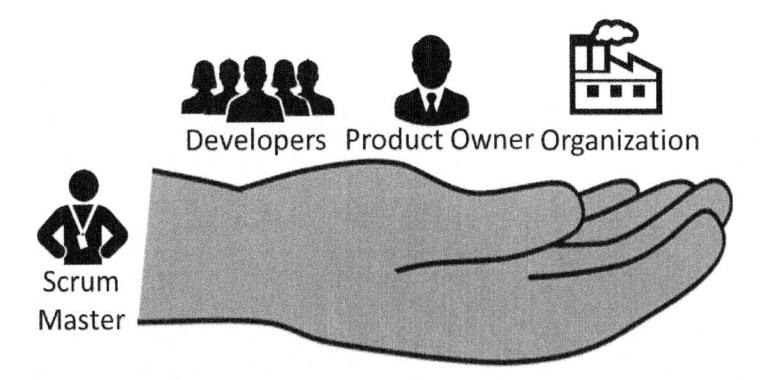

Figure 18 The Scrum Master serves the Scrum Team, Product Owner, and the organization.

7.4 Serving the Scrum Team

The Scrum Master serves the Scrum Team in several ways, including:

- *Coaching the team members in self-management and cross-functionality;*
- *Helping the Scrum Team focus on creating high-value Increments that meet the Definition of Done;*
- *Causing the removal of impediments to the Scrum Team's progress; and,*
- *Ensuring that all Scrum events take place and are positive, productive, and kept within the timebox.*

Figure 19 Coaching a team.

7.4.1 Coaching the team members in self-management and cross-functionality

One of the key responsibilities of the Scrum Master is to serve the Scrum Team by coaching team members in self-management and cross-functionality. This means that the Scrum Master helps the team develop their skills and capabilities to work more effectively together and achieve their goals.

Coaching team members in self-management involves helping them to become more autonomous and self-organizing. The Scrum Master encourages team members to take ownership of their work and to make decisions independently within the framework of Scrum. They help the team develop their decision-making skills so that they can make informed choices about how to approach their work and overcome obstacles that arise.

Coaching team members in cross-functionality involves helping them develop their skills in different areas to work more collaboratively and effectively as a team. The Scrum Master helps team members to identify their strengths and weaknesses and to work on developing their skills in areas where they may be less experienced. In addition, they encourage team members to share their knowledge and expertise so that everyone can contribute to the team's success.

For instance, disagreements, lack of decision, or confusion about a topic. The Scrum Master can bring the topic for discussion, facilitate, and allow the Scrum Team or Developers to determine what to do as a self-managing team.

Coaching the Scrum Team in self-management and cross-functionality is essential for the team's success. It helps team members become more autonomous, collaborative, and effective and ensures they can deliver value to the customer and the organization. The Scrum Master is critical in this process, providing guidance, feedback, and support to help the team continuously improve and optimize their performance.

For instance, if the Scrum Team wants to skip a Scrum event or skips tests from Definition of Done to deliver faster, the Scrum Master, instead of saying, "You must follow the Scrum Guide," or "Because Scrum says so," can ask powerful questions to make the team reflect on how the decision will affect the ability to inspect and adapt, what will be the risk or not meeting the goals, or what will the stability and quality of the product in the long term be and its consequences. People should believe in the change rather than imposing it.

7.4.1.1 GROW Coaching framework

The GROW coaching model is a widely used framework for coaching conversations that can help individuals or teams set and achieve their goals. The acronym stands for:

G	GOAL	Define a clear and specific goal that the coachee wants to achieve.
R	REALITY	Obstacles or challenges that prevent them from achieving their goal.
O	OPTIONS	Different options to overcome obstacles and move closer to the goal.
W	WILL	Specific actions that the coachee will take to achieve their goal.

1. Goal: The first step is clarifying the goal or objective the coachee wants to achieve. This helps the coach and the coachee to understand what they are working towards and why it's important.
2. Reality: The next step is to explore the current reality of the situation. This involves assessing the coachee's starting point, resources, strengths, weaknesses, and any obstacles or challenges that must be overcome.
3. Options: Once the goal and reality are clear, the coach and coachee can brainstorm potential options or strategies for achieving the goal. This step encourages creativity and generates a range of potential solutions.
4. Will: The final step is to help the coachee commit to a specific action. This involves selecting the most effective option and creating a plan for moving forward. The coach helps the coachee to identify the necessary steps, resources, and support needed to achieve their goal and to create a timeline for taking action.

The GROW model is a flexible and effective coaching framework that can be adapted to various coaching contexts and goals. It helps to structure coaching conversations, provide focus and direction, and support the coachee in achieving their goals.

7.4.1.2 Powerful questions

Powerful questions in coaching are open-ended questions that aim to stimulate deeper thinking, self-awareness, and reflection in the coachee. They encourage the coachee to explore their thoughts, beliefs, feelings, and actions and to gain insights into their challenges and goals. Powerful questions do not have a straightforward answer and help the coachee to see things from different perspectives and uncover underlying assumptions, biases, and patterns. They often help the coachee gain clarity, overcome obstacles, develop new strategies, and make decisions. Examples of powerful questions in coaching include:

- What would you do if you had no fear of failure?
- What assumptions are you making about this situation?
- How can you turn this challenge into an opportunity?
- What do you want to achieve, and why is that important?
- How can you apply your strengths to overcome this obstacle?
- What support do you need to achieve your goal?
- How would you describe your ideal outcome?
- What have you learned from this experience?

7.4.1.3 Five Strategies for using powerful questions in coaching

Strategies for using powerful questions in coaching include active listening, avoiding giving solutions and letting the coachee find their own solution and take action. This helps the coachee to develop problem-solving skills, take ownership of their actions, and build confidence in their abilities. The coach can also encourage the coachee to explore various options and weigh the pros and cons of each, to help them make an informed decision. Using powerful questions, the coach can guide the coachee towards discovering their solutions and owning their growth and development.

1. Ask open-ended questions: Powerful questions are open-ended questions that encourage exploration, creativity, and problem-solving. Avoid questions that can be answered with a simple "yes" or "no" and instead ask questions that begin with "what," "how," or "why."
2. Use reflective listening: Reflective listening involves paraphrasing what the coachee has said to ensure you understand them correctly. This demonstrates that you are listening actively and can help the coachee feel heard and understood.
3. Avoid leading questions: Leading questions can inadvertently guide the coachee toward a particular answer or solution. Instead, ask neutral questions that allow the coachee to explore all options and find and own their solution.
4. Allow for silence: Silence can be uncomfortable, but it can also be powerful. Giving the coachee space to think and reflect can lead to deeper insights and more meaningful conversations.
5. Follow up with action steps: Powerful questions can help the coachee gain clarity and insight, but it's important to follow up with actionable steps. Ask the

coachee what action steps they will take and how they will hold themselves accountable for progress towards their goals.

7.4.1.4 Powerful questions with GROW model

Powerful questions can be classified into many groups to address a conversation. However, combining them with the GROW model is a simple way to use them. You can use the following questions for a one-to-one conversation or with a team:

GOAL	REALITY
What is your desired outcome?	What is currently happening?
What would success look like?	What have you tried so far?
What are you hoping to achieve?	What is the biggest challenge you're facing?
What are your long-term goals?	What resources do you currently have?
How can you align your goals with the goals of the organization?	How do you feel about your current situation?

OPTIONS	WILL
What are some possible solutions?	Which option resonates most with you?
If it was up to you, what would you do?	What is one small step you can take to move closer to your goal?
How can it be more fun?	What action will you take next?
What might happen if you took a different path?	How will you hold yourself accountable for taking action?
What are some alternative ways of approaching this problem?	What support do you need to follow through on your plan?

7.4.1.5 Powerful questions at a team level

Now, we can also use the powerful questions when we look at the team to reflect and take action. Here are some examples of powerful questions designed to address a conversation with a team:

GOAL	REALITY
What are the key objectives we want to achieve as a team?	What are the biggest challenges we are currently facing as a team?
What impact do we want to have on our customers or stakeholders?	What is working well for us as a team?
	What are the root causes of our current challenges?

How will we know when we have achieved our goal?	What are the strengths and weaknesses of our team?
What is the vision we have for our team?	How do we communicate and collaborate as a team?
How can we ensure our goals align with the company's vision?	
OPTIONS	**WILL**
What are some potential solutions to our current challenges?	Which solution do we think is the best option for us to pursue?
What resources do we need to implement these solutions?	Who will be responsible for implementing the solution?
What are the risks associated with each solution?	What are the next steps we need to take to move forward?
What are the potential benefits of each solution?	How will we measure the success of our solution?
What would be the impact of not taking any action?	What can we do to stay committed to implementing our solution?

7.4.2 Help create high-value Increments

As a servant-leader, the Scrum Master serves the Scrum Team by helping them to focus on creating high-value increments that meet the Definition of Done. Here's how they do it:

1. Helping the team understand the Definition of Done: The Scrum Master ensures that the team understands what the Definition of Done means for the product and the increments they are creating. This means that they help the team to define what it means for an increment to be considered "done" and ensure that everyone on the team is on the same page. They can also facilitate creating and updating the Definition of Done as needed.
2. Encouraging the team to focus on high-value increments: The Scrum Master helps the team understand each increment's value and encourages them to focus on delivering high-value increments to the customer. They also work with the Product Owner to ensure that the Product Backlog is prioritized in a way that emphasizes high-value features.
3. Facilitating the team's work: The Scrum Master facilitates the team's work by helping to remove any impediments that may prevent the team from creating high-value increments. They also ensure the team has the necessary resources, skills, and tools to create high-value increments.
4. Ensuring that the team is continuously improving: The Scrum Master helps the team to continuously improve its practices by facilitating retrospectives, encouraging experimentation, and promoting a culture of continuous

improvement. By doing so, they help the team to create even higher-value increments over time.

In the end, the Scrum Master serves the Scrum Team by helping them to focus on creating high-value increments that meet the Definition of Done. Doing so ensures that the team delivers value to the customer and the organization and continuously improves its practices over time.

7.4.3 Removal of impediments

As a servant-leader, the Scrum Master serves the Scrum Team by causing the removal of impediments to the Scrum Team's progress. However, the Scrum Master does not typically remove impediments themselves. Instead, they facilitate the team's self-organization and help the team to find solutions to resolve the impediments.

The Scrum Master encourages the Scrum Team to work together to identify and resolve impediments on their own. They facilitate the team's decision-making and problem-solving processes and help them develop their skills and knowledge to become more self-organizing. By doing so, the Scrum Master empowers the team to take ownership of their work and to find creative solutions to overcome impediments.

Here's how they do it:

- Identifying impediments: The Scrum Master identifies impediments that may prevent the Scrum Team from progressing towards their Sprint Goal. These impediments can hinder the team's ability to deliver value to the customer, such as organizational bureaucracy, lack of resources, technical debt, or interpersonal conflicts.
- Facilitating the removal of impediments: Once the Scrum Master has identified an impediment, they work with the Scrum Team, the Product Owner, and other stakeholders to facilitate its removal. This may involve collaborating with other teams or departments, advocating for organizational changes, or finding creative solutions to overcome the impediment.
- Protecting the team from external disruptions: The Scrum Master also acts as a shield for the Scrum Team, protecting them from external disruptions that may impede their progress. They work to minimize interruptions and distractions, ensure the team has a quiet and focused work environment, and help the team maintain its focus on delivering high-quality increments.
- Supporting the team's self-organization: Finally, the Scrum Master supports the team's self-organization by empowering them to identify and remove impediments on their own. They encourage the team to collaborate, share knowledge and skills, and work together to solve problems.

Overall, the Scrum Master causes the removal of impediments to the Scrum Team's progress, which helps the team to achieve their Sprint Goals and deliver value to the customer. By doing so, they ensure that the team can work effectively and efficiently and that they are continuously improving their practices over time.

7.4.4 Ensuring positive Scrum Events

As a servant-leader, the Scrum Master serves the Scrum Team by ensuring that all Scrum events take place and are positive, productive, and kept within the timebox. Here's how they do it:

1. Ensuring that all Scrum events take place: The Scrum Master ensures that all the necessary Scrum events take place, including Sprint, Sprint Planning, Daily Scrum, Sprint Review, and Sprint Retrospective. In addition, they work with the Scrum Team to schedule these events and ensure that everyone knows when and where they will take place.
2. Facilitating positive and productive events: The Scrum Master also facilitates the Scrum events to ensure they are positive and productive. They help the team establish a collaborative and respectful environment, encourage active participation, and ensure that everyone has a chance to contribute their ideas and feedback.
3. Keeping events within the timebox: The Scrum Master also ensures that all Scrum events are kept within their timebox and teaches the Scrum Team to keep them within the time box. They help the team stay focused and on track and intervene if the discussion veers are off-topic or if there are any other distractions or disruptions.
4. Encouraging continuous improvement: Finally, the Scrum Master encourages continuous improvement of the Scrum events themselves. They work with the team to evaluate each event's effectiveness and identify ways to improve its structure, format, or content.
5. A guardian of transparency: The Scrum Team commits to upholding transparency. However, the team may miss the way. As a guardian of transparency, the Scrum Master ensures the artifacts are transparent for the Scrum Team and stakeholders. They ensure the right artifacts are inspected and adapted during the events with the commitments in mind, and the Scrum Team and stakeholders clearly understand the work being done and the progress being made.

Overall, the Scrum Master serves the Scrum Team by ensuring that all Scrum events take place and are positive, productive, and kept within the timebox. Doing so, they help the team to achieve their Sprint Goals and deliver value to the customer. They also promote a culture of continuous improvement, which is critical for the success of the team and the organization.

7.5 Serving the Product Owner

The Scrum Master serves the Product Owner in several ways, including:

- *Helping find techniques for effective Product Goal definition and Product Backlog management;*
- *Helping the Scrum Team understand the need for clear and concise Product Backlog items;*
- *Helping establish empirical product planning for a complex environment; and,*
- *Facilitating stakeholder collaboration as requested or needed.*

7.5.1 Effective Product Goal definition and Product Backlog management

As a servant-leader, the Scrum Master serves the Product Owner by helping them find techniques for effective Product Goal definition and Product Backlog management. Here's how they can do it:

1. Facilitating Product Goal definition: The Scrum Master can help the Product Owner define the Product Goal by facilitating discussions with stakeholders and team members to clarify the purpose of the product. For example, the Scrum Master can lead a workshop where the Product Owner and team members collaborate to create a Product Goal aligned with the organization's strategic objectives. They can also help the Product Owner to refine the Product Goal by applying the SMART criteria. For instance, if the Product Goal is to increase customer satisfaction, the Scrum Master can help the Product Owner to make it more specific by defining a measurable target such as "increase customer satisfaction rating from 4.5 to 4.8 out of 5 within the next 6 months."
2. Coaching on Product Backlog Management: The Scrum Master can coach the Product Owner on effective Product Backlog management by helping them to prioritize the Product Backlog based on customer value and business objectives. They can also help the Product Owner refine Product Backlog items with different techniques such as User Stories, Acceptance Criteria, Hypotheses, and experiments and ensure that they are clear, concise, and testable. For example, the Scrum Master can facilitate a refinement session where the Product Owner and team members collaborate to break down a User Story into smaller, more manageable pieces and define Acceptance Criteria that are specific and measurable.
3. Facilitating stakeholder engagement: The Scrum Master can help the Product Owner to engage with stakeholders and customers by facilitating feedback sessions, conducting user interviews, and analyzing market research data. For instance, the Scrum Master can organize a focus group where customers can provide feedback on the product and help the Product Owner to prioritize the Product Backlog based on their needs and expectations. They can also help the Product Owner to analyze customer data to identify trends and insights that can inform the product development process.

4. Find techniques to measure value: The Scrum Master can serve the Product Owner by helping them to identify metrics that reflect the current and potential product's value and the stakeholders' satisfaction. The Scrum Master also supports the Product Owner in analyzing these metrics and using them to guide the Product Backlog refinement process. For example, this may involve helping the Product Owner to prioritize backlog items based on value or identifying opportunities to improve the product based on stakeholder feedback.
5. Encouraging continuous improvement: The Scrum Master can improve Product Goal definition and Product Backlog management by facilitating retrospectives and encouraging the Product Owner to experiment with new techniques. For example, the Scrum Master can lead a retrospective session where the team reflects on the effectiveness of their Product Goal definition and Product Backlog management techniques and identifies areas for improvement. They can also encourage the Product Owner to experiment with new techniques, such as Value Stream Mapping or Impact Mapping, to improve their Product Backlog management effectiveness.

Generally, the Scrum Master serves the Product Owner by helping them to define the Product Goal and manage the Product Backlog effectively. Doing so helps ensure that the Scrum Team delivers value to the customer and that the product is aligned with the organization's strategy. They also promote a culture of continuous improvement, which is critical for the success of the product and the organization.

7.5.2 *Clear and concise Product Backlog items*

As a servant-leader, the Scrum Master serves the Product Owner by helping the Scrum Team understand the need for clear and concise Product Backlog items. Here are some examples of how they do it:

- Clarifying the role of Product Backlog items: The Scrum Master can help the Scrum Team understand the importance of clear and concise Product Backlog items by clarifying their role in the development process. They can explain that Product Backlog items represent customer requirements and are the basis for the team's Sprint Planning and Sprint Review. As a result, the Scrum Team can work more efficiently and effectively toward achieving the Sprint Goal by ensuring that Product Backlog items are clear and concise.
- Guiding non-mandatory techniques such as User Stories: The Scrum Master can guide the Scrum Team in creating clear and concise User Stories that accurately reflect customer requirements. For example, they can teach the team to use the INVEST criteria (Independent, Negotiable, Valuable, Estimable, Small, and Testable) to evaluate User Stories and ensure they are actionable and specific. By using this guidance, the Scrum Team can create Product Backlog items that are clear and concise, making it easier for them to plan and execute their work.
- Facilitating refinement sessions: The Scrum Master can facilitate refinement sessions where the Scrum Team and the Product Owner collaborate to refine

Product Backlog items. During these sessions, the Scrum Master can help the team clarify the requirements and ensure they are clear and concise. For example, they can encourage the team to ask questions and seek clarification from the Product Owner to ensure they have a shared understanding of the requirements.
- Feedback and coaching: The Scrum Master can also provide feedback and coaching to the Scrum Team on their Product Backlog items. They can review the items with the team, provide feedback on their clarity and conciseness, and coach the team on improving them. For example, they can teach the team to use a consistent format for User Stories or to break down large, complex requirements into smaller, more manageable pieces.

By helping the Scrum Team understand the need for clear and concise Product Backlog items, the Scrum Master can enable the team to work more efficiently and effectively toward achieving the Sprint Goal. In addition, they can provide guidance, facilitate refinement sessions, and provide feedback and coaching, all of which help to ensure that the Product Backlog items are clear, concise, and actionable.

7.5.3 Empirical product planning

As a servant-leader, the Scrum Master serves the Product Owner by helping establish empirical product planning for a complex environment. Here are some examples of how they can do it:

1. Collaborating on product vision: The Scrum Master can work with the Product Owner to establish a product vision aligned with the organization's goals and objectives. In addition, they can help the Product Owner understand the environment's complexity and develop a vision that is flexible enough to accommodate changes and adapt to new circumstances.
2. Facilitating stakeholder engagement: The Scrum Master can help the Product Owner engage with stakeholders and customers to gather feedback and insights to inform product planning. They can facilitate feedback sessions, conduct user interviews, and analyze market research data to help the Product Owner make informed decisions.
3. Coaching on prioritization: The Scrum Master can coach the Product Owner on prioritizing the Product Backlog based on customer value and business objectives. They can teach the Product Owner to use techniques such as Value-Based Prioritization or Cost of Delay to make informed decisions about which Product Backlog items to prioritize.
4. Facilitating Sprint Reviews and Retrospectives: The Scrum Master can facilitate Sprint Reviews and Retrospectives to help the Scrum Team reflect on the effectiveness of their product planning and make improvements. In addition, they can help the team identify improvement areas and develop action plans to address them in the next Sprint.
5. Encouraging experimentation: The Scrum Master can encourage the Product Owner to experiment with new approaches to product planning in a complex

environment. They can help the Product Owner to identify areas where experimentation may be beneficial, develop hypotheses and conduct experiments to test them. For example, the Product Owner may experiment with different pricing strategies to determine the most effective in a complex market.

In general, by helping establish empirical product planning for a complex environment, the Scrum Master can enable the Product Owner to make informed decisions and adapt to changing circumstances. In addition, they can collaborate on product vision, facilitate stakeholder engagement, coach on prioritization, facilitate Sprint Reviews and Retrospectives, and encourage experimentation.

7.5.4 Facilitating stakeholder collaboration

As a servant-leader, the Scrum Master serves the Product Owner by facilitating stakeholder collaboration as requested or needed. Here are some examples of how they do it:

1. Facilitating stakeholder feedback sessions: The Scrum Master can organize feedback sessions where stakeholders can provide feedback on the product and help the Product Owner to prioritize the Product Backlog based on their needs and expectations. The Scrum Master can facilitate these sessions, ensuring stakeholders understand the product and its goals clearly. They can also help the Product Owner to analyze feedback and identify trends and insights that can inform the product development process.
2. Facilitating stakeholder engagement: The Scrum Master can help the Product Owner engage with stakeholders to gather feedback and insights to inform product planning. They can organize focus groups, conduct user interviews, and analyze market research data to help the Product Owner make informed decisions. In addition, the Scrum Master can help the Product Owner to identify key stakeholders and develop strategies to engage them effectively.
3. Facilitating collaboration with cross-functional teams: The Scrum Master can help the Product Owner to collaborate with cross-functional teams to ensure that the product is aligned with the organization's goals and objectives. They can facilitate discussions between the Product Owner and other teams, such as marketing, sales, or engineering, to ensure everyone is aligned on the product vision and goals. This collaboration can help to identify potential obstacles and ensure that the product is developed in a way that meets the needs of all stakeholders.
4. Facilitating communication between the Product Owner and the Scrum Team: The Scrum Master can help the Product Owner communicate effectively with the Scrum Team to ensure everyone is aligned on the product vision and goals. They can facilitate conversations between the Product Owner and the team, helping to clarify requirements and ensure that the team understands what needs to be done. The Scrum Master can also help the team provide feedback to the Product Owner, ensuring that the product is developed to meet their needs.

To summarize, by facilitating stakeholder collaboration as requested or needed, the Scrum Master can help the Product Owner gather feedback and insights, align the product with the organization's goals and objectives, and ensure that everyone works together effectively to achieve the product vision and goals.

7.6 Serving the organization

The Scrum Master serves the organization in several ways, including:

- *Leading, training, and coaching the organization in its Scrum adoption;*
- *Planning and advising Scrum implementations within the organization;*
- *Helping employees and stakeholders understand and enact an empirical approach for complex work; and,*
- *Removing barriers between stakeholders and Scrum Teams.*

7.6.1 Leading the Scrum adoption

As a servant-leader, the Scrum Master serves the organization in leading, training, and coaching the organization in its Scrum adoption. Here are some examples of how they do it:

1. Leading Scrum adoption: The Scrum Master can lead the organization's adoption of Scrum by developing a plan for Scrum adoption, establishing Scrum roles and responsibilities, and defining Scrum processes and procedures. They can work with stakeholders to ensure that everyone understands Scrum principles and practices and that Scrum aligns with the organization's goals and objectives.
2. Training on Scrum principles and practices: The Scrum Master can train the organization on Scrum principles and practices by providing training sessions, workshops, and other educational opportunities. They can teach Scrum roles and responsibilities, Scrum events, artifacts, and other Scrum concepts to ensure that everyone understands Scrum and its benefits. They can also provide training on agile practices, such as continuous improvement and adaptive planning, to ensure that the organization can effectively adopt Scrum.
3. Coaching on Scrum implementation: The Scrum Master can coach the organization on Scrum implementation by working with Scrum Teams and other stakeholders to ensure that Scrum is implemented effectively. They can facilitate Scrum events, such as Sprint Reviews and Retrospectives, to ensure that the Scrum Team is working effectively and that the organization is continuously improving its Scrum adoption. They can also coach individual team members, Scrum Masters, and Product Owners to ensure they effectively carry out their roles and responsibilities.

4. Encouraging continuous improvement: The Scrum Master can encourage continuous improvement in the organization's Scrum adoption by identifying areas for improvement and developing action plans to address them. In addition, they can work with stakeholders to gather feedback and insights that can inform improvements to Scrum processes and procedures. They can also encourage experimentation with new approaches to Scrum implementation to help the organization continuously improve its Scrum adoption.

By leading, training, and coaching the organization in its Scrum adoption, the Scrum Master can help it implement Scrum effectively and achieve its goals. In addition, they can provide guidance, advocacy, and support and work with the organization to create a culture of continuous improvement and collaboration.

7.6.2 Planning Scrum implementations

As a servant-leader, the Scrum Master serves the organization in planning and advising Scrum implementations within the organization. Here are some examples of how they do it:

1. Planning Scrum implementations: The Scrum Master can help the organization to plan Scrum implementations by guiding how to implement Scrum effectively. They can work with key stakeholders to identify the benefits of Scrum and how it can benefit the organization. The Scrum Master can help to establish a framework for Scrum implementation, including training programs, Scrum events, and communication channels.
2. Advising on Scrum implementations: The Scrum Master can advise the organization on implementing Scrum effectively by providing workshops, training sessions, and coaching sessions. They can guide the Scrum framework, roles, and events and advise the organization on implementing Scrum effectively. They can also help establish Scrum metrics and advise the organization on measuring success.
3. Identifying potential obstacles: The Scrum Master can identify potential obstacles that may hinder successful Scrum implementation within the organization. They can work with key stakeholders to identify these obstacles and provide guidance on overcoming them. For example, if the organization has a rigid hierarchy, the Scrum Master can work with leaders to create a more flexible and collaborative culture.
4. Feedback and support: The Scrum Master can provide feedback and support to the organization as it implements Scrum. They can help identify areas where the organization struggles and guide it to improve. They can also provide feedback on the effectiveness of Scrum implementation and work with the organization to make adjustments as needed.

By planning and advising Scrum implementations within the organization, the Scrum Master can help the organization implement Scrum effectively and achieve its goals. In addition, they can provide guidance, identify potential obstacles, and provide feedback and support to the organization as it implements Scrum.

7.6.3 Helping stakeholders understand the empirical approach

As a servant-leader, the Scrum Master serves the organization by helping employees and stakeholders understand and enact an empirical approach to complex work. Here are some examples of how they do it:

1. Teaching the empirical approach: The Scrum Master can teach employees and stakeholders about the empirical approach by explaining the principles and values of Scrum. They can help create a continuous improvement culture and teach the organization to use feedback and data to make informed decisions. The Scrum Master can also teach the organization the importance of inspection, adaptation, and transparency in a complex work environment.
2. Facilitating empirical approaches: The Scrum Master can facilitate using empirical approaches by guiding how to use data and feedback to make decisions. They can help the organization create a feedback loop that enables them to gather and use feedback to improve. For example, the Scrum Master can facilitate a retrospective where the team reflects on the previous Sprint and identifies areas for improvement.
3. Encouraging experimentation: The Scrum Master can encourage the organization to experiment with new approaches to complex work by creating a safe environment for experimentation. They can help the organization identify areas where experimentation may be beneficial, develop hypotheses and conduct experiments to test them. For example, the organization may experiment with a new pricing strategy to determine its effectiveness.
4. Feedback and support: The Scrum Master can provide feedback and support to employees and stakeholders as they enact an empirical approach to complex work. They can help identify areas where the organization struggles and guide it to improve. They can also provide feedback on the effectiveness of the empirical approach and work with the organization to make adjustments as needed.

Overall, by helping employees and stakeholders understand and enact an empirical approach to complex work, the Scrum Master can create a culture of continuous improvement and enable the organization to make informed decisions based on data and feedback. In addition, they can teach the empirical approach, facilitate its use, encourage experimentation, and provide feedback and support.

7.6.4 Removing barriers between stakeholders and Scrum Teams

As a servant-leader, the Scrum Master serves the organization in removing barriers between stakeholders and Scrum Teams and understanding how to interact and get the most out of a Scrum Team.

For instance, the management may have expectations of the Scrum Team on how to do certain things, but it is the Scrum Team's responsibility to decide how. Then the Scrum Master can facilitate the discussion so both parties understand each other's needs and expectations.

Here are some examples of how they do it:

- Facilitating communication: The Scrum Master can facilitate communication between stakeholders and Scrum Teams to ensure that everyone is aligned on the product vision and goals. They can help to clarify requirements and ensure that the team has a clear understanding of what needs to be done. They can also help the team provide feedback to stakeholders, ensuring that the product is developed to meet their needs.
- Guiding Scrum practices: The Scrum Master can guide Scrum practices to stakeholders, helping them to understand how to interact with the Scrum Team effectively. For example, they can explain the purpose of Scrum events, such as the Sprint Review, and advise stakeholders on providing useful feedback to the Scrum Team. They can also help stakeholders to understand the roles and responsibilities of the Scrum Team and how to collaborate effectively with the team.
- Identifying and removing barriers: The Scrum Master can identify barriers that may hinder effective communication between stakeholders and the Scrum Team. For example, they may identify a lack of understanding between the Product Owner and the Developers or a lack of alignment between stakeholders and the Scrum Team. They can then work to remove these barriers by facilitating communication and providing guidance on how to work together effectively.
- Encouraging collaboration: The Scrum Master can encourage collaboration between stakeholders and the Scrum Team by creating a culture of trust and transparency. They can help establish open communication channels and encourage stakeholders to provide feedback to the Scrum Team. They can also help the Scrum Team work closely with stakeholders to ensure that the product is developed to meet their needs.

In the end, by removing barriers between stakeholders and Scrum Teams and helping stakeholders to understand how to interact and get the most out of a Scrum Team, the Scrum Master can enable effective collaboration and ensure that the product is developed in a way that meets the needs of all stakeholders. In addition, they can facilitate communication, provide guidance on Scrum practices, identify and remove barriers, and encourage collaboration between stakeholders and the Scrum Team.

7.6.5 Collaborating with other Scrum Masters

As a servant-leader, the Scrum Master serves the organization by working with other Scrum Masters to increase the effectiveness of applying Scrum in the organization. Here are some ways in which they do it:

- Collaboration and sharing best practices: The Scrum Master can collaborate with other Scrum Masters to share best practices and ideas to improve the organization's Scrum practices. They can share their experiences and challenges

and work together to find solutions for their respective teams. This can lead to an improvement in the overall effectiveness of Scrum within the organization.
- Coordinating and aligning Scrum efforts: The Scrum Master can work with other Scrum Masters to coordinate and align Scrum efforts within the organization. This can involve sharing information on Scrum events and activities, ensuring consistency in Scrum practices across different teams, and helping to resolve conflicts or issues that arise.
- Identifying opportunities for improvement: The Scrum Master can work with other Scrum Masters to identify opportunities for improvement in Scrum practices within the organization. This can involve conducting retrospectives across multiple teams, analyzing trends, and identifying areas where changes could be made to improve the effectiveness of Scrum.
- Supporting the adoption of Scrum: The Scrum Master can work with other Scrum Masters to support the adoption of Scrum in the organization. This can involve working with key stakeholders to help them understand the benefits of Scrum, providing training and coaching to teams, and helping to create a culture of continuous improvement and collaboration.

On the whole, by working with other Scrum Masters to increase the effectiveness of the application of Scrum in the organization, the Scrum Master can help to create a more cohesive and effective Scrum environment. In addition, they can collaborate and share best practices, coordinate and align Scrum efforts, identify opportunities for improvement, and support the adoption of Scrum.

7.7 The 8 Stances of a Scrum Master

Barry Overeem describes the eight stances of a Scrum Master in his whitepaper. These are the eight stances of a Scrum Master:

1. Servant Leader: The Scrum Master serves the Scrum Team by putting their needs before their own. They lead by example and prioritize the team's success above personal gain.
2. Facilitator: The Scrum Master facilitates the Scrum events, such as the Sprint Review and Retrospective, to ensure that they are productive and beneficial for the team. They guide the team through the process and help create a safe open communication environment.
3. Coach: The Scrum Master coaches the Scrum Team in the Scrum framework, practices, and values. They guide how to effectively use Scrum to meet the needs of the business and stakeholders.
4. Manager: The role of a Scrum Master is different from that of a traditional manager in that they do not have formal power over the Developers or their tasks. However, the Scrum Master is responsible for managing the Scrum process, ensuring that it is utilized effectively by people, teams, departments, and the organization as a whole. They are also accountable for ensuring that Scrum is understood and enacted correctly, removing impediments to the

Scrum Team's progress, and ensuring that everyone clearly understands goals, scope, and product domains. Despite not having formal power over the team, being a Scrum Master is a true management job with accountability, responsibility, and a specific sphere of influence. Unfortunately, this aspect of the Scrum Master's role is often overlooked or ignored.

5. Mentor: The Scrum Master mentors individual team members, helping them to grow and develop their skills. They guide and support team members, helping them achieve their goals.
6. Teacher: The Scrum Master teaches the Scrum Team about agile principles and practices. They help team members understand Scrum's value and how it can be used to improve their work.
7. Impediment Remover: The Scrum Master removes impediments that may be hindering the progress of the Scrum Team. They work with the team to identify obstacles and help to find solutions to overcome them.
8. Change Agent: The Scrum Master acts as a change agent, helping the organization to adopt and embrace the Scrum framework. They work to create a culture of continuous improvement and help the organization adapt to change.

The eight stances are intended to be a guideline for the various roles a Scrum Master may need to fulfill, but the specific balance of those stances will depend on the unique needs of the Scrum Team and the organization.

A Scrum Master may excel in some stances and have room for improvement in others, but as long as they are committed to continuously improving their skills and knowledge, they can be effective in their role. Additionally, Scrum Masters can work collaboratively with other Scrum Masters to leverage their strengths and support each other in areas needing improvement. Ultimately, what matters most is that the Scrum Master is committed to serving the Scrum Team and the organization and helping them to achieve their goals through the effective use of Scrum.

7.8 Anti-patterns of the Scrum Master

Here are some Scrum Master antipatterns:

1. Command and control: When the Scrum Master micromanages the team and makes all the decisions, it can reduce creativity, autonomy, and ownership within the team.
2. Lack of facilitation: When the Scrum Master fails to facilitate meetings effectively, it can lead to ineffective communication, misalignment, and confusion within the team.
3. Lack of collaboration: When the Scrum Master fails to collaborate with the team and other stakeholders effectively, it can lead to missed opportunities for improvement, reduced engagement, and suboptimal outcomes.
4. Focusing only on ceremonies: When the Scrum Master focuses solely on the Scrum events and fails to support the team with their ongoing work, it can lead

to missed opportunities for improvement, reduced productivity, and poor quality outcomes.
5. Lack of coaching: When the Scrum Master fails to coach the team and help them improve their skills and processes, it can lead to reduced autonomy, poor quality outcomes, and a lack of innovation.
6. Lack of agility: When the Scrum Master fails to adapt to changing circumstances, it can lead to missed opportunities, poor quality outcomes, and reduced engagement and productivity within the team.
7. Overprotecting the team: When the Scrum Master shields the team from all external influences and fails to challenge them, it can lead to a lack of innovation, poor quality outcomes, and reduced engagement and productivity within the team.
8. Lack of empathy: When the Scrum Master fails to understand the needs and perspectives of the team and other stakeholders, it can lead to miscommunication, poor collaboration, and suboptimal outcomes.
9. Allowing weak version of the Scrum framework: When the Scrum Master allows the team or stakeholders to modify the Scrum framework to suit their own needs, it can lead to confusion, reduced transparency, and suboptimal outcomes. The Scrum framework is designed to provide a clear set of roles, events, and artifacts. Changing it without a clear understanding of the implications can be detrimental to the effectiveness of the team and the Scrum process.
10. Telling the team what to do when they hesitate: Scrum Masters should avoid taking over their decision-making process by telling them what to do when they hesitate. Instead, they should use powerful questions to help the team explore the issue and develop solutions. Telling the team what to do can undermine their ownership and accountability for their work, leading to a lack of motivation and decreased productivity.

Part 8: Scrum Events

The Sprint is a container for all other events.

The Scrum Events are the Sprint, Sprint Planning, Daily Scrum, Sprint Review, and Sprint Retrospective.

The Product Backlog Refinement is not an event but an ongoing activity.

All Scrum events, work, and activities are contained within a Sprint.

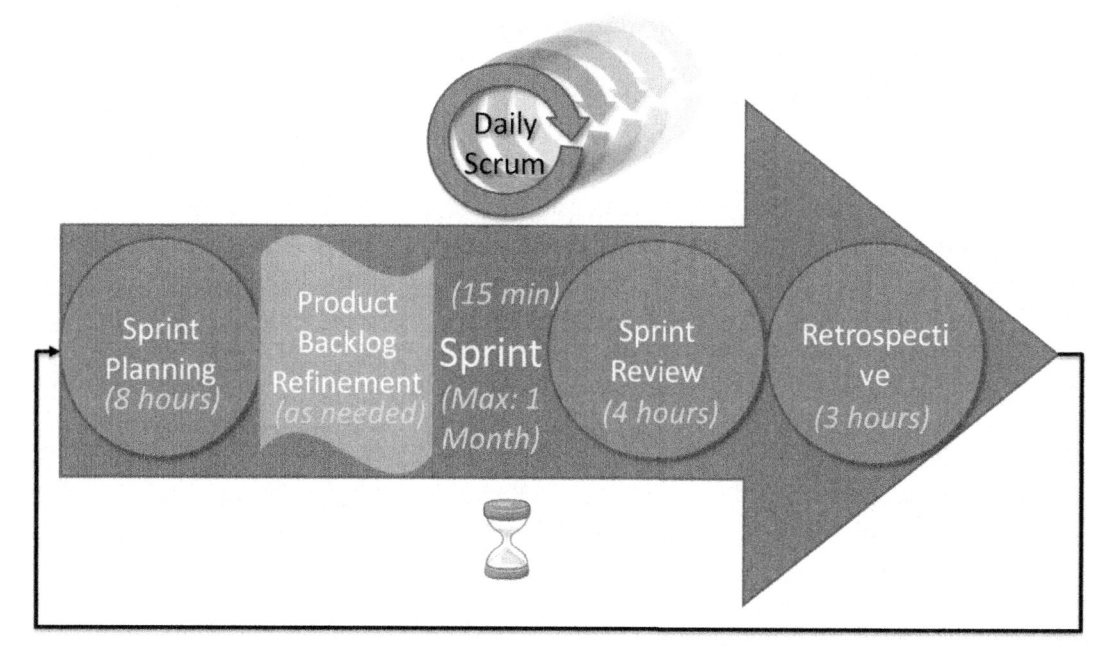

Figure 20 Scrum events.

8.1 Opportunities to inspect and adapt

> Each event in Scrum is a formal opportunity to inspect and adapt Scrum artifacts. These events are specifically designed to enable the transparency required. Failure to operate any events as prescribed results in lost opportunities to inspect and adapt. Events are used in Scrum to create regularity and to minimize the need for meetings not defined in Scrum.

In Scrum, each event is designed to provide the Scrum Team with a formal opportunity to inspect and adapt the Scrum artifacts, including the Product Backlog, Sprint Backlog, and Increment towards their commitments. These events are time-boxed and have specific objectives to ensure that the Scrum Team can work collaboratively and effectively to deliver valuable product Increments.

By inspecting and adapting Scrum artifacts during each event, the Scrum Team can gain transparency into their progress and identify areas for improvement. This allows them to continuously improve their processes and practices continuously, ultimately delivering higher quality, more valuable Increments.

However, if any event is not operated as prescribed, the Scrum Team may lose valuable opportunities to inspect and adapt its artifacts. For example, suppose the Sprint Review is not conducted or is conducted improperly. In that case, the Scrum Team may be unable to inspect the increment and gather feedback from stakeholders and may miss opportunities to improve the product. Similarly, suppose the Daily Scrum is not conducted or focused on synchronizing the work of the Scrum Team. In that case, the team may miss opportunities to identify and resolve obstacles to progress.

Considering all this, operating each event as prescribed is critical to the success of the Scrum Team and the delivery of valuable Increments. By taking advantage of the opportunities to inspect and adapt Scrum artifacts provided by each event, the Scrum Team can continuously improve their process and practices and deliver higher quality, more valuable Increments.

8.2 All events are timeboxed

A timebox is a fixed duration during which an activity or event occurs. Each Scrum event, including the Sprint, Sprint Planning, Daily Scrum, Sprint Review, and Sprint Retrospective, is timeboxed, meaning it has a fixed duration that cannot be exceeded.

Timeboxing is important in Scrum as a "boundary" for frequent inspection because it helps the Scrum Team focus on delivering high-quality, valuable work within a specific timeframe.

Additionally, timeboxing helps to create a sense of urgency and promotes better time management within the Scrum Team. Without a fixed duration, there may be a tendency to let events drag on, resulting in wasted time and reduced productivity.

This approach may not allow to finish or address all the topics but encourages individuals or teams to make the best possible decisions and focus their efforts within the constraints of the given time frame. Time-boxing offers several benefits, including:

1. Improved decision-making: Time boxes compel those familiar with the problem to make decisions more quickly and efficiently, as they know that time is limited. This helps to prevent analysis paralysis and encourages prioritizing the most critical aspects of the problem.
2. Enhanced focus: By allocating a specific time for a particular task or problem, individuals or teams can concentrate on that specific issue without getting sidetracked by other tasks or concerns. This focused approach leads to more productive and effective problem-solving.
3. Optimized time usage: Time-boxing ensures that the group's time is used effectively by concentrating their efforts on the task. This helps to prevent wasted time and keeps the team on track to meet its objectives.
4. Collaboration: When a group works within a time box, all members work simultaneously on the same problem, fostering collaboration and collective problem-solving. This shared experience can lead to more innovative and effective solutions.
5. Encouraging progress: Time-boxing helps break down larger tasks or projects into smaller, manageable segments. By focusing on completing these smaller tasks within a set time frame, team members can see tangible progress, boosting motivation and maintaining momentum throughout the project.

By timeboxing each event, the Scrum Team can maintain a predictable cadence and consistently deliver high-quality, valuable product Increments. In addition, this allows for better planning and forecasting and improved communication and collaboration among the Scrum Team and stakeholders.

Except for the Sprint, if the purpose of an event is achieved before the timebox is up, the Scrum Team can finish the event early.

8.2.1 Parkinson's Law

Parkinson's Law and timeboxing are related concepts in that they both emphasize the importance of setting specific timeframes for tasks to promote productivity and efficiency.

Parkinson's Law indicates that work will expand to fill the time available for completion, which can lead to wasted time and reduced productivity. On the other hand, timeboxing is a technique used in Scrum and other Agile frameworks to limit the duration of events or activities. By setting a specific timebox for a task or activity, individuals are forced to work more efficiently and effectively and are less likely to succumb to Parkinson's Law.

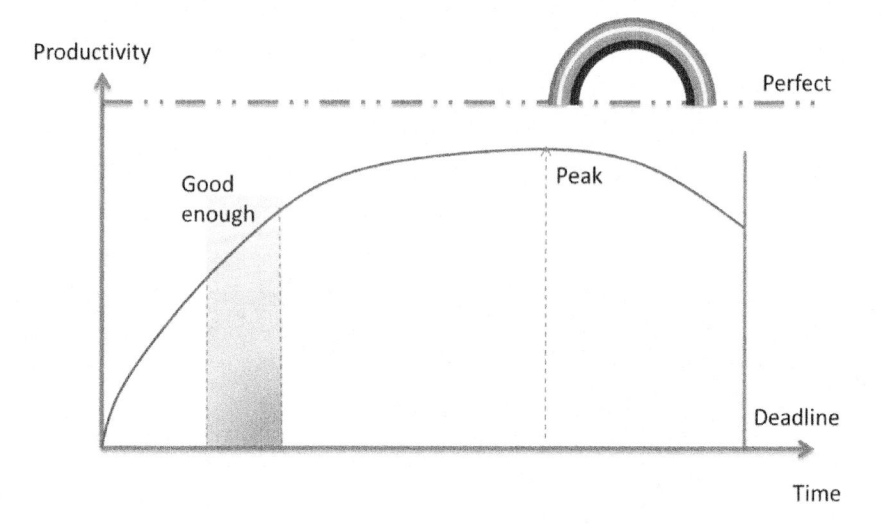

Figure 21 Parkinson's law and timebox.

Timeboxing is a proactive approach to avoid Parkinson's Law. Instead of allowing tasks to expand and fill available time, timeboxing provides a fixed time period during which a task or activity must be completed. This technique helps to ensure that tasks are completed within a specific timeframe and promotes efficiency, productivity, and focus.

In general, timeboxing is an effective technique to combat the effects of Parkinson's Law and promote productivity and efficiency. By setting specific timeframes for tasks and activities, individuals can work more efficiently and effectively, resulting in higher quality work and increased productivity.

8.2.2 Temporal motivation theory

Temporal Motivation Theory (TMT) is a theory that describes how time can influence motivation. According to TMT, people are more motivated to work on tasks with a deadline or a specific timeframe. In other words, the time pressure with a deadline can increase motivation and improve performance.

TMT suggests that people are more likely to focus and complete tasks when given a specific timeframe or deadline, similar to the concept of timeboxing. Setting a fixed time period for completing a task or activity can help create a sense of urgency and motivate individuals to work more efficiently and effectively.

In the end, the use of timeboxing in Scrum aligns with the principles of TMT, which suggest that people are more motivated to work when they have a specific deadline or timeframe. Therefore, by using timeboxing in Scrum, the Scrum Team can better stay focused, productive, and motivated, ultimately leading to higher quality, more valuable product Increments.

8.3 Optimally at the same time and place

Optimally, all events are held at the same time and place to reduce complexity.

The Scrum framework emphasizes the importance of communication and collaboration among the members of the Scrum Team, including the Product Owner, Developers, and Scrum Master. One way to facilitate this collaboration and reduce complexity is to hold all Scrum events at the same time and place.

By holding all Scrum events at the same time and place, the Scrum Team can avoid the need to coordinate multiple schedules and locations. This can reduce confusion, eliminate the need for additional coordination, and create a sense of consistency and predictability.

Additionally, holding events in the same location can help to create a sense of shared space and encourage team members to engage with one another. This can facilitate better communication and collaboration, ultimately leading to higher quality, more valuable work.

Notice that if the Developers need to meet online, in this context, the same place should use the same communication tool and setup.

While it is not always possible to hold all Scrum events at the same time and place, doing so can provide significant benefits for the Scrum Team. By minimizing complexity and improving communication and collaboration, the team can work together and deliver valuable Increments to the product.

8.3.1 Habits

Holding all Scrum events simultaneously and in place is also related to the concept of habits. By establishing a consistent routine for all Scrum events, the Scrum Team can create a habit of collaboration and communication that helps to promote efficiency and alignment.

In his book "The Power of Habit," author Charles Duhigg describes the habit loop, which consists of three components: a cue, a routine, and a reward. The cue is a trigger that prompts the behavior, the routine is the behavior itself, and the reward is the positive outcome reinforcing the behavior and making it more likely to occur.

In the case of the Daily Scrum, the cue is the consistent time and place of the meeting, which triggers the routine of collaboration and communication among the Developers. The reward is the progress made toward the Sprint Goal and the satisfaction of working together effectively as a team.

Just like with the Daily Scrum, holding all Scrum events at the same time and place provides a cue that triggers the routine of collaboration and communication among the Scrum Team. This routine can become a habit that helps to streamline the Scrum process and improve the team's overall effectiveness.

8.3.2 Impact of not holding scrum events at the same time and place

If Scrum events are not held at the same time and place, it can lead to several challenges and issues that can impact the effectiveness of the Scrum Team. Here are some potential consequences:

1. Increased complexity and confusion: When events are held at different times and locations, it can be challenging to coordinate schedules and ensure that all team members are present. This can lead to confusion, missed meetings, and product development progress delays.
2. Reduced collaboration: When team members are spread out in different locations, collaborating and communicating effectively can be more difficult. This can lead to miscommunication, misunderstandings, and decreased productivity.
3. Lower quality work: When team members cannot collaborate effectively, it can lead to lower quality work. This can be especially true for tasks requiring multiple team members' input and feedback.
4. Lack of consistency: Holding events at different times and locations can lead to a lack of consistency in the process and approach to Scrum. This can make it more difficult to establish a sense of team unity and shared goals.
5. Missed opportunities for improvement: If team members cannot attend all events, they may miss out on important opportunities to provide feedback and suggest improvements. This can limit the team's ability to adapt and improve its processes over time.

In summary, holding Scrum events at different times and locations can create challenges and obstacles that can impact the effectiveness of the Scrum Team. Therefore, to optimize collaboration and effectiveness, it is best to hold all events at the same time and place whenever possible.

8.3.3 Time Blocking

Time Blocking is not mentioned in the Scrum Guide but is related to timeboxing and holding the events simultaneously and in place.

Time blocking is a productivity technique that involves setting aside specific blocks of time for particular tasks or activities. Time blocking aims to help individuals focus their attention and energy on a specific task or project rather than allowing distractions and interruptions to interfere with their work.

Individuals typically start by creating a schedule that outlines their daily activities and tasks to implement time blocking. They then allocate specific blocks of time for each task, prioritizing the most important and time-sensitive activities.

Time blocking can be a useful technique in Scrum for implementing timeboxing and ensuring that events are held at the same time and place. By setting specific blocks of time for each event and holding them at the same time and place, the Scrum Team can optimize collaboration and reduce complexity.

For example, the Scrum Team may use time blocking to set aside specific blocks of time for Sprint Planning, Daily Scrum, Sprint Review, and Sprint Retrospective. By allocating specific time periods for each event, the team can ensure they are completed within the timebox and do not run over schedule.

Holding events at the same time and place can also be facilitated by time blocking, as team members can schedule their time more efficiently and avoid scheduling conflicts. By using time blocking to set aside specific time periods for Scrum events and ensuring that they are held at the same time and place, the Scrum Team can optimize their productivity and effectiveness and stay focused on delivering valuable increments of the product.

8.3.4 Example of a scheduled Sprint Events

The following is an example of a two-week Sprint of a team using time blocking in the team's calendar. The Sprint starts on Monday and finishes by Friday of the second week. The Product Backlog refinement is not an event, but the team decided to block some time for this activity and allow ad-hoc refinement as needed.

Figure 22 Example of a schedule of a two-week Sprint

Part 9: The Sprint

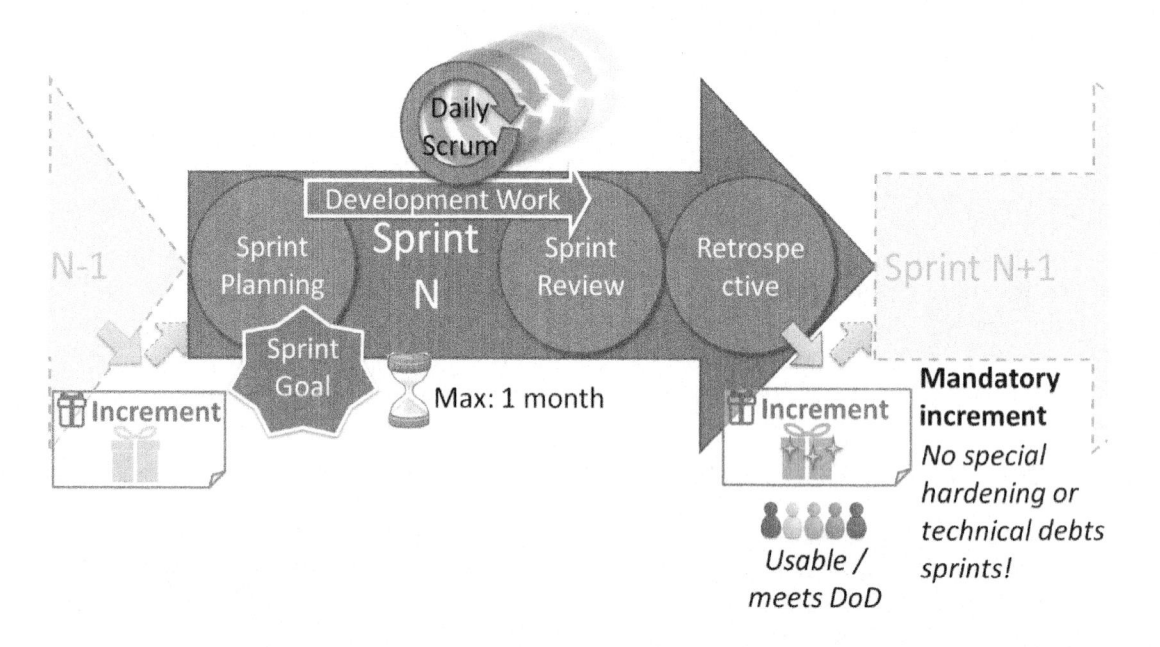

Figure 23 The Sprint.

> *Sprints are the heartbeat of Scrum, where ideas are turned into value.*

Sprints are a core element of the Scrum framework and are often called the heartbeat of Scrum. During a Sprint, the Developers work on a set of Product Backlog items selected during the Sprint Planning meeting. The Sprint aims to deliver a potentially shippable product increment that adds value to the end user.

Sprints are essential to the Scrum framework because they provide a regular cadence for the team to deliver value to the product. By focusing on a fixed set of work during a Sprint, the team can deliver value incrementally and respond to feedback and changes in requirements more effectively.

The outcome of the increment in a Sprint is typically affected by the following:

- The complexity of the Product Backlog Items.
- The complexity of technology.
- The working relationships and skills of the members of the Scrum Team.

The team's knowledge, skills, behaviors, unpredictable technology, and unpredictable requirements will impact its effectiveness in producing its increment, quality, and outcome.

9.1 The Sprint length

9.1.1 One month or less

> *They are fixed length events of one month or less to create consistency.*

Sprints are fixed-length events in Scrum that typically last between one and four weeks, with two weeks being a common duration. However, the Scrum Guide recommends that Sprints should be no longer than one month, as this allows for consistency in the development process and helps to maintain a regular cadence for the team.

The fixed length of Sprints serves several purposes in Scrum. Firstly, it helps to provide a predictable rhythm for the team, as they know when the Sprint begins and ends and can plan their work accordingly. This also helps to create a sense of urgency and focus within the team as they work to complete their commitments within the allotted time.

Second, the timeboxed nature of Sprints helps to maintain a sense of urgency and accountability within the team as they work to complete their commitments within the allotted time.

Additionally, the fixed length of Sprints makes it easier for the team to plan their work and estimate how much work they can realistically complete during a Sprint. This helps avoid over-committing or under-delivering and ensures the team can deliver a potentially shippable product increment at the end of each Sprint.

In a nutshell, the fixed length of Sprints is a fundamental aspect of Scrum and helps to create consistency and predictability in the development process while enabling the team to deliver value to the product regularly and incrementally.

9.1.2 Immutable length

Once a Sprint has started, its length cannot be modified. This is because the Sprint length is an important constraint that helps to establish a regular cadence and rhythm for the team, and changing it mid-Sprint could disrupt the team's focus and momentum.

However, it is worth noting that the Sprint length is not set in stone and can be adjusted between Sprints. Therefore, teams may experiment with different Sprint lengths to find the best one. This experimentation can help the team to optimize their workflow and increase their ability to deliver value regularly.

That being said, once a Sprint length has been established, it is generally recommended to keep it consistent over time unless there is a compelling reason to change. This consistency helps establish a regular rhythm for the team, increasing predictability and improving their ability to plan and deliver work effectively.

In summary, once a Sprint length has been established, it is generally best to keep it consistent by maintaining a regular cadence and improving predictability.

9.1.3 No time between Sprints

> *A new Sprint starts immediately after the conclusion of the previous Sprint.*

A new Sprint starts immediately after the conclusion of the previous Sprint. There is no timebox between Sprints. This means that as soon as the current Sprint ends, the team should start planning and preparing for the next Sprint. This helps to establish a regular cadence and rhythm for the team and ensures that progress is made regularly.

Starting a new Sprint immediately after the previous one also helps minimize downtime and ensures the team can maintain momentum. It also helps to establish a regular feedback loop, as the team can review the results of each Sprint and use that information to plan the next Sprint.

Overall, the immediate start of a new Sprint after the conclusion of the previous Sprint is a key aspect of the Scrum framework, helping to ensure that the team is able to work effectively and deliver value regularly.

> *All the work necessary to achieve the Product Goal, including Sprint Planning, Daily Scrums, Sprint Review, and Sprint Retrospective, happen within Sprints.*

Some people think the Sprint starts after the Sprint Planning, but on the contrary, the Sprint Planning occurs during the Sprint as its first event. There are no events or work between Sprints. The Scrum Team does all the work and holds the Scrum events between the start and end of the Sprint.

According to the Scrum framework, all the work necessary to achieve the Sprint Goal and pursue the Product Goal, including Sprint Planning, Daily Scrums, Sprint Review, and Sprint Retrospective, happens within Sprints. This means that during the time-boxed period of a Sprint, the Scrum Team is responsible for planning, executing, and reflecting on all the activities necessary to deliver a potentially releasable product increment.

9.1.4 No "Special" Sprints

Hardening Sprints, technical debt Sprints, Sprint 0, testing Sprints, QA Sprints, bug fixing Sprints, Release Sprints, or special Sprints are not part of the Scrum framework.

There may be many reasons a team decides to run a "special" Sprint that adds no new value to the product, but none are valid in the Scrum Framework. For example:

1. A team may schedule a "hardening Sprint" at the end of a release cycle to focus on bug fixing, stabilization, and performance optimization. This Sprint would not add any new features or functionality but instead, focus on ensuring the product is stable and ready for release.
2. A team decides to start the first Sprint with a "Sprint 0" to work on the initial phase of a project where, instead of delivering an increment, the team focuses on activities such as setting up the development environment, defining initial requirements, and establishing team norms and processes.
3. Similarly, a team may schedule a "technical debt Sprint" to address accumulated technical debt in the codebase. This Sprint would not add new features but instead focus on improving the quality and maintainability of the code.

These special Sprints are not a core part of the Scrum framework. Instead, the entire Scrum Team is accountable for creating a valuable, useful Increment for every Sprint that meets the Definition of Done.

The decision of these examples may be because:

- The team has a weak Definition of Done
- Developers can't meet the Definition of Done. For instance, because it is too hard, there is too much technical debt, the requirements and technology are too big or complex, or they don't have the skills to meet it.
- Developers are struggling to build usable increments.
- The Scrum Team has an upfront architectural, analysis, and design mindset instead of an emergent design mindset to use an iterative and incremental approach to deliver small pieces of functionality and value.

In summary, the problem with Special Sprints is that they change the rules of Scrum. The Sprint rules apply to all Sprints from the first one.

9.2 Rules during the Sprint

During the Sprint:

> - *No changes are made that would endanger the Sprint Goal;*
> - *Quality does not decrease;*
> - *The Product Backlog is refined as needed; and,*
> - *Scope may be clarified and renegotiated with the Product Owner as more is learned.*

9.2.1 No changes are made that would endanger the Sprint Goal

During a Sprint, the Scrum Team works towards achieving the Sprint Goal agreed upon during the Sprint Planning. The Sprint Goal represents the overall objective that the team will work towards during the Sprint and serves as a unifying theme or focus for the work that will be done.

To ensure that the team can effectively achieve the Sprint Goal, no changes are made during the Sprint that would endanger or compromise the ability of the team to deliver on the Sprint Goal. This means that the Sprint Backlog, which contains the list of items to be completed during the Sprint, can be changed to reflect the work needed to achieve the Sprint Goal but should not be changed in a way that would jeopardize the team's ability to meet the Sprint Goal.

For example, imagine a software Scrum Team working on a new e-commerce platform. During the Sprint, the team has committed to delivering features allowing customers to search for products and add them to their cart. However, midway through the Sprint, the Product Owner comes to the team with a request to add a new payment gateway to the checkout process. If the team were to stop working on their original commitment and switch their focus to adding the new payment gateway, this could jeopardize their ability to deliver on the original Sprint Goal within the allocated time frame. Therefore, the Scrum Master would work with the Product Owner to prioritize the new request and determine whether it can be added to the Product Backlog for the next Sprint or if it is critical enough to halt the current Sprint and start a new one with a new Sprint Goal.

9.2.2 Changes to the Sprint Goal

It is generally not recommended to change the Sprint Goal during the Sprint as it can disrupt the focus of the Scrum Team and potentially lead to failure to achieve the original Sprint Goal. However, if there is a compelling reason to change the Sprint Goal, it can be done with the agreement of the entire Scrum Team.

For instance, if the Sprint Goal's wording is unclear or needs to be improved for readability, it is generally acceptable to make changes during the Sprint. Still, changing the essence or objective of the Sprint Goal is not recommended. However, any changes to the Sprint Goal should be communicated clearly and transparently to the Scrum Team, Product Owner, and stakeholders to avoid confusion or misalignment.

On the other hand, if the Sprint Goal becomes obsolete, it may be preferable to cancel the Sprint altogether rather than try to salvage it with a revised goal. Canceling a Sprint is a serious decision that should only be made in exceptional circumstances. Canceling a Sprint can be disruptive, but it is important to remember that the ultimate goal is to deliver a high-quality product that meets the needs of the stakeholders.

9.2.3 Quality does not decrease

During the Sprint, the quality of the product being developed mustn't decrease. The quality standards defined in the Definition of Done (DoD) should be met to ensure that the increment of the product delivered at the end of the Sprint is potentially releasable and meets the needs of the stakeholders.

For example, if a Scrum Team is working on a new feature for a mobile application during a Sprint, one of the items in the Definition of Done is to conduct thorough user acceptance testing (UAT) before the feature is considered done. However, due to time constraints, the team skipped the UAT to deliver the feature faster.

This may seem like a good idea in the short term, as it allows the team to meet the Sprint deadline and deliver the feature on time. However, it can lead to quality and user satisfaction issues in the long term. For example, defects or other issues may impact the user experience if the feature is not thoroughly tested, leading to negative feedback and lower adoption rates.

If the team identifies these quality issues later on, addressing them may take more time and effort than conducting UAT in the first place. For example, the team may need to spend additional time debugging and fixing defects, or they may need to conduct additional rounds of testing to ensure that the feature is working as intended. This can delay future Sprints and impact the team's overall productivity.

In conclusion, it is important to prioritize quality during the Sprint and ensure that all items in the Definition of Done are met to deliver a potentially releasable increment of the product that meets the needs of the stakeholders. Skipping quality checks or taking shortcuts in the short term can lead to issues in the long term and impact the overall product's success.

9.2.3.1 The broken window theory

The concept of "quality does not decrease" during a Sprint can be related to the Broken Window Theory in that ignoring small issues or allowing quality to decrease during a Sprint can lead to larger problems down the line.

The Broken Window Theory suggests that if a broken window in a building is not repaired, it can signal to others that no one cares about the building, leading to more damage and destruction. Similarly, suppose quality standards are not upheld during a Sprint. In that case, it can signal to the team and stakeholders that quality is not a priority, leading to more issues in the future.

For example, if a team omits a part of the Definition of Done to deliver a feature faster, it may lead to future technical debt or quality issues. If these issues are not addressed promptly, they can accumulate and eventually lead to a significant decrease in quality or even project failure.

Therefore, it is important to prioritize quality and uphold the Definition of Done during each Sprint to prevent small issues from becoming larger problems down the line, similar to how repairing a broken window can prevent further damage to a building.

9.2.4 The Product Backlog is refined as needed

Product Backlog refinement is an ongoing activity, not a specific Scrum event. Therefore, the Product Backlog refinement is not timeboxed. The Scrum Team decides how much time they need to spend on refinement, as long as it does not endanger the current Sprint Goal.

For example, during a Sprint, the Developers may identify a Product Backlog item that is too large and complex to be completed in a single Sprint. Then, during the Sprint, they may break down that item into smaller, more manageable pieces. Refining the Product Backlog item allows the team to estimate more accurately, identify dependencies and risks, and improve their understanding of the work required.

The team may spend time during the Sprint refining the Product Backlog items for the next Sprint, such as reviewing and clarifying details or adding new items to the Product Backlog. However, they must ensure this activity does not jeopardize the current Sprint Goal.

Briefly, refining the Product Backlog is an important activity that helps ensure the success of the Sprint and the product. The Scrum Team needs to manage this activity effectively and balance it with other work to ensure they meet their Sprint commitments.

9.2.5 Scope may be clarified and renegotiated with the Product Owner as more is learned

During a Sprint, as the Scrum Team works on the Product Backlog items, they may discover new information or learn more about the requirements of the product. As a result, the scope of the Sprint Goal or individual Product Backlog items may need to be clarified or renegotiated with the Product Owner. It is common for requirements to be unclear from the beginning of a Sprint.

9.2.5.1 New ideas during the Sprint

Let's say the Scrum Team is working on an e-commerce website, and their Sprint Goal is to implement a new payment gateway. During the Sprint, the Product Owner realizes that customers should be able to cancel their orders, but this feature is not in the Sprint Backlog. The Scrum Team and the Product Owner discuss the options and agree to reduce the scope of another feature planned for the current Sprint, to add the new tracking feature and meet the Sprint Goal by the end of the Sprint.

Later in the Sprint, one of the Developers had a great idea for a new feature that could enhance the checkout process. The Developers discuss it, believing this feature could be implemented in the current Sprint without endangering the Sprint Goal. First, however, they must negotiate with the Product Owner to add it to the Sprint.

After a discussion, the Product Owner decides that the new feature does not add enough value to the product right now, and they choose not to add it to the Sprint. Instead, the Product Owner adds it to the Product Backlog for future consideration.

At the end of the Sprint, the Scrum Team successfully implemented the new payment gateway and the cancel order feature, delivering a high-quality product increment according to the Definition of Done. In addition, they focused on changing the scope, respecting the Sprint Goal, keeping quality standards, keeping pace, and working within their capacity for the Sprint.

In summary, during the Sprint, the scope may be clarified and renegotiated with the Product Owner as more is learned. The Scrum Team needs to negotiate with the Product Owner on any changes that could affect the Sprint Goal, and the Product Owner ultimately decides what is valuable for the product. Changes in scope can be time-consuming, so the Scrum Team needs to carefully consider the impact of any changes before negotiating with the Product Owner. If a Scrum Team spends considerable time negotiating big scope changes every Sprint, it may be a topic to address during the Sprint Retrospective.

9.2.5.2 Too much work to complete the Sprint Backlog

If the Developers realize that they cannot meet the Sprint Goal during the Sprint, they should immediately inform the Product Owner. The Scrum Team should then work together to evaluate the situation and determine what steps should be taken to get back on track.

For example, let's say that during the Sprint, the Developers realize that the work of the Sprint Backlog will take more time than expected, and it is unlikely that they will be able to complete all the items within the Sprint. In this case, the Scrum Team would discuss the situation and develop a plan to ensure they can still meet the Sprint Goal.

One possible solution might be to renegotiate the scope of the Sprint by removing some of the less critical items from the Sprint Backlog to ensure that the team can focus on completing the most important work related to the Sprint Goal.

The Scrum Team should not extend the Sprint length but instead look for ways to meet the Sprint Goal within the remaining time. This may involve negotiating with the Product Owner to adjust the scope or finding ways to work more efficiently as a team. Maintaining the Sprint length and normal working hours help ensure a consistent cadence and allows for more accurate planning and forecasting in the future.

Ultimately, the Scrum Team should work together to develop a plan to enable them to achieve the Sprint Goal while still maintaining the quality and value of the work being produced.

9.2.5.3 Unplanned work: critical bugs

Let's say that during a Sprint, a critical production bug is reported by a customer. Upon learning about this, the Product Owner determined that fixing this bug is of the utmost importance and needs to be included in the current Sprint. The Product Owner communicates this to the Developers, and they agree to renegotiate the Sprint Goal to include the critical bug fix.

To achieve this, the Scrum Team must put aside some of the lower-priority items from the Sprint Backlog to free up capacity for the critical bug fix. Then, the Product Owner and the Developers collaborate to adjust the Sprint Backlog accordingly and ensure that the Sprint Goal is still achievable while fixing the bug within the remaining time of the Sprint.

This negotiation and adjustment of scope allow the Developers to focus on the most important work for the Sprint and deliver a potentially shippable product increment that meets the revised Sprint Goal.

9.2.5.4 Unplanned work, but not critical

Let's say that during a Sprint, a customer report a critical bug to the Product Owner, which would require significant time and effort from the Developers to address. The Product Owner evaluates the bug and determines that while it is important, it is not so critical and would endanger the Sprint Goal of the current Sprint. The Product Owner adds the bug to the Product Backlog for consideration in a future Sprint. The Developers continue working on the items in the current Sprint Backlog to achieve the Sprint Goal. The Product Owner communicates their decision and arguments to the customer and how the bug will be addressed.

By making this decision, the Product Owner can maintain the focus on the current Sprint Goal and ensure that the team does not get distracted by adding significant work mid-Sprint that may endanger their ability to achieve the Sprint Goal. At the same time, the Product Owner can keep the bug in mind for future Sprints and address it when appropriate and does not jeopardize the progress of the current Sprint.

9.3 Predictability

> *Sprints enable predictability by ensuring inspection and adaptation of progress toward a Product Goal at least every calendar month.*

By breaking down the work into Sprints, the Scrum Team can regularly inspect and adapt their progress toward the Product Goal. This enables them to make course corrections as needed and ensure they are on track to deliver the desired outcomes.

In addition, the timeboxed nature of the Sprint provides a predictable cadence for the Scrum Team and stakeholders. By setting a fixed timeframe for each Sprint, the team can plan their work accordingly and ensure they can deliver a potentially releasable product increment at the end of each Sprint.

In simple words, Sprints in Scrum enable predictability by providing a regular cadence for inspection and adaptation and breaking down the work into manageable chunks that can be planned and executed within a fixed timeframe. This helps ensure the team stays on track and delivers value to stakeholders promptly and predictably.

9.3.1 Short vs. long Sprints

> *When a Sprint's horizon is too long the Sprint Goal may become invalid, complexity may rise, and risk may increase. Shorter Sprints can be employed to generate more learning cycles and limit risk of cost and effort to a smaller time frame.*

Short Sprints, typically between one to two weeks, allow for more frequent opportunities to gather stakeholder feedback, inspect and adapt the product, and pivot if necessary. This can be particularly helpful when building a product or service in a rapidly changing market or when there is a high degree of uncertainty regarding customer needs and preferences. Short Sprints also provide a sense of urgency and focus, as there is a constant deadline looming for the next Sprint Review. If the business requires constant adaptation to the market, it is easier to set a new meaningful Sprint Goal every Sprint.

On the other hand, long Sprints, typically between three to four weeks, may provide more time for the team to plan and execute a larger set of features or functionality. This can be particularly helpful when building complex or intricate systems requiring more design, development, and testing time. Longer Sprints may also be helpful when working with a distributed team or when significant dependencies on other teams or systems may require more coordination time.

However, longer Sprints also carry the risk of building the wrong product or not satisfying stakeholder expectations, as there may be less frequent opportunities to gather feedback and inspect and adapt the product. This can result in significant rework or a complete shift in direction if the product does not meet the customer's needs or the market. Additionally, longer Sprints may result in a loss of focus or urgency, as the deadline for the Sprint Review may seem further away and less pressing. Finally, if the business requires constant adaptation to the market, it is harder to adapt Sprint to new inputs, and the Sprint Goal may become meaningless.

Ultimately, the decision to use short or long Sprints should be based on the needs of the project and the product being developed, as well as the preferences and capabilities of the team. It may be helpful to experiment with different Sprint lengths and gather feedback from stakeholders and the team to determine what works best for the specific situation.

9.3.2 A Sprint is like a short project

> *Each Sprint may be considered a short project.*

Many people feel a change of mindset, purpose, meaning of value, and impact on users by using the term "Product" instead of "Project." This is positive, and it can be used to inspire people. However, "project" is not a bad word.

In Scrum, each Sprint is considered a short project because it has a defined goal, a set of requirements, a plan for execution, and a defined timeframe for completion.

Consider each Sprint as a short project to achieve a valuable goal of the Product and part of a bigger project to achieve the Product Goal and vision of the Product.

Like a project, the Sprint has a defined start and end date, a specific goal or outcome that the team is working towards, and a set of tasks or activities that must be completed to achieve that goal. Sprint is also managed using Scrum events and artifacts to inspect the progress and adapt as necessary.

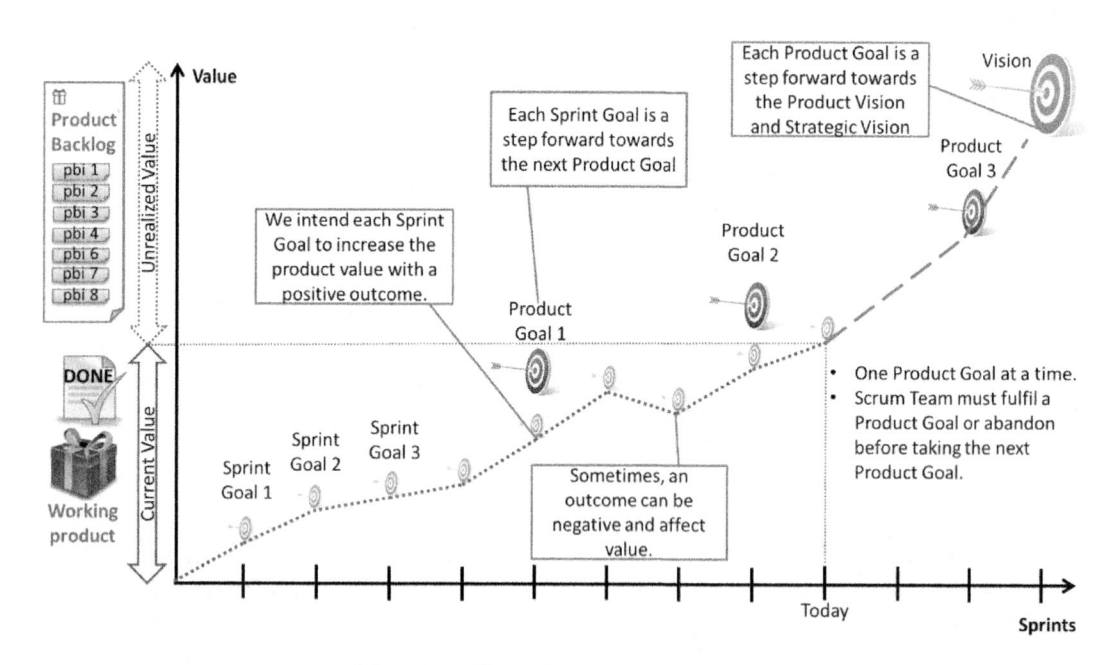

Figure 24 Adding value to each Sprint towards goals.

Notice that the vision is not required in Scrum, but Products typically have a Product Vision, or the organization may have a strategic vision overarching the Product Goals.

9.3.3 Experimentation and learning

Shorter Sprints also enable the team to generate more learning cycles and adapt their approach as needed.

Low-risk experiments, fail fast, pivot, and learning cycles are important concepts in Scrum that enable teams to innovate and improve their approach over time. Here's how these concepts compare in short Sprints vs. long Sprints:

Short Sprints:

- Low-risk experiments: Short Sprints are ideal for low-risk experiments that can be completed within the time frame of the Sprint. By focusing on a small experiment, the team can quickly gather feedback and make any necessary adjustments.
- Fail fast: Short Sprints enable the team to learn from their mistakes quickly. The team can quickly pivot and adjust their approach in the next Sprint by taking an iterative approach.
- Pivot: If an experiment does not produce the desired outcome, the team can quickly pivot and adjust their approach in the next Sprint. By working iteratively and incrementally, the team can refine its approach over time to achieve the desired outcome.
- Learning cycles: Short Sprints enable more frequent learning cycles, allowing the team to quickly adapt to changes in the business environment and improve their approach over time.

Long Sprints:

- Low-risk experiments: Longer Sprints can be used for more complex experiments that require more time and resources. By taking a longer-term approach, the team can gather more data and insights to inform their approach.
- Fail fast: Even in longer Sprints, it is still important to fail fast and learn quickly from mistakes. Then, if an experiment does not produce the desired outcome, the team can pivot and adjust their approach in the current or next Sprint.
- Pivot: If an experiment does not produce the desired outcome, the team can pivot and adjust their approach in the current or next Sprint. By working iteratively and incrementally, the team can refine its approach over time to achieve the desired outcome.
- Learning cycles: Longer Sprints enable the team to gather more data and insights over a longer time frame, which can be used to inform their approach and improve their outcomes.

Essentially, both short and long Sprints enable the team to leverage low-risk experiments, fail fast, pivot, and learning cycles to innovate and improve their approach over time. The key difference is that short Sprints enable more frequent learning cycles, while longer Sprints enable more in-depth data gathering and analysis. The choice of Sprint length depends on the complexity of the work and the level of risk involved.

9.3.4 Monitoring Sprint Progress

> *Various practices exist to forecast progress, like burn-downs, burn-ups, or cumulative flows. While proven useful, these do not replace the importance of empiricism. In complex environments, what will happen is unknown. Only what has already happened may be used for forward-looking decision making.*

The Developers decide how to track, manage, and monitor the progress during the Sprint.

Developers can sum the total work remaining in the Sprint Backlog at any time in a Sprint. Then, the Developers can track this total work remaining at least for every Daily Scrum to forecast the likelihood of achieving the Sprint Goal. By tracking the remaining work throughout the Sprint, the Developers can manage their progress, inspect it during the Daily Scrum, and take corrective actions.

In Scrum, empiricism is a fundamental principle that underpins the entire framework. It is making decisions based on observable evidence rather than relying on assumptions or speculation. Scrum leverages empiricism to enable teams to regularly inspect and adapt their approach based on the feedback they receive from stakeholders.

While various practices exist to forecast progress, such as burn-downs, burn-ups, Kanban metrics, or cumulative flows, these are not mandatory and are not meant to replace the importance of empiricism. Instead, these practices provide visibility into progress and identify potential issues or risks that must be addressed.

For example, a burn-down chart represents the amount of work remaining in the Sprint Backlog, whereas a burn-up chart shows the total work completed over time. Both of these charts can be used to forecast progress, identify potential issues, and make data-driven decisions.

Similarly, a cumulative flow diagram is a tool for visualizing the flow of work through the Scrum process, which can help teams to identify bottlenecks and optimize their workflow.

However, it's important to remember that these practices are only as useful as the data used to create them. Empiricism is still the foundation of Scrum, and teams should always seek ways to gather and analyze data to improve their process and outcomes.

Finally, besides any technique, the Daily Scrum is a key event for the Developers to inspect their progress toward the Sprint Goal and adapt.

9.4 Canceling a Sprint

> *A Sprint could be cancelled if the Sprint Goal becomes obsolete. Only the Product Owner has the authority to cancel the Sprint.*

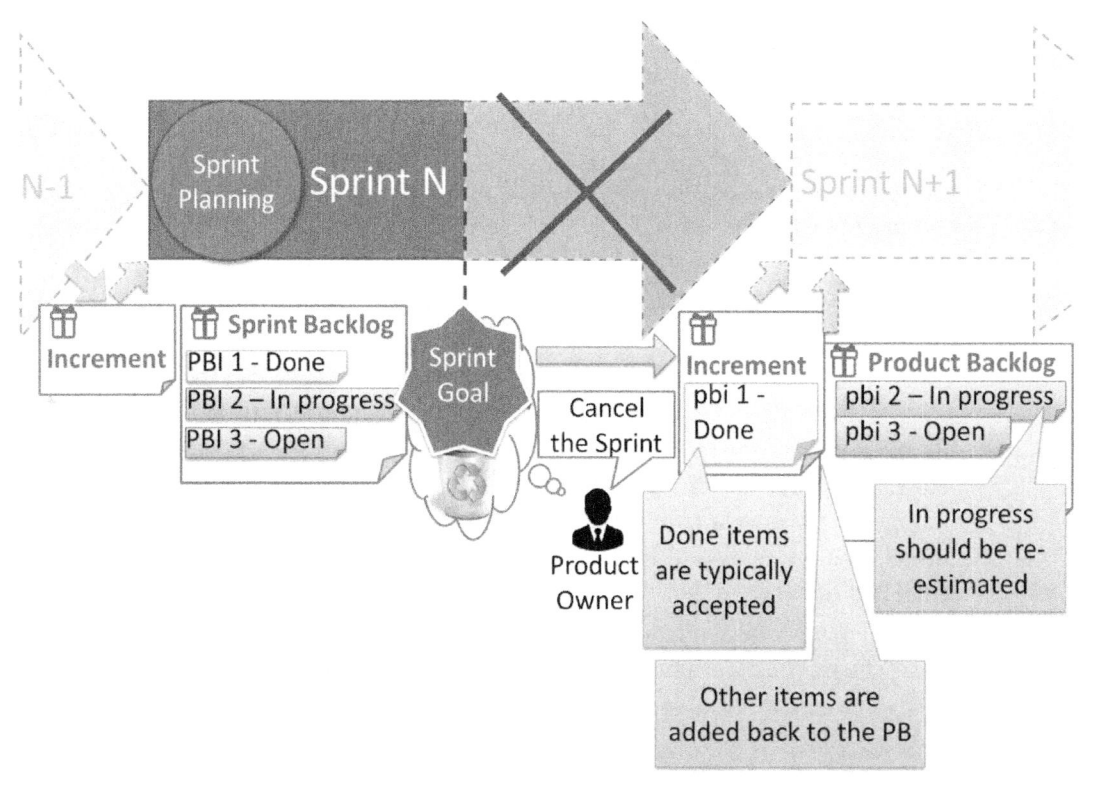

Figure 25 Canceling a Sprint.

If the Sprint Goal becomes obsolete or no longer provides value to the team during a Sprint, then it may be necessary to cancel the Sprint. However, canceling a Sprint is an extreme measure and should only be done when there is no other way to achieve the Sprint Goal.

Because the Product Owner decides what is valuable or not for the Product, only the Product Owner can cancel a Sprint.

However, canceling a Sprint should not be done unilaterally by the Product Owner. Instead, it should be done in consultation with the Developers and the Scrum Master. The Developers can provide insights into the progress made towards the current Sprint Goal, technical impact, consequences, and other aspects. The Scrum Master can guide how to proceed and ensure that the Scrum framework is followed when canceling the Sprint.

9.4.1 Reasons Why a Sprint Goal may become obsolete

There are various reasons why a Sprint Goal can become obsolete during a Sprint. Here are some examples:

- Change in business priorities: A change in business priorities can lead to a shift in the Product Backlog items, which may make the Sprint Goal obsolete. For instance, a new business requirement that is way more critical than the current Sprint Goal may emerge during the Sprint.

- Technical challenges: Technical challenges may arise during the Sprint, making it difficult for the Developers to achieve the Sprint Goal. In such cases, the Sprint Goal may need to be re-evaluated to ensure it is still achievable, given the technical constraints.
- Changes in customer needs: Customer needs may change during the Sprint, making the original Sprint Goal irrelevant. For instance, customer feedback may reveal that a particular feature is no longer needed, and the Sprint Goal may need to be modified to reflect this change.
- Higher costs: If, during the Sprint, the Developers realize that the cost for such Sprint Goal is much higher than expected, then the value vs. cost ratio may become unattractive for the Product Owner compared to other business goals.
- Unforeseen circumstances: Unforeseen circumstances such as a pandemic, natural disaster, or unforeseen technical issue may arise during the Sprint, making it impossible to achieve the original Sprint Goal. In such cases, the Sprint Goal may need to be re-evaluated, and the Sprint may need to be cancelled or rescheduled.
- Dependencies: Dependencies on external teams or systems may cause delays or issues during the Sprint, making it impossible to achieve the original Sprint Goal. The Sprint Goal may need to be revised to consider the dependencies.

In summary, the Sprint Goal can become obsolete for various reasons, such as changes in business priorities, technical challenges, customer needs, unforeseen circumstances, or dependencies. Therefore, the Scrum Team must remain flexible and adapt to changes during the Sprint to ensure that the Sprint Goal remains relevant and achievable.

9.4.2 Why not just adapt the Sprint Goal?

While changing the Sprint Goal is a common way to adapt to changing circumstances during a Sprint, there may be situations where canceling the Sprint is the most appropriate course of action. However, big changes in the essence of the Spring Goal and difficulties after the Sprint Planning. If the new Sprint Goal is different, it may need different work to achieve. Therefore, it is better to go to new Sprint Planning by canceling the current Sprint and starting a new Sprint to forecast the work with realistic expectations.

Here are some reasons why canceling Sprint may be necessary:

- The Sprint Goal is no longer relevant: If the Sprint Goal is no longer relevant, and no alternative goals can be pursued, then canceling the Sprint may be the most appropriate course of action. For example, this could happen if the original goal is no longer needed due to changes in business priorities or if it is technically impossible to achieve the original goal.
- The Sprint Goal cannot be achieved within the Sprint time-box: If it becomes clear during the Sprint that the Developers will not be able to achieve the Sprint Goal within the time box, then canceling the Sprint may be the best option. For example, this could happen if the team encounters unexpected technical

challenges or dependencies or if external factors make it impossible to complete the work within the Sprint time-box.
- The cost of continuing the Sprint outweighs the benefits: If it becomes clear that continuing the Sprint would be more costly than the benefits of achieving the Sprint Goal, then canceling the Sprint may be the best option. For example, this could happen if the team encounters unexpected technical challenges requiring significant additional resources or changes in business priorities that make achieving the Sprint Goal less valuable.
- The Developers and Product Owner cannot agree on a revised Sprint Goal: If the Scrum Team and Product Owner cannot agree on a revised Sprint Goal that is relevant and achievable, then canceling the Sprint may be the best option. For example, this could happen if there are significant disagreements between the team and the Product Owner about what is feasible or valuable.

In summary, while changing the Sprint Goal is often the most appropriate course of action when circumstances change during a Sprint, there may be situations where canceling the Sprint is the best option. The decision to cancel the Sprint should be made in consultation with the Developers, Product Owner, and Scrum Master, considering the costs and benefits of continuing the Sprint and the feasibility of achieving the Sprint Goal within the time box.

9.4.3 *Costs and Impact of Cancelling a Sprint*

Canceling a Sprint in Scrum can cost and impact the project and the team. Here are some examples:

- Time and effort: Cancelling a Sprint can result in wasted time and effort spent on work that will not be completed. The team may need to start over with new work or refocus on other priorities.
- Reduced productivity: Cancelling a Sprint can disrupt the team's momentum and reduce productivity. The team may need time to regroup and refocus on new priorities, which can delay the project's progress.
- Loss of stakeholder confidence: Cancelling a Sprint can erode stakeholder confidence in the project and the team's ability to deliver. Stakeholders may question the team's ability to manage the project and may have concerns about delays and additional costs.
- Delayed time-to-market: Cancelling a Sprint can delay the time-to-market for the product. The team may need to reschedule work and adjust timelines, which can delay product delivery to customers.
- Additional costs: Cancelling a Sprint can result in additional costs, such as wasted resources and time spent on replanning and rescheduling work. These costs can impact the project's budget and may require additional funding to complete the project.
- Team morale: Cancelling a Sprint can harm team morale. The team may feel demotivated or frustrated by the delay or priority changes.

In summary, canceling a Sprint can have high costs and impacts on the project and team. The decision to cancel a Sprint should be made carefully, in consultation with the Developers, Product Owner, and Scrum Master, considering the costs and benefits of continuing the Sprint and the feasibility of achieving the Sprint Goal within the time box. The Scrum Team should work together to minimize the impact of canceling a Sprint and to develop a plan to move forward.

9.4.4 Communicating Sprint Cancellation

Communicating a Sprint cancellation is important and should be transparent and clear. These are some steps that you can follow when communicating a Sprint cancellation:

1. Notify the team: The first step in communicating a Sprint cancellation is to notify the Developers, Scrum Master, and Product Owner as soon as possible. This can be done in person or through a group communication tool, such as a messaging app or email.
2. Explain the reasons: The team should be given a clear explanation of the reasons for canceling the Sprint, such as changes in business priorities, technical challenges, or external factors that make it impossible to achieve the Sprint Goal within the time box.
3. Discuss the impact: The team should be informed of the impact of canceling the Sprint, including any delays or changes to project timelines and any additional costs or resource requirements.
4. Answer questions: The team may have questions about the cancellation, and it is important to answer them honestly and openly. The Scrum Master or Product Owner may need to provide additional information or clarification to ensure that everyone understands the situation.
5. Plan next steps: Once the Sprint is canceled, the team should work together to plan the next steps, such as rescheduling work or adjusting timelines. The Scrum Master may need to facilitate discussions to ensure the team is aligned on the new plan.
6. Communicate to stakeholders: Depending on the impact of the Sprint cancellation, it may be necessary to communicate to stakeholders, such as customers or sponsors, to inform them of the delay or changes to project timelines. The Scrum Master or Product Owner should be responsible for communicating with stakeholders and ensuring that they understand the situation.

In summary, communicating a Sprint cancellation requires transparency, clarity, and open communication. The Scrum Team should work together to understand the impact of the cancellation and plan the next steps to minimize the impact on the project and team morale. In addition, the Scrum Master and Product Owner should be responsible for communicating with stakeholders and ensuring they are informed of any changes to project timelines or deliverables.

9.5 Anti-patterns of the Sprint

Anti-patterns are common mistakes or bad practices that can hinder the effectiveness of Sprint in Scrum. Here are some examples of Sprint antipatterns:

1. Overcommitment: The Scrum Team should avoid overcommitting to the work they can complete in a Sprint. Overcommitment can lead to low-quality work, delays, and burnout.
2. Scope creep: The Scrum Team should avoid adding new requirements that were not agreed upon during the Sprint Planning or changing the scope of the Sprint during the Sprint without the agreement of the Scrum Team. This practice can disrupt the team's focus and hinder progress. For example, if a Developer adds a feature that was not agreed upon, even if he thought it was a great idea, the Product Owner did not assess its value and must be removed from the Increment for Sprint Review.
3. Lack of collaboration: The Sprint is a collaborative effort, and the Scrum Team should work together to achieve the Sprint Goal. Lack of collaboration can lead to delays, misunderstandings, and low-quality work.
4. Micromanagement: The Scrum Master should avoid micromanaging the Scrum Team during the Sprint. Micromanagement can lead to low morale and hinder creativity and innovation.
5. Lack of transparency: The Scrum Team should ensure transparency in their work during the Sprint. Lack of transparency can lead to misunderstandings, miscommunication, and a lack of trust among team members.
6. Poor prioritization: The Scrum Team should prioritize their work during the Sprint based on the Product Backlog and the Sprint Goal. Poor prioritization can lead to delays, low-quality work, and a failure to achieve the Sprint Goal.
7. Technical debt: The Scrum Team should avoid accumulating technical debt during the Sprint. Technical debt can lead to low-quality work, delays, and a failure to achieve the Sprint Goal.

To avoid these antipatterns, the Scrum Master should ensure that the Scrum Team follows the Scrum framework and establishes clear guidelines for the Sprint. In addition, they should encourage collaboration, transparency, and focus and work with the Product Owner to ensure that the Sprint Goal and Product Backlog are well-defined and prioritized. This will help ensure that Sprint is an effective tool for delivering value to the product's customers and promoting continuous improvement within the Scrum Team.

Part 10: Sprint Planning

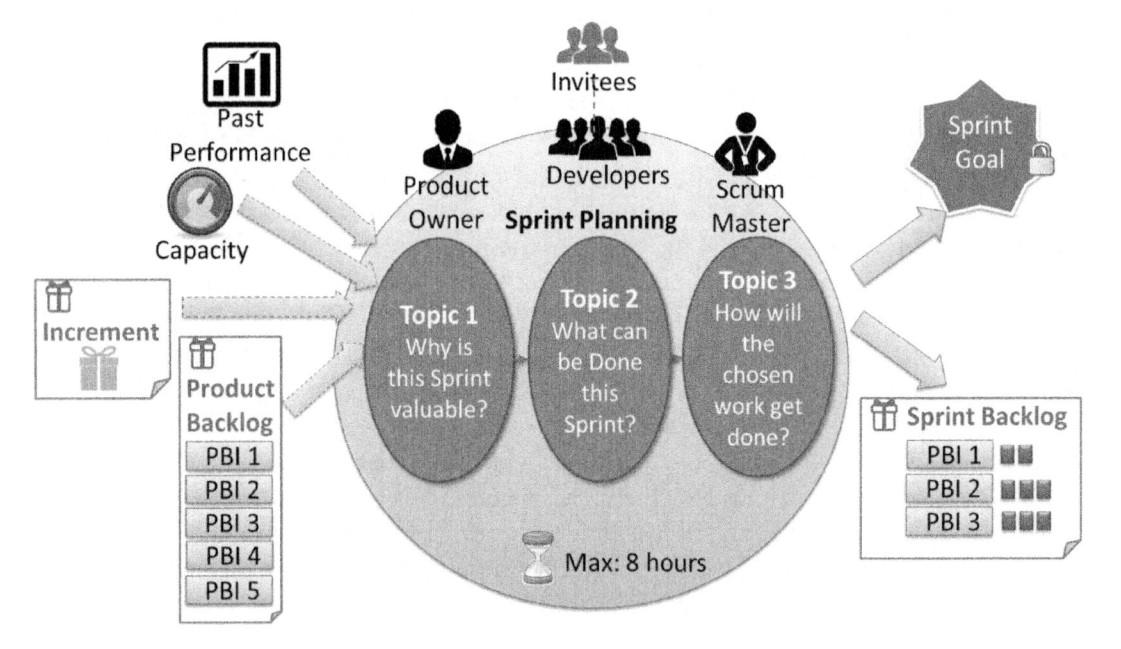

Figure 26 Sprint Planning.

10.1 Collaborative planning

Sprint Planning initiates the Sprint by laying out the work to be performed for the Sprint.

Sprint Planning is a crucial event in Scrum that initiates the Sprint. Therefore, Sprint and Sprint Planning start at the same time.

10.2 The first event of the Sprint

This resulting plan is created by the collaborative work of the entire Scrum Team.

In Scrum, Sprint Planning is a collaborative effort of the entire Scrum Team, which includes the Product Owner, the Developers, and the Scrum Master. During the Sprint Planning, the Scrum Team works together to create a plan for the upcoming Sprint with a meaningful Sprint Goal for the business that will guide their work towards achieving such a goal.

10.3 Focus on the Product Goal

> *The Product Owner ensures that attendees are prepared to discuss the most important Product Backlog items and how they map to the Product Goal.*

In Sprint Planning, the Product Owner plays a critical role in ensuring that the team is focused on delivering the most valuable work for the Sprint. In addition, the Product Owner ensures that all attendees are prepared to discuss the most important Product Backlog items that will contribute to achieving the Product Goal.

This means that the Product Owner must clearly understand the Product Backlog items that are likely to be worked on during the Sprint and their priority order. In addition, they should be able to explain the rationale behind the priority order and how each item contributes to the Product Goal.

During the Sprint Planning meeting, the Scrum Team collaborates to determine which items will be included in the upcoming Sprint. The Product Owner guides the priority of the items, while the Developers provide input on the feasibility and effort required to complete each item. Together, they create a plan for the Sprint that is realistic and aligned with the Product Goal.

Let's say that during Sprint Planning, the Product Owner ensures that all attendees have a clear understanding of the Product Goal and business goals that need to be achieved to fulfill that vision. They may remind the team of the Product Goal and provide additional context on why certain Product Backlog items are more important than others.

The Scrum Team collaborates to craft the Sprint Goal based on the Product Goal, business goals, and the most important Product Backlog items already refined and ready for Sprint Planning. Then, the Scrum Team uses this information to guide their discussions on what work will be performed during the Sprint and how they will achieve the Sprint Goal.

By ensuring that everyone clearly understands the Product Goal and business goals, the team can make informed decisions about which backlog items to prioritize and how to plan the work for the Sprint. This helps to ensure that the Sprint Goal is achievable and aligned with the Product Goal, ultimately driving the product towards success.

10.4 Invitees to the Sprint Planning

> *The Scrum Team may also invite other people to attend Sprint Planning to provide advice.*

Sometimes, the Scrum Team may find it valuable to invite others to attend the Sprint Planning meeting to provide advice and insights.

For example, the team might invite a subject matter expert to help clarify some technical or domain aspects of a feature they plan to work on during the Sprint. Or they might invite a UX designer to provide input on improving the user experience for a particular feature.

In another scenario, the team might invite a customer or end-user representative to attend the Sprint Planning meeting to provide feedback on the planned features. Again, this can help ensure that the team is building the right thing and that the product is meeting the needs of its intended audience.

Regardless of who is invited to the Sprint Planning meeting, it's important to remember that the Scrum Team is ultimately responsible for deciding what work will be performed during the Sprint. Of course, the input and advice provided by external attendees should be considered, but the Scrum Team has the final say on what work will be done.

10.5 Three topics: Why, what, and how

Sprint Planning addresses the following topics:

- *Topic One: Why is this Sprint valuable?*
- *Topic Two: What can be Done this Sprint?*
- *Topic Three: How will the chosen work get done?*

10.5.1 Topic One: Why is this Sprint valuable?

Topic One: Why is this Sprint valuable?

The Product Owner proposes how the product could increase its value and utility in the current Sprint. The whole Scrum Team then collaborates to define a Sprint Goal that communicates why the Sprint is valuable to stakeholders. The Sprint Goal must be finalized prior to the end of Sprint Planning.

In this part of Sprint Planning, the Product Owner and the Scrum Team work together to define the purpose and value of the upcoming Sprint. The Product Owner proposes ideas on how to increase the value and utility of the product, and the Scrum Team discusses and collaborates to define a clear and specific Sprint Goal that communicates the value of the Sprint to stakeholders.

For example, suppose the product is an online grocery store. In that case, the Product Owner might want to increase the speed and accuracy of order fulfillment and propose to add features such as automated order tracking, optimizing the inventory management system, and streamlining the order fulfillment process. The Scrum Team would then work together to define a Sprint Goal as "Increase the speed and accuracy of order fulfillment to improve customer satisfaction" and forecast if the Developers can deliver these features within the Sprint while maintaining the overall quality of the product.

It is important to note that the Sprint Goal must be finalized before the end of Sprint Planning to ensure that everyone on the team clearly understands what needs to be accomplished during the Sprint. In addition, the Sprint Goal also serves as a guide throughout the Sprint, helping the team stay focused and aligned with the overall vision of the product.

10.5.2 Topic Two: What can be Done this Sprint?

> *Topic Two: What can be Done this Sprint?*
>
> *Through discussion with the Product Owner, the Developers select items from the Product Backlog to include in the current Sprint. The Scrum Team may refine these items during this process, which increases understanding and confidence.*
>
> *Selecting how much can be completed within a Sprint may be challenging. However, the more the Developers know about their past performance, their upcoming capacity, and their Definition of Done, the more confident they will be in their Sprint forecasts.*

During the second topic of Sprint Planning, the Scrum Team discusses what work they can complete during the upcoming Sprint. In this phase, the Developers work with the Product Owner to select items from the refined Product Backlog that align with the Sprint Goal and that they believe they can complete within the Sprint time-box. Again, the team may refine these items during the discussion to increase their understanding and confidence in the work.

For example, in the online grocery shop, the Scrum Team may select items from the Product Backlog that focus on improving customer experience during the checkout process, such as optimizing the payment gateway and improving the user interface. The team may also consider items that address technical debt, such as refactoring code for better maintainability.

Selecting how much work the team can realistically complete during the Sprint can be challenging. To help forecast how much work they can complete, the Developers can consider their past performance, upcoming capacity, and Definition of Done. By doing so, they can forecast how much work they can complete during the Sprint and commit to a realistic goal that aligns with the Sprint Goal.

- Past performance refers to the team's ability to complete work in previous Sprints. By reviewing their past performance, the Developers can get an idea of how much work they can typically complete in a Sprint. For instance, some Scrum Teams review their velocity. Notice that velocity is an optional metric not part of the Scrum Framework.
- Upcoming capacity refers to the Developers' time and resources available for the upcoming Sprint. This includes factors such as team availability, holidays, and any other commitments that may impact the team's ability to complete work.

- Finally, the Definition of Done is a shared understanding of what it means for a Product Backlog item to be "done" and ready to ship. By clearly defining the criteria for completing a task, the Developers can more accurately estimate the effort required to complete it.

For example, in an online grocery shop, the Developers can review their past performance in completing tasks related to the website's user interface. They could also compare the estimated sizes of the desired features for this Sprint and how much similar work they completed in previous Sprints. They can also consider any upcoming availability issues, such as an upcoming holiday season that may increase website traffic, a team member taking days off, and another team member attending a three-day programming conference. Finally, they can review their Definition of Done to ensure they have a shared understanding of all the work required to complete tasks related to the desired features without reducing the expected level of quality defined in the Definition of Done. By considering these factors, the Developers can make a good forecast of how much work they can complete during the upcoming Sprint.

10.5.3 Topic Three: How will the chosen work get done?

> *Topic Three: How will the chosen work get done?*
>
> *For each selected Product Backlog item, the Developers plan the work necessary to create an Increment that meets the Definition of Done. This is often done by decomposing Product Backlog items into smaller work items of one day or less. How this is done is at the sole discretion of the Developers. No one else tells them how to turn Product Backlog items into Increments of value.*
>
> *The Sprint Goal, the Product Backlog items selected for the Sprint, plus the plan for delivering them are together referred to as the Sprint Backlog.*

Once the Product Backlog items have been selected for the Sprint, the Developers plan the work required to turn them into an Increment of value that meets the Definition of Done. This planning process typically involves breaking down each Product Backlog item into smaller, more manageable tasks that can be completed in one day or less.

The specific techniques and tools used to plan and manage this work are at the Developers' discretion.

The Sprint Goal is an overarching objective that guides the work of the Developers during the Sprint. It should be clear and concise and should align with the larger goals of the product and the organization. The Sprint Goal may be adjusted or refined throughout the Sprint as the Developers better understand the work required to achieve it.

The Sprint Backlog is the plan of the Developers for the Sprint. It is a list of the tasks and activities required to turn the selected Product Backlog items into an Increment of value that meets the Definition of Done. It includes all the tasks required to design, develop, test, and deploy the software and any other activities required to meet the Definition of Done.

During the Sprint, the Developers work on the tasks and activities in the Sprint Backlog, intending to complete all of them by the end of the Sprint. The Sprint Backlog created during the Sprint Planning is not a definitive or detailed plan, but good enough to start the Sprint with a clear understanding of the effort needed to achieve the Sprint Goal. Developers may adjust their plan and the Sprint Backlog as needed throughout the Sprint to ensure they remain on track to achieve the Sprint Goal.

At the end of the Sprint, the Developers should have created an Increment of value that meets the Definition of Done and contributes to the overall goals of the product and the organization. This Increment is then reviewed by the Product Owner and other stakeholders, who provide feedback and identify any additional work that needs to be done in future Sprints.

A non-mandatory way to validate if there is a plan for the Sprint is to ask the Developers if they can explain their plan for the Sprint to the Product Owner and the Scrum Master.

10.5.4 Forecast vs. Commit

The Developers "forecast" the items they can complete during a Sprint, and they "commit" to the Sprint Goal.

"Forecasting" the items of a Sprint refers to estimating how much work the Developers believe they can complete during the Sprint based on their past performance, upcoming capacity, and Definition of Done. This is not a commitment but rather a prediction. The term "forecast" in Scrum indicates that the team anticipates the future while planning; not everything is certain. As a result, the Developers cannot guarantee that the plan will remain unaltered, as it is a projection based on the available information now.

On the other hand, "committing" to a Sprint Goal means that the Developers are dedicated to achieving the agreed-upon goal by the end of the Sprint, as defined by the Sprint Backlog. It is a firm commitment to achieving the goal rather than just predicting how much work can be completed.

A forecast can fail if the work takes longer than anticipated or unexpected impediments or issues occur. However, if the Developers communicate these issues with the Product Owner, they can renegotiate the scope to ensure that the Sprint Goal is still achievable. In that case, the Scrum Team can achieve the Sprint Goal with fewer features of high quality.

In contrast, if the Developers commit to a Sprint Goal but cannot achieve it, this can lead to a failure to deliver value to stakeholders. Therefore, the Developers must communicate to the Product Owner as soon as possible if they realize they cannot achieve the Sprint Goal. This allows the Product Owner to communicate with stakeholders, renegotiate expectations, or find a workaround to minimize the business impact.

It is better to communicate any issues or concerns early in the Sprint so that the team can work together to find a solution and adjust the scope or Sprint Goal if necessary. In addition, the Scrum framework is designed to encourage transparency, so it is important for the team to communicate openly and honestly with each other and with the Product Owner.

Therefore, it is important for the Developers to carefully consider their capacity and ability to achieve the Sprint Goal before committing to it.

10.6 Max Timebox: 8 hours

> *Sprint Planning is timeboxed to a maximum of eight hours for a one-month Sprint. For shorter Sprints, the event is usually shorter.*

Sprint Planning is a time-boxed event and should be no more than eight hours for a one-month Sprint. The length of the Sprint itself influences the timebox for Sprint Planning.

The timebox for Sprint Planning is usually shorter for shorter Sprints. For example, a two-week Sprint might have a timebox of four hours for Sprint Planning, while a one-week Sprint might have a timebox of two hours. However, this is not a formula. While a four-hour timebox for Sprint Planning sounds reasonable for a two-week Sprint, the Scrum Team may choose to use a longer or shorter timebox based on their specific needs and circumstances. In any case, the maximum timebox is 8 hours.

For instance, in a two-week Sprint, a mature Scrum Team may be fine with a 2-hour Sprint Planning, while a newly formed Scrum Team may need a 5-hours Sprint Planning.

The specific timebox for Sprint Planning can be adjusted as needed to ensure that the event is efficient and effective while still providing enough time for the Scrum Team to plan and organize their work for the upcoming Sprint.

10.7 Communicating the Sprint Goal

The Scrum Framework does not mandate communication of the Sprint Goal.

However, the Sprint Goal is an important communication tool for the Scrum Team and stakeholders, as it helps everyone understand the purpose of the Sprint and the expected outcomes.

After the Sprint Planning event, The Product Owner may want to communicate the Sprint Goal and the features that will be worked on during the Sprint to the stakeholders. This can be done through a variety of communication channels, including:

- Sprint Review: The Sprint Review is an event at the end of the Sprint where the Scrum Team presents the results of their work to stakeholders. This is an opportunity to showcase the features worked on during the Sprint and discuss progress toward the Sprint Goal.
- Product Backlog: The Product Backlog is a prioritized list of features and items the Scrum Team will work on over time. It is vital for the Scrum Team to keep

the Product Backlog up-to-date and to communicate changes and updates to the stakeholders.
- Status updates: The Scrum Team can update stakeholders throughout the Sprint to inform them of progress toward the Sprint Goal. This could include regular reports or updates on the status of specific features or items.
- Meetings or presentations: The Scrum Team may also schedule meetings or presentations with stakeholders to discuss the Sprint Goal and features. This could include meetings with customers or user groups to gather feedback or presentations to management or other stakeholders to discuss progress and next steps.

The Scrum Framework does not impede stakeholders from giving feedback during the Sprint before the Sprint Review. On the contrary, an agile principle says that "Business people and Developers must work together daily throughout the project." However, in some environments that are not always possible or could affect the focus, the Sprint Review is a mandatory event to collaborate with stakeholders.

10.8 Anti-patterns of the Sprint Planning

Antipatterns are common mistakes or bad practices that can hinder the effectiveness of Sprint Planning in Scrum. Here are some examples of Sprint Planning antipatterns:

1. Lack of preparation: The Scrum Team should adequately prepare for Sprint Planning to ensure the meeting is productive. Lack of preparation can lead to delays, misunderstandings, and a failure to achieve the Sprint Goal.
2. Lack of focus: Sprint Planning should focus on the Sprint Goal and the work required to achieve it. Discussions about unrelated topics or tasks can distract from the meeting's purpose.
3. Over-analysis: The Scrum Team should avoid over-analyzing the work required to achieve the Sprint Goal. Over-analysis can lead to delays and a lack of progress.
4. Over-commitment: The Scrum Team should avoid committing to more work than they can complete in the Sprint. Over-commitment can lead to low-quality work, delays, and burnout.
5. Lack of collaboration: Sprint Planning is a collaborative effort, and the Scrum Team should work together to achieve the Sprint Goal. Lack of collaboration can lead to misunderstandings, delays, and a failure to achieve the Sprint Goal.
6. Lack of flexibility: The Scrum Team should be flexible during Sprint Planning and willing to adapt to the Product Backlog or Sprint Goal changes. Lack of flexibility can lead to delays and a failure to achieve the Sprint Goal.
7. Poor time management: Sprint Planning is time-boxed, and the Scrum Team should manage their time effectively to ensure they achieve the Sprint Goal. Poor time management can lead to delays and a failure to achieve the Sprint Goal.

To avoid these antipatterns, the Scrum Master should ensure that the Scrum Team follows the Scrum framework and establishes clear guidelines for Sprint Planning. They should encourage collaboration, flexibility, and focus and work with the Product Owner to ensure the Product Backlog is well-defined and prioritized. This will help ensure that Sprint Planning is an effective tool for achieving the Sprint Goal and delivering value to the product's customers.

Part 11: Daily Scrum

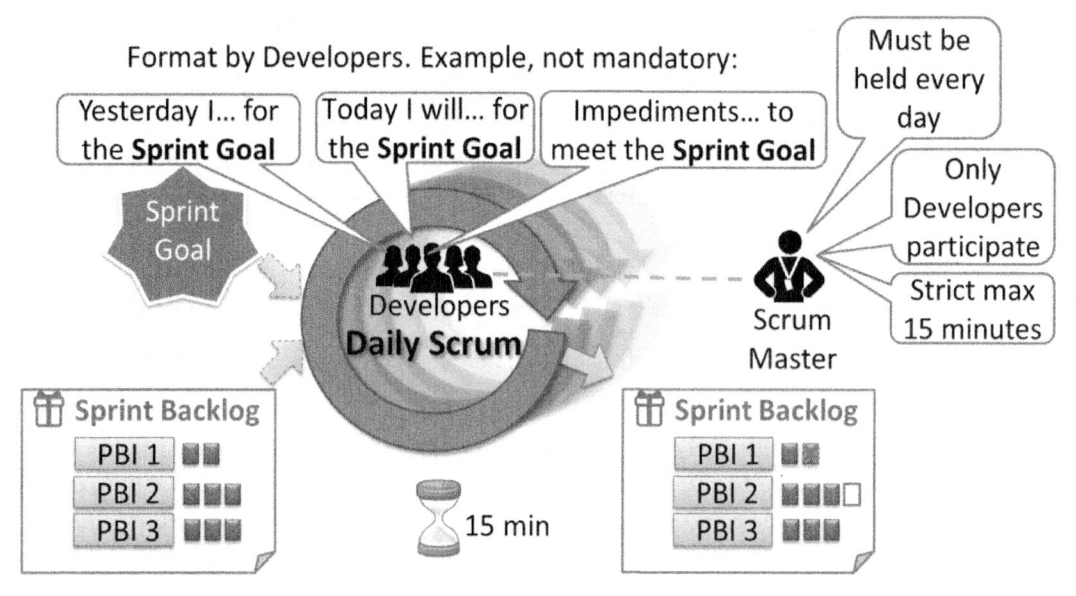

Figure 27 Daily Scrum.

The purpose of the Daily Scrum is to inspect progress toward the Sprint Goal and adapt the Sprint Backlog as necessary, adjusting the upcoming planned work.

During the Sprint Planning, Developers committed to achieving the Sprint Goal by the end of the Sprint. No one manages the Developers' progress because they manage their progress themselves. The Daily Scrum is a inspect and adapt meeting where the Developers inspect their progress to it and adapt the plan or Sprint Backlog.

The Daily Scrum is an event for the Developers and by the Developers. It is not a report session.

It is important to mention that the Daily Scrum is not a report session. The purpose of the meeting is not to provide detailed reports or status updates on individual tasks or items in the Sprint Backlog. Instead, it is a collaborative meeting where the team works together to plan their work and identify any potential issues that need to be addressed.

11.1 Timebox: 15 minutes

> *The Daily Scrum is a 15-minute event for the Developers of the Scrum Team.*

The 15-minute timebox for the Daily Scrum is intended to keep the meeting short and focused and to encourage the team to stay on track and avoid going into too much detail or getting sidetracked by unrelated topics. It is also intended to encourage the team to communicate frequently and stay up-to-date on each other's progress and activities.

However, it's important to note that the 15-minute timebox is a guideline, not a hard rule. The team may choose to use a shorter timebox of the Daily Scrum based on their specific needs and circumstances, as long as they are able to achieve the purpose of the meeting and remain focused on the Sprint Goal.

The timebox for the Daily Scrum is not directly dependent on team size but rather on the purpose of the meeting and the needs of the Developers. However, team size can be a factor in determining how the timebox is used and how the meeting is conducted.

11.1.1　*Is the size of the team a factor?*

For example, if a Scrum Team is very large, it may take longer for each team member to participate and for the team to set actions for any issues or impediments. In this case, the timebox may need 15 minutes to accommodate the larger team size.

Similarly, if a Scrum Team is very small, it may not take the full 15 minutes to complete the Daily Scrum, as there may be fewer updates and issues to discuss. In this case, the timebox may be shortened to ensure that the meeting remains efficient and effective.

Ultimately, the Developers should determine the Daily Scrum's timebox based on their specific needs and circumstances. The important thing is that the meeting is timeboxed, focused on the Sprint Goal, and provides an opportunity for the team to collaborate towards a plan to meet the Sprint Goal and communicate effectively.

11.2 Same time and place

> *To reduce complexity, it is held at the same time and place every working day of the Sprint.*

While with the Scrum events, Scrum says, "Optimally, all events are held at the same time and place to reduce complexity," the Daily Scrum makes a bigger remark that "it is held at the same time and place," as it is a daily meeting and changing time or place would break the habit.

The team can establish a routine and ensure that everyone can attend and participate by holding the meeting at a consistent time and location. This can help to promote a habit of collaboration and communication among team members and to ensure that everyone is aligned on the Sprint Goal and working together to achieve it.

The Developers decide the best time and place to have the Daily Scrum.

In addition to reducing complexity, holding the Daily Scrum at a consistent time and place can also help to improve efficiency and focus. Team members can plan their work around the meeting and arrive prepared with updates and any issues or impediments that need to be addressed.

11.3 No need to solve the problems during the Daily Scrum

Typically, the Developers do not try to solve all the problems during the event but instead, identify and create a plan to address these problems during the day as fast as possible.

In this way, the Daily Scrum helps the team to stay focused on the Sprint Goal and to adapt their work as necessary to ensure that they are making progress toward that goal. In addition, it allows the team to identify and address any potential impediments or issues on time and to collaborate and work together to achieve the Sprint Goal.

11.4 Participation of Scrum Master and Product Owner

> *If the Product Owner or Scrum Master are actively working on items in the Sprint Backlog, they participate as Developers.*

If the Product Owner or Scrum Master are also taking Developers' accountabilities or actively working on items in the Sprint Backlog, they participate in the Daily Scrum as Developers. This means they provide an update on their progress, plans, and obstacles, just like any other Developer.

11.5 Attend vs. participate

In general, the term "attend" refers to someone who joins a meeting as a passive listener. In contrast, "participate" refers to someone who joins the meeting and participates actively during the meeting. "Attendees" refers to all the people joining a meeting, whether they are passive listeners or actively participating.

In Scrum, the Daily Scrum is an event where the Developers plan their work for the upcoming day.

There is a difference between attending and participating in the Daily Scrum. Here's what it means:

- Attend: To attend the Daily Scrum means to be present at the meeting as an observer. This could include the Product Owner, Scrum Master, stakeholders, or other team members who are not Developers. These individuals may be present to observe the meeting, listen to updates, offer support or guidance to the Developers, or the Developers ask them to join to address progress issues faster.
- Participate: To participate in the Daily Scrum means to be an active member of the Developers and to provide updates on progress, plans, and obstacles. Only Developers are expected to participate in the meeting in this way.

It is important to note that while attendees are welcome at the Daily Scrum, only the Developers are responsible for planning their work for the upcoming day. Therefore, the meeting is not intended to be a status update for stakeholders or an opportunity for the Product Owner or Scrum Master to give direction to the team. Instead, it is a collaborative meeting where the Developers work together to plan their work and identify potential issues or obstacles.

11.6 The Scrum Master in the Daily Scrum

The Scrum Master is not required to attend the Daily Scrum. However, typically join regularly to facilitate and ensure the meeting is positive.

Here are some key aspects of the Scrum Master's role in the Daily Scrum:

- Facilitate the meeting: The Scrum Master is responsible for facilitating the Daily Scrum and ensuring that the meeting stays focused and productive. This includes keeping the meeting within the time box and encouraging active participation from all members of the Developers. Additionally, if others are present, the Scrum Master ensures they do not disrupt the meeting.
- Make Developers accountable: The Scrum Master ensures that the Developers have the meeting, but the Developers are responsible for conducting the Daily Scrum in the long term. The Scrum Master teaches the Developers to keep the Daily Scrum within the 15-minute time-box. Scrum Master coaches Developers to manage their own progress, and Scrum Masters make themselves useless during the Daily Scrum in the long term.
- Observe and identify issues: While the Scrum Master does not actively participate in the Daily Scrum as a Developer, they may observe the meeting and identify any issues or obstacles that need to be addressed. The Scrum Master may use this information to guide the team in problem-solving or provide needed coaching or support.
- Ensure adherence to Scrum framework: The Scrum Master is responsible for ensuring that the Daily Scrum is conducted following the Scrum framework. This includes ensuring that the meeting is held at the same time and place each

day, that all members of the Developers participate, and that the meeting focuses on planning the work for the upcoming day.
- Progress awareness: The Scrum Master may use the Daily Scrum to create awareness of monitoring the Developers' progress and identify any potential risks or issues that must be addressed. They may use this information to guide the team in problem-solving or to provide coaching or support as needed.
- Help remove obstacles: The Scrum Master is responsible for helping to remove any obstacles or issues preventing the Developers from achieving their goals. They may use the information gathered during the Daily Scrum to identify and address these obstacles and to provide support or guidance to the team as needed.

If others are present, the Scrum Master ensures they do not disrupt the meeting.

11.7 Developers decide the structure

> *The Developers can select whatever structure and techniques they want, as long as their Daily Scrum focuses on progress toward the Sprint Goal and produces an actionable plan for the next day of work. This creates focus and improves self-management.*

Because the Developer manages the Sprint progress, the structure of the Daily Scrum is decided by the Developers, not by the Scrum Master or Product Owner.

Here are some ways that the Developers can decide on the structure of the Daily Scrum:

- Determine the format: The Developers can determine the format of the Daily Scrum, such as whether it will be held in person, virtually, or a combination of both. They may also decide on the specific tools or technologies that will be used to facilitate the meeting.
- Choose the order: The Developers can decide on the order in which each team member will provide their update during the meeting. This can help ensure the meeting stays on track and everyone can participate.
- Set the agenda: The Developers can set the agenda for the Daily Scrum, such as the specific questions that will be asked during the meeting or the topics that will be discussed. This can help ensure the meeting stays focused and everyone clearly understands what will be covered.
- Review and adjust: The Developers should review and adjust the structure of the Daily Scrum as needed to ensure that it remains effective and productive. They may make changes based on feedback from team members, observations of the meeting, or changes in the project or team dynamics.

It is important to note that while the Developers decide the structure of the Daily Scrum, the Scrum Master may provide guidance or suggestions to help ensure that the meeting stays focused and productive. However, ultimately, it is up to the Developers to determine the Daily Scrum's structure and ensure that it supports their goals and objectives.

11.7.1 The three questions are not mandatory

While the Daily Scrum is intended to be a focused and productive meeting, no set format or specific questions must be asked. However, many teams find using standard questions to guide the meeting helpful.

The most commonly used set of questions in the Daily Scrum is:

1. What did you do yesterday?
2. What are you planning to do today?
3. Are there any obstacles that are preventing you from achieving your goals?

These questions are designed to help team members provide updates on their progress, plans, and obstacles and to help the team stay aligned on their goals and objectives.

It is important to note that while these questions are commonly used, they are not mandatory. Some teams may choose to use a different set of questions or to forego questions altogether. The goal of the Daily Scrum is to help the Developers plan their work for the upcoming day, and the team should determine the specific format of the meeting to support their needs and objectives best.

Furthermore, while the three questions can be useful for some Developers, they may not be useful for others. For example, some team members may prefer to provide updates in a different format, such as a visual display or a written update. It is up to the Developers to determine the best approach for their specific needs.

11.7.2 Answers by the end of the Daily Scrum

Because the purpose of Daily Scrum is to inspect the progress toward the Sprint Goal, create a plan for the day, and adapt the Sprint Backlog to achieve it, by the end of the Daily Scrum, the Developers should be able to answer the following questions:

1. What is our progress toward the Sprint Goal?
2. What changes should we make to the Sprint Backlog?
3. What is the action plan for today?

These three questions at the end of the Daily Scrum are a good way for the Developers to validate if they achieved the purpose of the Daily Scrum.

Notice that we are not referring to mandatory questions but questions that the Developers should answer naturally and without hesitation if the Daily Scrum is successful.

The desired outcome of the Daily Scrum is to create daily actions to meet the Sprint Goal.

11.8 It is not a report meeting

In Scrum, the Daily Scrum is an event designed for the Developers to plan their work for the upcoming day. It is not a report meeting for the Product Owner, Scrum Master, or stakeholders.

While the Product Owner and Scrum Master may attend the Daily Scrum as observers or participants, they listen and observe rather than report on their progress or ask for updates. The Daily Scrum focuses on the Developers and their work, and it is not intended to be a status meeting for other stakeholders.

Stakeholders may be interested in the progress of the project and the work being done by the Developers. Still, the Daily Scrum is not the appropriate forum for providing detailed updates. Instead, stakeholders may receive updates through other channels, such as Sprint Reviews or regular communication with the Product Owner.

Ensuring that the Daily Scrum remains focused on the Developers and their work is important. This helps to keep the meeting short and productive and ensures that the team has the time and space they need to plan their work and identify any obstacles or issues that need to be addressed.

11.9 Daily Scrum eliminates the need for other meetings

> *Daily Scrums improve communications, identify impediments, promote quick decision-making, and consequently eliminate the need for other meetings.*

There are several benefits to conducting a Daily Scrum, including improved communication, identifying impediments, promoting quick decision-making, and reducing the need for other meetings.

Here's how the Daily Scrum can help teams achieve these benefits:

- Improve communication: The Daily Scrum allows the Developers to communicate with each other and ensure that everyone is aligned on their goals and objectives. In addition, by providing a regular forum for updates and discussions, the Daily Scrum can help to improve communication and collaboration among team members.
- Identify impediments: The Daily Scrum provides a platform for team members to identify any obstacles or impediments preventing them from achieving their goals. By raising these issues early on, the team can work together to address them and ensure they do not become larger problems.
- Promote quick decision-making: The Daily Scrum helps to promote quick decision-making by allowing the team to quickly identify any issues or obstacles and work together to address them. In addition, by ensuring that everyone is

aligned on their goals and priorities, the team can make decisions more quickly and effectively.
- Reduce the need for other meetings: By providing a regular forum for updates and discussions, the Daily Scrum can help to reduce the need for other meetings. Because the team is regularly communicating and collaborating, there may be less need for separate status meetings or other types of gatherings.
- Increase focus during the day: By removing the need for other meetings. The Developers can focus on making progress during the day according to the agreed day plan.

11.10   Do not skip it

Skipping or canceling the Daily Scrum is unacceptable simply because the team has too many meetings. The Daily Scrum is a crucial event in Scrum, where the Developers collaborate and plan for the day ahead. It allows the team to synchronize their work, identify any impediments, and make quick decisions to keep the Sprint on track.

If the team has too many meetings, they should consider ways to streamline their process and optimize their time. For example, they could review their meeting schedule and identify any meetings that could be shortened, combined, or eliminated. They could also consider using asynchronous communication methods like email or chat to reduce the need for in-person meetings.

However, it is important to recognize the value of the Daily Scrum and ensure that it is not sacrificed due to scheduling conflicts. If necessary, the team could adjust the timing or location of the Daily Scrum to accommodate other meetings, but the event should not be skipped entirely.

In Scrum, the events are designed to support the team's collaboration and alignment toward a shared goal. Skipping or canceling events can lead to miscommunication, missed opportunities, and a lack of progress toward the Sprint Goal. Therefore, it is important to prioritize the events and optimize the team's time while ensuring that the Scrum framework is followed.

Skipping or reducing the frequency of the Daily Scrum can have several negative consequences for the Scrum Team and the Sprint:

1. Lack of alignment: The Daily Scrum is a critical event for the Scrum Team to synchronize their work and ensure everyone is aligned towards the Sprint Goal. Skipping or reducing the frequency of the event can lead to misalignment and a lack of shared understanding of the work being done.
2. Increased risk of impediments: The Daily Scrum allows the Scrum Team to identify and address any impediments blocking their progress. Skipping or reducing the event frequency can increase the risk of impediments going unnoticed or unaddressed, leading to delays in the Sprint.
3. Decreased transparency: The Daily Scrum promotes transparency by allowing the Scrum Team to share updates and progress towards the Sprint Goal.

Skipping or reducing the event frequency can decrease transparency and make it harder for the team to identify issues or opportunities for improvement.
4. Reduced collaboration: The Daily Scrum fosters collaboration and encourages the Scrum Team to work together towards a shared goal. Skipping or reducing the event frequency can reduce collaboration and make it harder for the team to work together effectively.
5. Decreased accountability: The Daily Scrum promotes accountability by requiring each team member to share their daily progress and plans. Skipping or reducing the frequency of the event can decrease accountability and make it harder to track progress toward the Sprint Goal.

11.11   Don't wait until the next Daily

> *The Daily Scrum is not the only time Developers are allowed to adjust their plan. They often meet throughout the day for more detailed discussions about adapting or re-planning the rest of the Sprint's work.*

While the Daily Scrum provides a regular forum for updates and discussions, it is not the only time the Developers can adjust their plan.

It is common for the Developers to meet throughout the day for more detailed discussions about adapting or re-planning the rest of the Sprint's work. Team members may initiate these meetings or be scheduled by the Scrum Master or Product Owner to address specific issues or concerns.

Some examples of when these more detailed discussions may be necessary include:

- When a team member encounters an unexpected obstacle or issue that requires input or collaboration from other team members.
- When a team member needs to work on a task that depends on other tasks or requires coordination with other team members.
- When the team needs to adjust its plan in response to project or product requirements changes.
- When the team needs to refine their understanding of the work to be done to ensure that they are meeting the Sprint Goal.

In other words, if the team members encounter problems during the day, there is no need to wait until the next day to raise them during the Daily Scrum.

It is important to note that while the Daily Scrum provides a regular forum for updates and discussions, it is not intended to be a detailed planning meeting. Instead, the Developers should use the Daily Scrum to plan their work for the upcoming day and identify any obstacles or issues that must be addressed. Still, they may need to hold additional meetings throughout the day to address more detailed planning or coordination.

11.12 Anti-patterns of the Daily Scrum

Antipatterns are common mistakes or bad practices that can hinder the effectiveness of the Daily Scrum in Scrum. Here are some examples of Daily Scrum antipatterns:

Status update: The Daily Scrum is not a status update meeting; each team member should not just give a progress report. This practice can lead to long meetings that do not provide value or promote collaboration.

1. Monologue: The Daily Scrum is a collaborative event, and team members should not deliver monologues or speak for an extended period. The meeting should allow team members to share information and collaborate to solve problems.
2. Problem-solving: The Daily Scrum is not a problem-solving meeting, and team members should not try to solve problems during the meeting. Instead, they should raise issues and discuss potential solutions after the meeting.
3. Late attendance: Team members who arrive late to the Daily Scrum can disrupt the meeting and waste valuable time. Punctuality is critical to ensure the meeting is effective and everyone can participate.
4. Lack of focus: The Daily Scrum should focus on the progress made since the last meeting and what team members plan to work on next. Discussions about unrelated topics or tasks can distract from the meeting's purpose.
5. Blaming: Team members should avoid blaming others for problems or delays during the Daily Scrum. Instead, they should focus on identifying the root cause of the issue and work together to find a solution.
6. Lack of engagement: Team members not engaged during the Daily Scrum can slow down the meeting and prevent progress. Each team member should actively participate and contribute to the meeting.
7. Skipping the Daily Scrum: Skipping or canceling events can lead to miscommunication, missed opportunities, and a lack of progress towards the Sprint Goal.

To avoid these antipatterns, the Scrum Master should ensure that the Daily Scrum remains focused, collaborative, and valuable for the team. In addition, they should encourage team members to follow the Scrum framework and establish clear guidelines for the meeting. This will help ensure that the Daily Scrum is an effective tool for promoting collaboration, transparency, and progress within the Scrum Team.

Part 12: Sprint Review

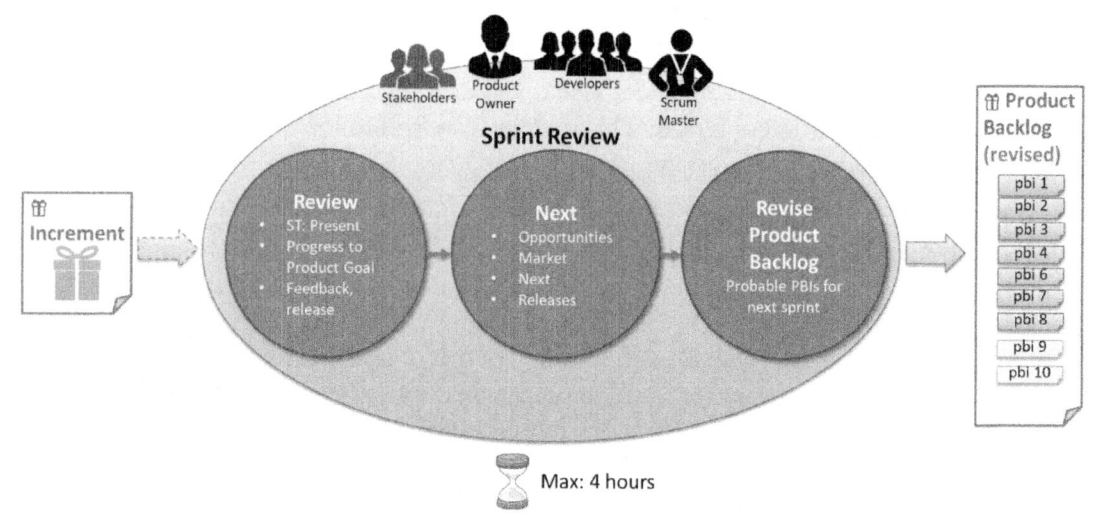

Figure 28 Sprint Review.

12.1 Collaboration with Stakeholders toward goals

> The purpose of the Sprint Review is to inspect the outcome of the Sprint and determine future adaptations. The Scrum Team presents the results of their work to key stakeholders and progress toward the Product Goal is discussed.
>
> During the event, the Scrum Team and stakeholders review what was accomplished in the Sprint and what has changed in their environment. Based on this information, attendees collaborate on what to do next. The Product Backlog may also be adjusted to meet new opportunities.

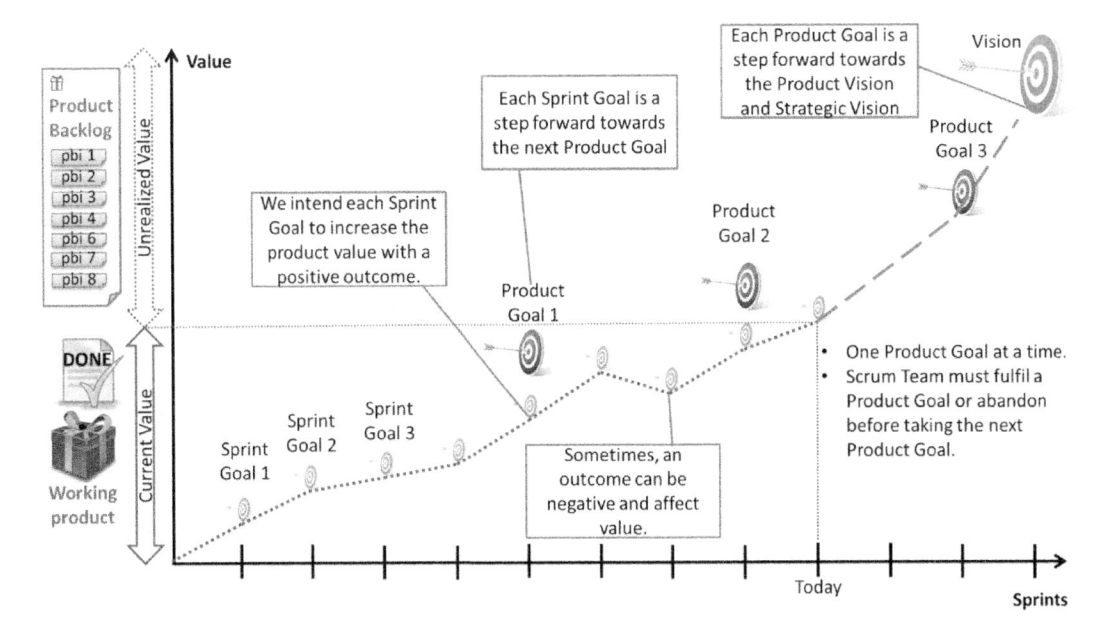

Figure 29 Adding value to each Sprint towards goals.

In Scrum, the Sprint Review is an event that occurs at the end of each Sprint.

Here are some key aspects of the Sprint Review:

- Inspect the outcome of the Sprint: The Sprint Review is an opportunity for the Scrum Team to demonstrate the outcome of the Sprint to key stakeholders. This includes any completed product increments or features worked on during the Sprint. For instance, understand how the Sprint Goal may translate into real value for end users and how to measure it.
- Review what has changed in the environment: Attendees also discuss any changes that have occurred in the environment since the start of the Sprint. This could include changes in the market, changes in customer needs, or changes in technology.
- Determine future adaptations: The Sprint Review is also an opportunity for the Scrum Team to reflect on the Sprint and determine future adaptations. This includes discussing any improvements that could be made to the process or product and identifying any obstacles or impediments that need to be addressed in the next Sprint.
- Present results to stakeholders: The Scrum Team presents the results of their work to key stakeholders, such as the Product Owner, customers, or other members of the organization. This allows stakeholders to see the progress made and provide feedback on the product.
- Discuss progress toward the Product Goal: The Sprint Review is an opportunity to discuss progress toward the Product Goal, which is the long-term objective for the product. The Scrum Team can discuss how the work

completed during the Sprint aligns with the Product Goal and identify any next steps needed to move closer to achieving the goal.
- Collaborate on what to do next: Attendees collaborate on what to do next based on the information reviewed during the event. This includes identifying any next steps needed to move closer to achieving the Product Goal. The Scrum Team may also identify any improvements that could be made to the process or product.
- Adapt the Product Backlog: The Sprint Review is also an opportunity to adapt the Product Backlog based on the feedback and insights gained during the Sprint. The Product Owner works with the Scrum Team and stakeholders to prioritize and refine the Product Backlog based on the outcomes of the Sprint Review.

In simple terms, the Scrum Team and stakeholders review the product.

In summary, the Sprint Review is an important event in Scrum that provides an opportunity to inspect the outcome of the Sprint and determine future adaptations. In addition, the Scrum Team presents the results of their work to key stakeholders and progress toward the Product Goal is discussed. By reflecting on the Sprint and identifying areas for improvement, the Scrum Team can continuously improve their process and product.

12.1.1 Effects of absent stakeholders

If stakeholders do not attend the Sprint Retrospective, there can be negative impacts on the product, value, and risk.

Firstly, stakeholders who do not attend the retrospective miss the opportunity to provide feedback and insight on the Sprint. This feedback can be crucial in determining whether the product meets their needs and expectations. Without this feedback, the product may not deliver the expected value, and there is a higher risk of not meeting the stakeholders' needs.

Secondly, if stakeholders are not present to understand the Sprint Review and the Increment, they may be unable to make informed decisions regarding the product's future direction. This lack of knowledge can lead to increased risk, as stakeholders may push for changes or features that are not aligned with the current product direction or may not deliver the expected value.

In summary, the absence of stakeholders from the Sprint Retrospective can lead to a lack of collaboration and communication between the Scrum Team and stakeholders, negatively impacting the product's value and increasing risk. Therefore, it is essential to ensure that stakeholders attend the retrospective to maintain alignment and transparency and achieve the best possible outcomes for the product.

12.2 Stakeholders' Feedback Before the Sprint Review

The Scrum Framework does not impede stakeholders from giving feedback during the Sprint before the Sprint Review. On the contrary, an agile principle says that "Business people and Developers must work together daily throughout the project." However, in some environments, that are not always possible or could affect the focus of the Developers, so the Sprint Review is a mandatory event to collaborate with stakeholders.

Here are some other ways the Scrum Team can engage with stakeholders and gather feedback throughout the Sprint:

- User feedback sessions: The Scrum Team can also conduct user feedback sessions to gather input on specific features or items being developed during the Sprint. This can be done through user testing or other forms of user research.
- Regular status updates: The Scrum Team can provide regular status updates to stakeholders to inform them of progress and any changes to the plan. These updates can be delivered through regular reports, email updates, or other forms of communication.
- Collaborative design sessions: The Scrum Team can also engage stakeholders in collaborative design sessions to gather input on the design of specific features or items. This can be done through workshops or other collaborative sessions.
- Measure user satisfaction: The Scrum Team can also measure user satisfaction and the success of previous Sprint goals through surveys, feedback forms, or other methods. This information can help the team identify improvement areas and make data-driven decisions about the next steps for the product.

12.3 It's not a plan for the next Sprint

It is important to note that the Sprint Review is not a plan or commitment for the next Sprint.

While the Sprint Review provides an opportunity for the Scrum Team and stakeholders to discuss what to do next, any commitments or plans for the next Sprint should be made during the Sprint Planning event, which occurs at the beginning of each Sprint.

During the Sprint Planning event, the Scrum Team plans the work that will be done during the upcoming Sprint. First, they identify the Sprint Goal and select the Product Backlog items they will work on. This includes creating a plan for accomplishing the work and determining the Sprint's outcome.

In contrast, the Sprint Review is focused on inspecting the outcome of the Sprint and determining future adaptations. Therefore, while the Scrum Team may identify areas for improvement or next steps during the Sprint Review, they should not make commitments or plans for the next Sprint during this event.

In summary, the Sprint Review is an important event in Scrum that provides an opportunity to inspect the outcome of the Sprint and determine future adaptations. However, any plans or commitments for the next Sprint should be made during the Sprint Planning event, which occurs at the beginning of each Sprint.

12.4 It's not a "Demo"

> *The Sprint Review is a working session and the Scrum Team should avoid limiting it to a presentation.*

It is important to note that the Sprint Review is not a demo but a working session where the Scrum Team and stakeholders collaborate and provide feedback on the product.

While the Scrum Team will showcase completed work during the Sprint Review, it is important to avoid limiting the event to a simple presentation. Instead, the Sprint Review should be a collaborative session where the Scrum Team and stakeholders engage in a two-way conversation to review progress and gather feedback.

Here are some ways the Scrum Team can avoid limiting the Sprint Review to a presentation:

1. Encourage dialogue: The Sprint Review should be a dialogue between the Scrum Team and stakeholders. Encourage stakeholders to ask questions, provide feedback, and converse about the product.
2. Solicit feedback: The Scrum Team should actively solicit feedback from stakeholders during the Sprint Review. This could be done through surveys, group discussions, or other methods.
3. Collaborate on the next steps: The Sprint Review is an opportunity for the Scrum Team and stakeholders to collaborate on the next steps for the product. This could include identifying new features to add to the Product Backlog, refining existing features, or changing the product direction toward the Product Goal.
4. Focus on the Sprint Goal: Throughout the Sprint Review, it is important to keep the Sprint Goal in mind. The Scrum Team and stakeholders should evaluate progress toward the Sprint Goal and identify any areas for improvement.

In summary, the Sprint Review is not a demo but a working session where the Scrum Team and stakeholders collaborate and provide feedback on the product. By encouraging dialogue, soliciting feedback, collaborating on the next steps, and focusing on the Sprint Goal, the Scrum Team can ensure that the Sprint Review is a productive and valuable event for everyone involved.

12.5 Do not cancel it

Canceling the Sprint Review is unacceptable simply because the Developers could not deliver an increment or meet the Sprint Goal. The Sprint Review is a crucial event in Scrum, where the Scrum Team presents the work completed during the Sprint to stakeholders and receives feedback. It is an opportunity to showcase progress, demonstrate the value delivered, and gather input for future product development.

Suppose the Developers could not deliver an increment or meet the Sprint Goal. In that case, the Scrum Team should still hold the Sprint Review and use the opportunity to discuss the reasons for the shortfall and explore ways to improve their performance in the future. In addition, the stakeholders should be informed of the challenges the Scrum Team faces, and the Scrum Team can discuss any changes to the product roadmap or the Sprint Backlog.

By canceling the Sprint Review, the Scrum Team misses the opportunity to gather valuable feedback from stakeholders and improve their product development process. Therefore, if the Sprint Review is canceled, it is important to reschedule it as soon as possible and ensure that the Scrum Team is prepared to present a progress update and receive feedback.

12.6 Timebox: 4 hours

> *The Sprint Review is the second to last event of the Sprint and is timeboxed to a maximum of four hours for a one-month Sprint. For shorter Sprints, the event is usually shorter.*

In Scrum, the Sprint Review is an important event that occurs at the end of each Sprint. The purpose of the Sprint Review is to inspect the outcome of the Sprint and determine future adaptations. The Sprint Review is the second to last event of the Sprint and is timeboxed to a maximum of four hours for a one-month Sprint. For shorter Sprints, the event is usually shorter.

For example, if the Sprint is two weeks long, the Sprint Review might be timeboxed to two hours. If the Sprint is one week long, the Sprint Review might be timeboxed to one hour. However, this is not a rule. A two-week Sprint can still have a Sprint Review of four hours and still be within the rules of the Scrum Framework. However, that decision is unlikely.

It's important to note that the timebox for the Sprint Review is not a formula that applies to every situation. The duration of the Sprint Review should be determined based on the needs of the Scrum Team and stakeholders, as well as the length and complexity of the Sprint. The goal is a focused and productive event that allows for a thorough review of the work completed during the Sprint.

12.6.1 Understanding timebox restrictions

During the Sprint Review, the Scrum Team presents the Increment developed during the Sprint to the stakeholders. This event is time-boxed to four hours for a one-month Sprint, and the purpose is to inspect the Increment and adapt the Product Backlog accordingly. The time-box restriction ensures that the presentation of new features is focused and efficient and that all stakeholders have an equal opportunity to provide feedback.

The Scrum Master can coach the Developers with time management techniques to ensure that the most valuable functionalities are presented first and that the presentation stays within the time box. This helps to maximize the value of the Sprint Review and ensure that the stakeholders understand the most important features of the Increment.

Additionally, the Scrum Master can coach the stakeholders to understand Scrum and the importance of time-boxing all events, including the Sprint Review. Allowing the event to extend beyond the time box can disrupt the team's work and cause delays in delivering value to the stakeholders. By understanding and adhering to the time-box concept, the stakeholders can actively participate in the event and help the team achieve the Sprint Review's goals.

12.7 Antipatterns of the Sprint Review

Antipatterns are common mistakes or bad practices that can hinder the effectiveness of the Sprint Review in Scrum. Here are some examples of Sprint Review antipatterns:

1. No customer involvement: The Sprint Review is an opportunity to get feedback from customers or stakeholders, and their absence can lead to misunderstandings and missed opportunities for improvement.
2. Lack of preparation: The Scrum Team should prepare adequately for the Sprint Review to ensure the meeting is productive. Lack of preparation can lead to delays, misunderstandings, and a failure to achieve the Sprint Goal.
3. Focus on the wrong metrics: The Sprint Review should focus on the value delivered to customers, not just on technical metrics or the completion of tasks. Focusing on the wrong metrics can lead to missed opportunities for improvement and a failure to meet customer needs.
4. Lack of collaboration: The Sprint Review is a collaborative effort, and the Scrum Team should work together to present their work and get feedback. Lack of collaboration can lead to misunderstandings, delays, and a failure to achieve the Sprint Goal.
5. Overemphasis on defects: While defects should be discussed during the Sprint Review, focusing too much on them can create a negative atmosphere and detract from the value delivered.
6. Demo mindset: When the Sprint Review is used solely as a demo, it can lead to a lack of engagement from stakeholders and a failure to incorporate valuable insights and feedback, which can result in a product that does not meet

stakeholder needs or expectations. Additionally, this approach may result in missed opportunities for innovation and collaboration, as stakeholders are not given the opportunity to provide input and share their ideas during the review process. No action items: The Sprint Review should result in action items that the Scrum Team can use to improve their work in the next Sprint. A lack of action items can lead to a lack of improvement and a failure to meet customer needs.

7. Long and unproductive meetings: The Sprint Review should be time-boxed and focused on achieving the Sprint Goal. Long and unproductive meetings can lead to delays, misunderstandings, and a lack of progress.

To avoid these antipatterns, the Scrum Master should ensure that the Scrum Team follows the Scrum framework and establishes clear guidelines for the Sprint Review. In addition, they should encourage collaboration, focus on value delivered to customers, and work with the Product Owner to ensure that the Sprint Goal is well-defined and aligned with customer needs. This will help ensure that the Sprint Review is an effective tool for getting feedback and delivering value to the product's customers.

Part 13: Sprint Retrospective

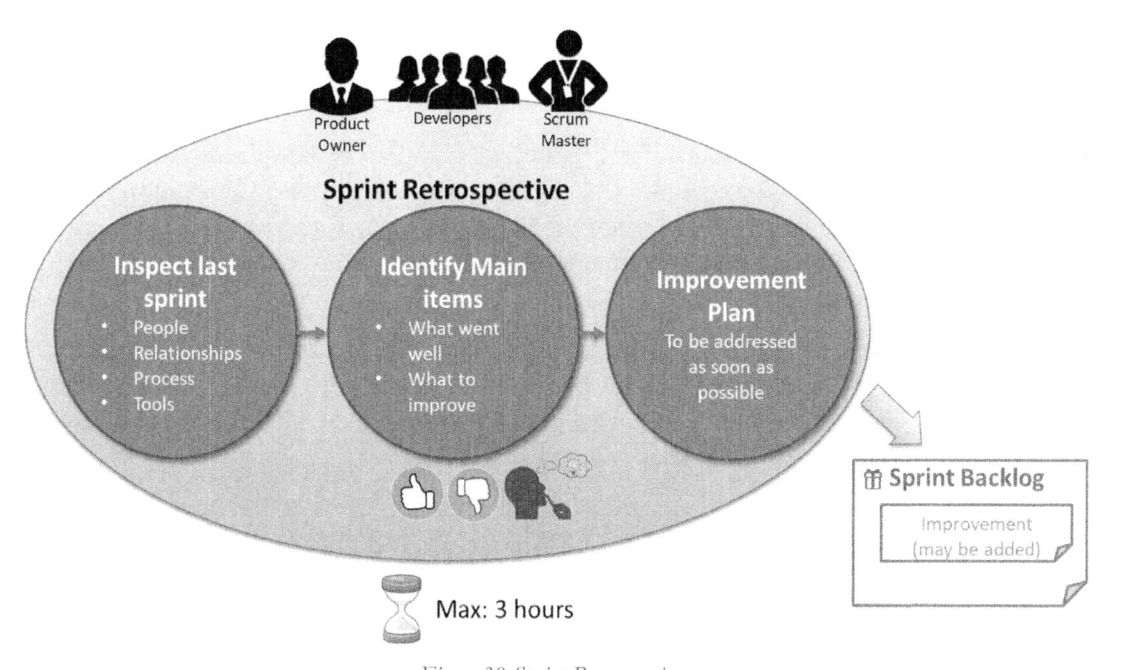

Figure 30 Sprint Retrospective.

The purpose of the Sprint Retrospective is to plan ways to increase quality and effectiveness. The Scrum Team inspects how the last Sprint went with regards to individuals, interactions, processes, tools, and their Definition of Done. Inspected elements often vary with the domain of work. Assumptions that led them astray are identified and their origins explored.

In simple terms, the Scrum Team reviews its process privately. Some call it a pain-oriented workshop, where team members expose their pains and find the cure.

During the Sprint Retrospective, the Scrum Team comes together to reflect on the previous Sprint and identify ways to improve their performance going forward. One of the key objectives of the Sprint Retrospective is to discuss what went well during the Sprint, what problems were encountered, and how those problems were (or were not) solved.

The Scrum Team might start by discussing what went well during the Sprint, such as successful collaborations or meeting the Definition of Done. By discussing these successes, the team can build confidence and reinforce the positive aspects of their work.

They might then discuss the problems they encountered during the Sprint, such as missed deadlines or quality issues. By openly discussing these issues, the Scrum Team can identify their root causes and work together to find solutions.

Finally, the Scrum Team might discuss how those problems were solved (or not solved). They might discuss the effectiveness of their solutions, whether they were implemented promptly, and whether there were any unintended consequences. This discussion can help the Scrum Team identify areas for improvement in their problem-solving process.

By discussing what went well and what didn't go well during the Sprint, the Scrum Team can gain a deeper understanding of their performance and identify opportunities for improvement going forward. In addition, by continuously inspecting and adapting their process, the Scrum Team can deliver a high-quality product that meets customer needs.

For example, they might discuss whether they were able to collaborate effectively, whether they encountered any roadblocks, whether they followed their Definition of Done, and whether they used the most appropriate tools and processes. By identifying areas for improvement, the Scrum Team can plan ways to increase quality and effectiveness in future Sprints.

It's important to note that the Sprint Retrospective is not just about identifying problems but also about celebrating successes and recognizing the contributions of team members. The Scrum Team can build a positive, collaborative team culture that fosters continuous improvement.

13.1 Individuals, interactions, processes, and tools

During the Sprint Retrospective, the Scrum Team comes together to reflect on the previous Sprint and identify ways to improve their performance going forward. In addition, the Sprint Retrospective is an opportunity to inspect various aspects of the Scrum process, including individuals, interactions, processes, and tools.

For example, the Scrum Team might discuss the following:
- Individuals: Whether team members could effectively collaborate and work together during the Sprint. They might discuss whether everyone understood

their accountabilities and whether there were any communication or interpersonal dynamics issues. They could also discuss if they have all the skills to be on a cross-functional team.
- Interactions: The Scrum Team could interact with stakeholders and other teams during the Sprint effectively. They might discuss any issues with communication or feedback and whether there were any missed opportunities for collaboration. They could discuss dependencies, boundaries, and how to become a more cross-functional and self-managing team.
- Processes: Whether the Scrum process was effective and efficient during the Sprint. They might discuss whether they could deliver the expected value within the Sprint timeframe and whether they encountered any roadblocks or bottlenecks during the process. In addition, they could discuss the purpose, effectiveness, time, and place of meetings.
- Tools: Whether the tools and technologies used during the Sprint were effective and supported the team's work. They might discuss whether they had all the necessary tools and resources and whether any improvements could be made to their tooling and infrastructure.

By inspecting these various aspects of the Scrum process, the Scrum Team can identify areas for improvement and plan ways to increase quality and effectiveness in the future. This can include changing team structure or communication processes, adopting new tools or technologies, or refining their overall approach to Scrum. By continuously inspecting and adapting its process, the Scrum Team can improve its ability to deliver a high-quality product that meets customer needs.

13.2 The Role of the Scrum Master

There are three possible ways the Scrum Master can participate in the Sprint Retrospective:

- Facilitating the Sprint Retrospective: The Scrum Master is responsible for facilitating the Sprint Retrospective meeting, which involves guiding the Scrum Team through reflecting on the previous Sprint and identifying areas for improvement. The Scrum Master creates a safe and open environment for the team members to share their opinions and feedback and ensures that everyone participates and contributes equally. The Scrum Master also helps the team to stay focused on the goals of the Sprint Retrospective and encourages the team to identify actionable improvements.
- Joining the Sprint Retrospective as a Scrum Team member: The Scrum Master is also a member of the Scrum Team and can participate in the Sprint Retrospective as a peer team member. In this role, the Scrum Master shares their feedback and ideas for improvement, just like any other team member. However, the Scrum Master should avoid dominating the conversation and instead encourage the rest of the team to share their own feedback and ideas.

- Assisting the Scrum Team in identifying and improving the most beneficial adjustments to increase its efficacy: The Scrum Master also helps the team to identify and prioritize the most beneficial adjustments that can be made to increase the team's efficacy. The Scrum Master assists the team in creating an action plan to address the identified improvements and helps the team to stay accountable for implementing the plan. The Scrum Master also encourages the team to continuously reflect on their performance and identify areas for further improvement.

However, notice that facilitating and participating as a member can be challenging and affect the focus of both. Typically, a facilitator should act neutral and focus on facilitation to guide the group to fulfill the purpose of the meeting rather than creating content and actively discussing.

13.3 Inspecting the Definition of Done

Inspecting and adapting the Definition of Done allows the Scrum Team to increase the quality of the product in its process as they need.

Let's say that during the Sprint Retrospective, the Scrum Team identified that they had been encountering too many bugs and issues with their product during testing and deployment. They realized that one of the reasons for this was that they did not have a clear and comprehensive Definition of Done in place.

To address this issue, the Scrum Team might work together to define a new and more robust Definition of Done that includes specific criteria for testing, quality assurance, and deployment. They might also agree on specific tools and processes that they will use to ensure that their work meets these criteria.

For example, their new Definition of Done might include criteria such as:

- All code is fully tested and passes automated tests before being submitted for review
- All code reviews are completed, and any identified issues are addressed before the code is merged
- All features are tested on multiple devices and platforms to ensure compatibility
- All deployments are fully tested in a staging environment before being deployed to production
- All documentation is complete and up-to-date before the feature is considered "done."

By defining these specific criteria for quality and completeness, the Scrum Team can ensure that they are consistently delivering high-quality work that meets customer needs. In addition, by adhering to these criteria and continuously improving their processes, they can reduce the number of bugs and issues that arise during testing and deployment and increase the overall quality of their product.

13.4 Improvements

> *The Scrum Team identifies the most helpful changes to improve its effectiveness. The most impactful improvements are addressed as soon as possible. They may even be added to the Sprint Backlog for the next Sprint.*

Like in the Sprint, there is not enough timebox to build all the nice-to-have features, but at least the most important features we need now. The timebox of the Sprint Retrospective does not allow us to fix all the pains of the team, but at least the most critical ones.

Creating a detailed solution for improvement during the Sprint Retrospective is not mandatory. The objective of the Sprint Retrospective is to reflect on the previous Sprint and identify ways to improve the Scrum Team's performance going forward. Therefore, the Scrum Team may discuss various issues they encountered during the Sprint but are not obligated to develop specific solutions during the Retrospective.

Instead, the Scrum Team may use the insights gained during the Retrospective to plan how they will address the issues they identified. They may also experiment with new approaches to address the issues and see how they work. Creating an action item with the general idea of improvement to be addressed during the Sprint would be enough.

The Sprint Retrospective is a time-boxed event, and the Scrum Team should use the time available to identify and discuss the most important issues affecting their performance. The focus should be on identifying areas for improvement and discussing potential solutions rather than creating a detailed plan for every improvement. The Scrum Team can continue to refine their approach and adapt as necessary as they work through the Sprint and beyond.

13.5 Managing the improvements

There is no mandatory way of managing the improvements identified during the Sprint Retrospective. However, the Scrum Team should address the most impactful improvements as soon as possible, and typically, it may add them to the Sprint Backlog for the next Sprint. Doing so ensures that the improvements are prioritized and given the necessary resources and attention.

Less impactful improvements may be disregarded or added to the Product Backlog.

For example, suppose the Scrum Team identified during the Sprint Retrospective that they experienced delays in their development process due to issues with their testing infrastructure. In that case, they might prioritize improving their testing environment in the next Sprint. This could include implementing new testing tools, increasing testing resources, or optimizing testing processes.

The Scrum Team can continuously improve its effectiveness and deliver a high-quality product that meets customer needs by addressing the most impactful improvements as soon as possible. This approach also supports the Scrum principle of "inspect and adapt," as the team continuously reflects on their performance and makes changes to improve their process.

13.6 The end of the Sprint

> *The Sprint Retrospective concludes the Sprint.*

The Sprint Retrospective is the last event of the Sprint and marks the end of the current Sprint. During the Retrospective, the Scrum Team reflects on their performance during the Sprint and identifies ways to improve their process going forward.

The Sprint Retrospective is held at the end of the Sprint after the Sprint Review, so the Scrum Team has all the information to reflect on what is performed during the Sprint.

The Scrum Retrospective allows the team to celebrate their successes, learn from their mistakes, and plan for future improvements. In addition, the insights gained during the Retrospective are used to improve the Scrum Team's performance in the next Sprint.

Once the Sprint Retrospective is complete, the Scrum Team moves on to the next Sprint with a new Sprint Planning meeting.

13.7 Timebox: 3 hours

> *It is timeboxed to a maximum of three hours for a one-month Sprint. For shorter Sprints, the event is usually shorter.*

The length of the Sprint Retrospective usually depends on the length of the Sprint itself. The Scrum Guide states that the Sprint Retrospective is timeboxed to a maximum of three hours for a one-month Sprint. However, for shorter Sprints, the event is usually shorter. For example, a Sprint Retrospective of two hours or less might be good enough for a two-week Sprint and keeping a good cadence. A Scrum Team with a two-week Sprint will rarely need a longer timebox, but it is not forbidden.

The Sprint Retrospective's timeboxing helps ensure the event is focused and productive. Limiting the time available allows the Scrum Team to focus on the most important issues affecting their performance and identify actionable improvements.

The timebox for the Sprint Retrospective is designed to promote efficiency and focus while allowing the Scrum Team to reflect on their performance and identify ways to improve continuously.

13.8 Do not skip the Retrospective

Some typical excuses to skip Sprint Retrospectives in Scrum may include:
1. Lack of time: Due to other commitments or deadlines, the Scrum Team may feel they do not have enough time to hold a Sprint Retrospective.
2. Lack of value: The Scrum Team may feel that previous Sprint Retrospectives did not result in significant improvements or did not provide value.
3. Complacency: The Scrum Team may feel they are already performing well enough and do not need to hold a Sprint Retrospective.
4. Lack of participation: The Scrum Team may feel that some members are not actively participating in the Sprint Retrospective, making it seem like a waste of time.

However, skipping the Sprint Retrospective is a bad idea for several reasons. First, the Sprint Retrospective is an essential tool for the Scrum Team to identify areas for improvement and continuously improve their work. Skipping the Sprint Retrospective can lead to complacency and a failure to meet customer needs.

Second, the Sprint Retrospective is a collaborative effort, and all members of the Scrum Team should participate to ensure that everyone's perspectives are heard. Skipping the Sprint Retrospective can lead to misunderstandings and a lack of progress.

The consequences of skipping the Sprint Retrospective can include failing to meet customer needs, lacking improvement, and lacking trust within the Scrum Team. These consequences can ultimately lead to decreased product quality, lower customer satisfaction, and a failure to meet business goals.

To avoid skipping the Sprint Retrospective, the Scrum Master should emphasize the importance of the meeting and work with the Scrum Team to address any concerns or issues hindering participation or progress. This will help ensure that the Sprint Retrospective is an effective tool for improving the Scrum Team's work and delivering value to the product's customers.

13.9 Anti-patterns of the Sprint Retrospective

Antipatterns are common mistakes or bad practices that can hinder the effectiveness of the Sprint Retrospective in Scrum. Here are some examples of Sprint Retrospective antipatterns:
1. Lack of focus: The Sprint Retrospective should focus on the work done in the previous Sprint and identify opportunities for improvement. Discussions about unrelated topics or tasks can distract from the meeting's purpose.
2. Lack of participation: All members of the Scrum Team should participate in the Sprint Retrospective to ensure that everyone's perspectives are heard. Lack of participation can lead to misunderstandings and a lack of progress.

3. Lack of action items: The Sprint Retrospective should result in action items that the Scrum Team can use to improve their work in the next Sprint. A lack of action items can lead to a lack of improvement and a failure to meet customer needs.
4. Lack of trust: The Sprint Retrospective is an opportunity for the Scrum Team to discuss their work and identify areas for improvement openly. A lack of trust can lead to misunderstandings and a lack of progress.
5. Blame and finger-pointing: The Sprint Retrospective should focus on opportunities for improvement and not on assigning blame for past mistakes. Blame and finger-pointing can lead to a negative atmosphere and detract from the value of the meeting.
6. No follow-up: The action items identified during the Sprint Retrospective should be followed up in the next Sprint. A lack of follow-up can lead to a lack of improvement and a failure to meet customer needs.
7. Long and unproductive meetings: The Sprint Retrospective should be timeboxed and focused on achieving the Sprint Goal. Long and unproductive meetings can lead to delays, misunderstandings, and a lack of progress.

To avoid these antipatterns, the Scrum Master should ensure that the Scrum Team follows the Scrum framework and establishes clear guidelines for the Sprint Retrospective. In addition, they should encourage participation, focus on opportunities for improvement, and work with the Product Owner to ensure that action items are aligned with customer needs. This will help ensure that the Sprint Retrospective is an effective tool for improving the Scrum Team's work and delivering value to the product's customers.

Part 14: Scrum Artifacts

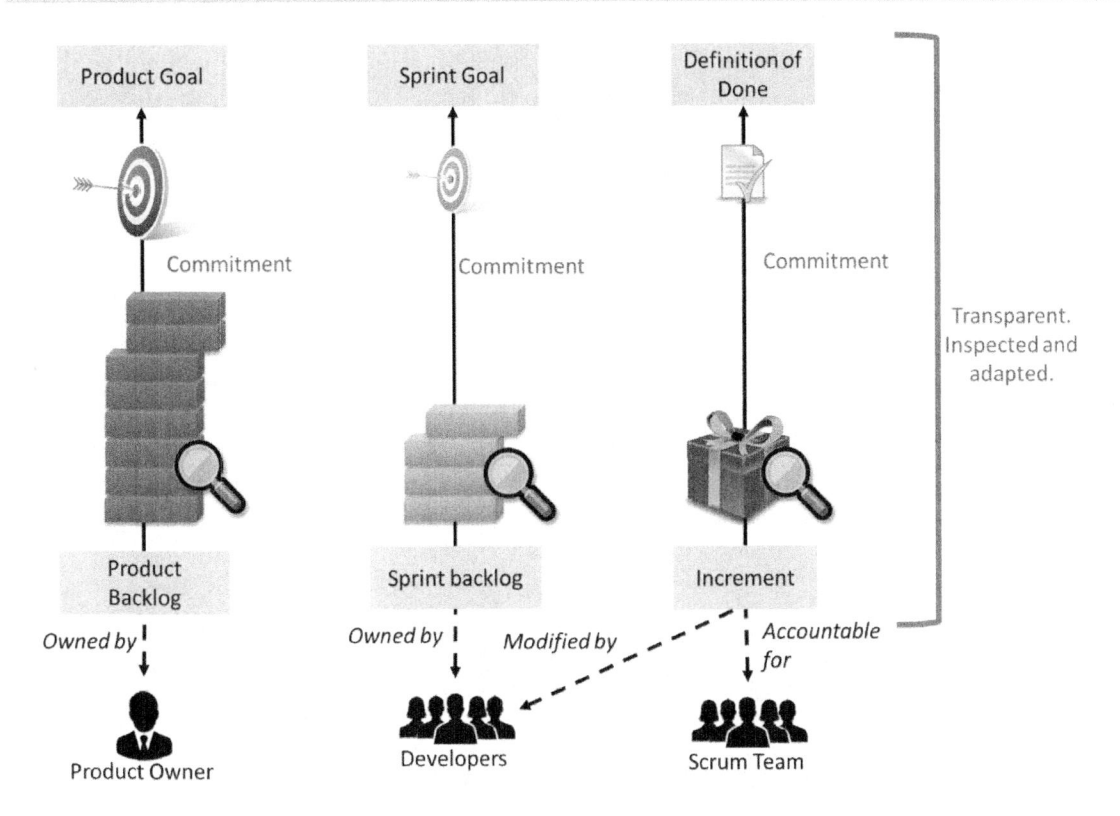

Figure 31 Scrum artifacts.

14.1 Artifacts represent works of value

Scrum's artifacts represent work or value.

Scrum's artifacts represent work or value because Scrum is an empirical process control framework. This means that Scrum relies on transparency, inspection, and adaptation to enable the Scrum Team to improve the product and the process continuously.

The artifacts in Scrum are designed to represent the work or value being produced by the Scrum Team.

- The Product Backlog represents the work that needs to be done to create the product.
- The Sprint Backlog represents the work the Scrum Team plans to complete during the current Sprint.
- The Increment represents the value delivered to the product's customers.

By focusing on work or value, the Scrum Team can ensure they deliver the highest possible value to the product's customers. They can prioritize the most important work and ensure that the work being done is aligned with the product's overall vision and goals.

Furthermore, by representing work or value, the artifacts in Scrum enable the Scrum Team to make informed decisions about what to do next. They can inspect the artifacts and adapt their plans based on the information provided. This enables them to continuously improve the product and the process and deliver more value to their customers over time.

To wrap up, the focus on work or value in Scrum's artifacts enables the Scrum Team to create a transparent and adaptable process that continuously improves the product and the process.

14.2 Artifacts maximize transparency

> *They are designed to maximize transparency of key information. Thus, everyone inspecting them has the same basis for adaptation.*

Artifacts in Scrum are designed to maximize transparency of key information, making them visible and accessible to everyone involved in the Scrum process. By doing so, the Scrum Team ensures that everyone who inspects the artifacts has access to the same information, which forms the basis for adaptation and decision-making.

For example, the Product Backlog is a key artifact in Scrum that represents the work needed to create the product. It contains a prioritized list of product requirements or features that the Scrum Team needs to work on, and it is constantly evolving based on feedback from stakeholders and the Scrum Team. By making the Product Backlog transparent and accessible to everyone, the Scrum Team ensures everyone involved in the process has the same basis for adaptation. This means they can make informed decisions about what to prioritize and work more effectively towards the product's overall vision and goals.

Similarly, the Sprint Backlog is another artifact in Scrum that represents the work the Scrum Team plans to complete during the current Sprint. By making the Sprint Backlog transparent and accessible, the Scrum Team ensures everyone is aware of the progress and can collaborate effectively toward the Sprint Goal.

Finally, the Increment is the sum of all the completed product requirements or features at the end of each Sprint. By making the Increment transparent and accessible to everyone, the Scrum Team ensures everyone is aware of the progress toward the product's overall vision and goals.

14.3 Commitments

> *Each artifact contains a commitment to ensure it provides information that enhances transparency and focus against which progress can be measured:*
>
> - *For the Product Backlog it is the Product Goal.*
> - *For the Sprint Backlog it is the Sprint Goal.*
> - *For the Increment it is the Definition of Done.*
>
> *These commitments exist to reinforce empiricism and the Scrum values for the Scrum Team and their stakeholders.*

In Scrum, each artifact is designed to provide specific information that enhances transparency and focus. This is essential for the Scrum Team to be able to measure progress and make informed decisions. Additionally, each artifact is associated with a commitment that ensures that it provides the necessary information.

The Scrum values - commitment, courage, focus, openness, and respect - are essential for the Scrum Team to work effectively together and deliver value to the product's customers. The commitments associated with each artifact help to reinforce these values by ensuring that the Scrum Team is working towards a shared objective, staying focused on the Sprint Goal, and delivering a potentially releasable Increment at the end of each Sprint.

This promotes collaboration, transparency, and a culture of continuous improvement, which are essential for the success of the Scrum process.

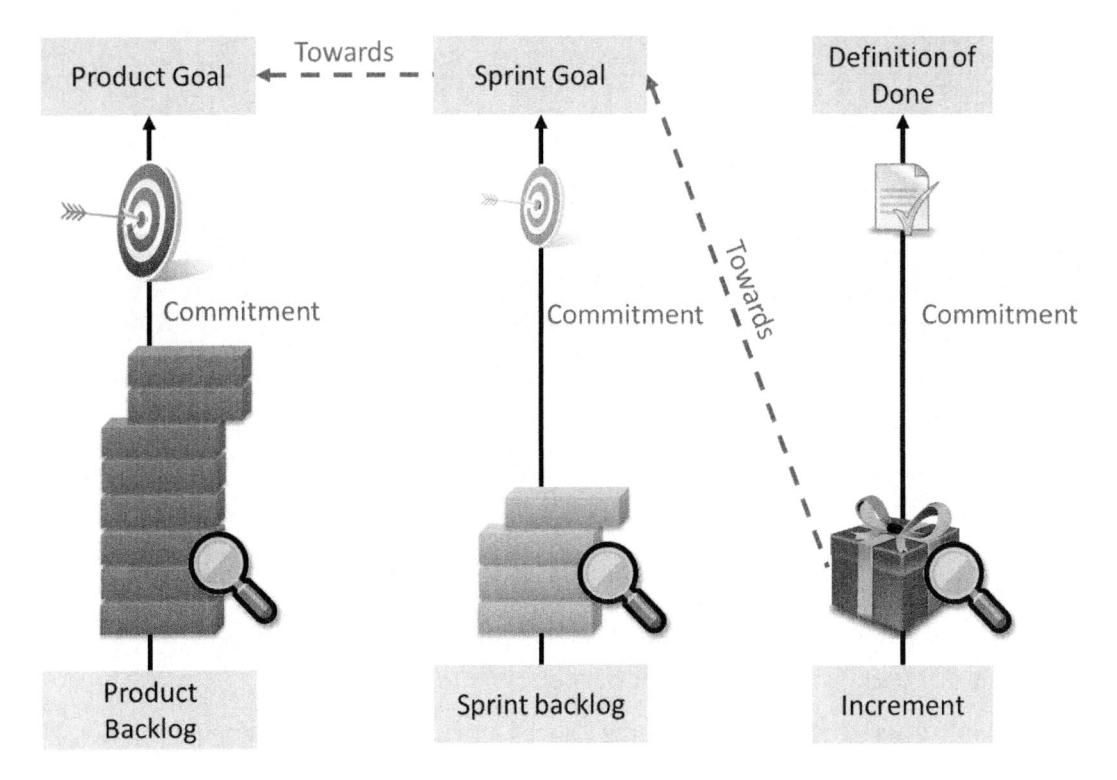

Figure 32 Scrum artifacts and commitments.

Each Increment is created according to the Definition of Done as a step toward the Sprint Goal and the Product Goal. Likewise, each Sprint Goal is created as a step towards the Product Goal.

Inspect and adapt:

- Inspect the Product Backlog and adapt it to meet the Product Goal.
- Inspect the Sprint Backlog and adapt it to meet the Sprint Goal.
- Inspect the Increment and adapt it to meet the Definition of Done.

Part 15: Product Backlog

15.1 It is emergent and ordered

The Product Backlog is an emergent, ordered list of what is needed to improve the product.

The Product Backlog in Scrum is an essential artifact that captures all the work needed to deliver the desired product or service. It is an ordered list of product features, enhancements, and bug fixes that represent the work to be completed by the Scrum Team.

The Product Backlog is dynamic, never complete, and evolves as the product or service evolves.

The Product Backlog is emergent because it evolves, and new items are added or removed as the product evolves. The Scrum Team continually reviews and refines the Product Backlog to ensure that it accurately reflects the current state of the product and the customer's needs. Therefore, you can see the Product Backlog as a draft of ideas that will constantly evolve.

The Product Backlog is also ordered, with the most important items at the top of the list. The order of the Product Backlog is based on the value each item will bring to the product or service. The Product Owner is responsible for prioritizing the Product Backlog based on input from stakeholders and the Scrum Team.

Usually, higher-ordered Product Backlog items are clearer and more detailed than lower-ordered ones. Similarly, Developers typically can assess the size and effort of the higher-ordered items better than the lower-ordered ones because of their greater clarity and increased detail.

In other words, the items on the top are more refined, typically ready for Sprint Planning, and likely to be added to the next Sprint because of their importance.

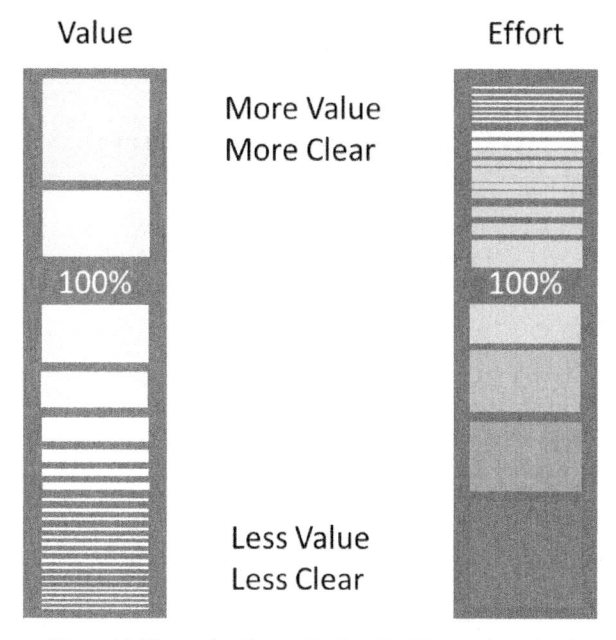

Figure 33 Example of how a Product Backlog can be ordered.

15.2 It is the single source of work for all Sprints

It is the single source of work undertaken by the Scrum Team.

The Product Backlog is the single source of work undertaken by the Scrum Team. It represents all the work the Scrum Team needs to do to deliver the product or service. The Scrum Team works on the items in the Product Backlog in order, from top to bottom, and completes as many items as possible during each Sprint.

In Scrum, the Product Backlog is the single source of work undertaken by the Scrum Team. This means that the Product Backlog represents all the work needed to deliver the product or service, and the Scrum Team works on the items in the Product Backlog in order, from top to bottom, until the Sprint Goal is met.

In other words, all the items added to a Spring Backlog must come from the Product Backlog. All new work or ideas must be added to the Product Backlog first.

15.3 Is it a list of User Stories?

While user stories are a popular way to capture requirements, they are not mandatory in Scrum. The Scrum Guide does not mention user stories or any technique explicitly. Instead, it describes the Product Backlog as an ordered list of items representing the work required to deliver the product or service. The items in the Product Backlog can take many forms, including user stories, technical requirements, design specifications, and others. The Scrum Team should work with the Product Owner to ensure that the items in the Product Backlog are clear, concise, and actionable.

15.4 Types of Product Backlog items

Scrum does not mandate any technique or approach for Product Backlog items.

The Product Backlog in Scrum typically contains various items representing the work required to deliver a product or service. Some of the most common types of items in the Product Backlog are:

1. Features: These are new capabilities added to the product to deliver new value to customers or stakeholders.
2. Enhancements: These are improvements to existing features, often made in response to feedback or issues that have arisen.
3. Bugs: These are defects or errors in the product that needs to be fixed to improve its quality.
4. Technical debt: This represents work that needs to be done to improve the underlying technology or infrastructure of the product, such as refactoring code or upgrading libraries.
5. Infrastructure improvements: These are changes to the underlying infrastructure of the product, such as setting up new servers or improving network performance.
6. Research and development: These items require exploration or investigation before they can be added to the product, such as prototyping or user testing.

7. User stories: These are brief, plain-language descriptions of a feature or functionality from an end user's perspective.
8. Non-functional requirements: These are requirements that do not relate to specific features or functions of the product but rather to its overall performance, usability, security, or other non-functional aspects.
9. Spikes: These are time-boxed investigations or research activities that help the Scrum Team better to understand a complex problem, technology, or requirement.

The types of items in the Product Backlog may vary depending on the product, the industry, and the needs of the stakeholders. The Product Owner is responsible for ensuring that the Product Backlog includes all the necessary items to deliver the product or service and prioritizing them based on their value. The Scrum Team works on the items in the Product Backlog to achieve the Sprint Goal and deliver value to the customers and stakeholders.

15.5 Non-functional Requirements in PB or DoD

The Product Owner can add Non-functional requirements as Product Backlog items and discuss with the Scrum Team to add Non-functional requirements as part of the Definition of Done.

Non-functional requirements refer to a product's aspects that are not directly related to its features or functionality but rather to its performance, usability, reliability, security, and other similar characteristics. Examples of non-functional requirements include load time, response time, user interface design, accessibility, scalability, and security features.

Non-functional requirements can be added to the Product Backlog anytime as part of new features or as standalone items. They can also be included in the Definition of Done, a formal description of the Increment state when it meets the product's required quality measures. Including non-functional requirements in the Definition of Done ensures that they are considered part of the overall quality of the product and are not overlooked in a rush to deliver new features.

Adding non-functional requirements to the Product Backlog or as part of the Definition of Done can also help ensure they are given the same attention and priority as functional requirements. This can help ensure that the product meets the needs of all stakeholders, including end-users and customers, and that it can perform effectively in real-world scenarios.

Here are examples of non-functional requirements that could be added to the Product Backlog as a standalone item or as part of the Definition of Done:

1. Adding a Non-functional Requirement as a Product Backlog Item:
    - Example: Improve load time for the home page by 50%
    - Explanation: This non-functional requirement is a standalone item added to the Product Backlog. It outlines the specific goal of improving

the load time of web pages by a certain percentage. The team will need to work on implementing changes to the product to achieve this goal.
  2. Adding a Non-functional Requirement as Part of the Definition of Done:
     - Example: All new features must meet accessibility standards.
     - Explanation: This non-functional requirement is added to the Definition of Done for all new features. It ensures that all new features are designed and developed with accessibility in mind rather than being an afterthought. This requirement will be met with every new feature and will not need to be added as a separate item to the Product Backlog each time.

Here's an example of a non-functional requirement that could be added as a Product Backlog item to update existing previously developed features and as part of the Definition of Done for all new features:

1. Adding a Non-functional Requirement as a Product Backlog Item to Update Existing Previously Developed Features:
   a. Example: Implement HTTPS encryption for all previously developed features.
   b. Explanation: This non-functional requirement is added to the Product Backlog as a standalone item to update previously developed features. It outlines the specific goal of implementing HTTPS encryption for all previously developed features. The team will need to work on updating the features to achieve this goal.
2. Adding the Same Non-functional Requirement as Part of the Definition of Done for All New Features:
   a. Example: All new features must have HTTPS encryption implemented.
   b. Explanation: This non-functional requirement is also added as part of the Definition of Done for all new features. It ensures that all new features are designed and developed with HTTPS encryption in mind from the outset. This requirement will be met with every new feature and will not need to be added as a separate item to the Product Backlog each time.

In Summary,

- A Non-functional Requirement that applies to one or a few features and will be developed one time will typically be added to the Product Backlog.
- A Non-functional Requirement that applies to all new Product Backlog items should be added as part of the Definition of Done.
- A Non-functional Requirement can also be added as a Product Backlog item to update previously developed features and as part of the Definition of Done for all new product features.

15.6 A PBI is a Hypothesis of value

In Scrum, requirements are not real value. Instead, they are hypotheses of potential value. That hope of value must be validated through experiments. Therefore, rather than treating requirements as a firm belief of value with fixed and immutable definitions, the Scrum Team can use an iterative approach to refine and test their understanding of the customer's needs.

From the EBM Framework:

> *Organizations can spend a lot of money implementing features and other requirements in products, only to find that customers don't share the company's opinion on their value; beliefs in what is valuable are merely assumptions until they are validated by customers. This is where hypotheses and experiments are useful.*
>
> *In simplified terms, a hypothesis is a proposed explanation for some observation that has not yet been proven (or disproven). In the context of requirements, it is a belief that doing something will lead to something else, such as delivering feature X will lead to outcome Y. An experiment is a test that is designed to prove or reject some hypothesis.*
>
> *Every feature and every requirement really represent a hypothesis about value. One of the goals of an empirical approach is to make these hypotheses explicit and to consciously design experiments that explicitly test the value of the features and requirements. The entire feature or requirement need not actually be built to determine whether it is valuable; it may be sufficient for a team to simply build enough of it to validate critical assumptions that would prove or disprove its value.*
>
> *Explicitly forming hypotheses, measuring results, and inspecting and adapting goals based on those results are implicit parts of an agile approach.*

We often hear that the Product Backlog will be prioritized by business value. In reality, the items of the Product Backlog have no real value, but they have the potential or expectation of bringing value once they are in the hands of the users. Releasing an increment or feature is just an output and not an outcome. We can only measure and confirm the value of a feature once the user has interacted enough with it and generated a tangible positive or negative outcome.

Here's how requirements can be viewed as hypotheses and experiments in Scrum:

1. Hypotheses: In Scrum, the Product Backlog is a list of items that describe the work to be done. Each item in the Product Backlog can be viewed as a hypothesis about what the customer needs and its expected value. The Scrum Team should treat these hypotheses as starting points for further exploration and experimentation.
2. Experiments: Once a hypothesis has been identified, the Scrum Team can design experiments to test it. These experiments should be designed to validate or invalidate the hypothesis and to provide feedback on the customer's needs. The experiments can take various forms, such as user testing, A/B testing, or prototyping.

3. Results: Based on the results of the experiments, the Scrum Team can refine their understanding of the customer's needs and the likelihood of its value and update the Product Backlog accordingly. If the experiment validates the hypothesis, the requirement can be prioritized higher in the Product Backlog. Conversely, the requirement can be removed or de-prioritized if the experiment invalidates the hypothesis.

Here's an example of a hypothesis of value for a Product Backlog item, an experiment to test it, and the measured results:

- Hypothesis: Adding a new payment gateway to our e-commerce platform will increase conversion rates by 10%.
- Experiment: To test this hypothesis, we will add a new payment gateway to the checkout process for a subset of users. We will measure the conversion rates for this subset of users and compare them to the conversion rates for users who use the existing payment gateway.
- Measured Results: After running the experiment, we found that the conversion rates for users who used the new payment gateway were lower than those who used the existing payment gateway. The conversion rate for users who used the new payment gateway was only 5%, while the conversion rate for users who used the existing payment gateway was 12%. Based on these results, we concluded that our hypothesis was invalid, and we removed the requirement for the new payment gateway from the Product Backlog.

By treating requirements as hypotheses and experiments, the Scrum Team can ensure they build the right product for the customer. This approach helps to reduce the risk of building a product that doesn't meet the customer's needs and enables the team to learn and adapt as they work continuously. It also encourages collaboration between the Product Owner, the Developers, and the customer, which is critical for the product's success.

15.7 Owned by the Product Owner

The Product Backlog is created and owned by the Product Owner, who is responsible for prioritizing the items in the Product Backlog based on the value they bring to the product or service. The Scrum Team works with the Product Owner to understand the requirements and dependencies of the items in the Product Backlog.

Others could update the Product Backlog only if the Product Owner authorized them. The Product Owner may delegate part or total management of the Product Backlog, allowing team members to make changes such as ordering, creating, or clarifying items. However, the Product Owner remains accountable for any of those changes and the positive or negative impact on the Product's value.

15.8 Ready items

> *Product Backlog items that can be Done by the Scrum Team within one Sprint are deemed ready for selection in a Sprint Planning event. They usually acquire this degree of transparency after refining activities.*

Product Backlog items that can be Done by the Scrum Team within one Sprint are deemed "ready" for selection in a Sprint Planning event. This means they have been refined and are sufficiently well-understood to be estimated and included in the upcoming Sprint. In other words, they are in a state of readiness that allows the Scrum Team to commit to delivering them within the Sprint.

The basic condition in Scrum to consider that a Product Backlog item is "ready" to be added to a Sprint Backlog is that the Developers can forecast confidently that they can get it done within one Sprint.

Some Scrum Teams may define a Definition of Ready to strengthen this basic condition of items that can be added to a Sprint, but this is not required or mentioned by the Scrum Framework.

Scrum's concept of "ready" can be related to being ready to start a race. In the context of Scrum, "ready" means that a Product Backlog item is sufficiently well-defined and understood by the Scrum Team so that it can be estimated and included in a Sprint. You may not have all the details, but you have a good understanding to start working on the item.

Similarly, runners must be physically and mentally prepared when they are getting ready to start a race. They must stretch, warm up, and get the right mindset to run the race. They also need to ensure they have the right equipment and clothing and are familiar with the race course.

In both cases, being "ready" is essential to achieving success. For example, if a Product Backlog item is not "ready" for inclusion in a Sprint, it may lead to delays, misunderstandings, or incomplete work. Similarly, if a runner is not "ready" to start a race, they may not be able to perform at their best or achieve their goals.

15.9 Product Backlog Refinement

> *They usually acquire this degree of transparency after refining activities. Product Backlog refinement is the act of breaking down and further defining Product Backlog items into smaller more precise items. This is an ongoing activity to add details, such as a description, order, and size. Attributes often vary with the domain of work.*

Product Backlog refinement is not an event. Instead, Product Backlog refinement is the ongoing activity of breaking down and further defining Product Backlog items into smaller, more precise items. This is done to ensure that each item is well-understood and transparent so that it can be estimated or sized and included in a Sprint.

Product Backlog items usually acquire the "ready" degree of transparency after refinement activities. During this process, the Scrum Team and the Product Owner work together to add details to the items in the Product Backlog. This may include a description, order, size, and any other attributes relevant to the work domain. The goal is to ensure that each item is sufficiently well-defined to be estimated and included in a Sprint.

Refining Product Backlog items is an ongoing activity that continues throughout the product's life. As new information becomes available or the product evolves, the Product Backlog may need to be updated and refined to ensure it remains transparent and well-understood.

Product Backlog refinement can occur at any time during Sprint and as much as the team needs. However, the Scrum Team should prioritize the time of the Sprint to meet the Sprint Goal.

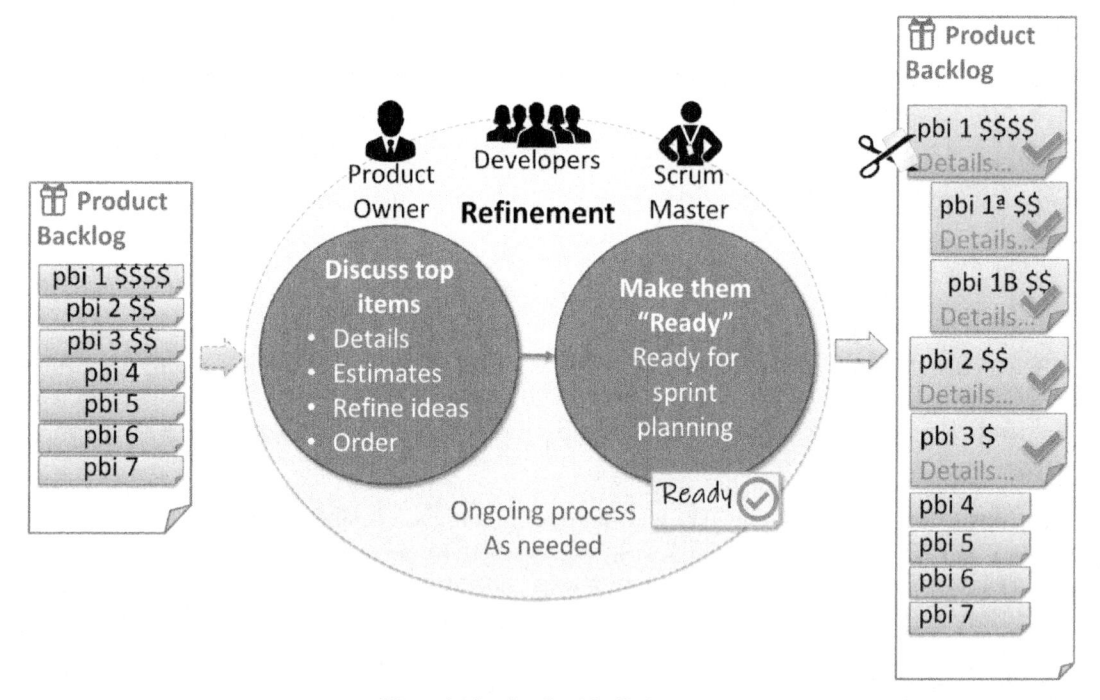

Figure 34 Product Backlog Refinement.

Typically, during the Sprint, the Scrum Team will refine the items that will likely be added to the next Sprint.

15.9.1 Who must participate in the Product Backlog refinement?

The Scrum Team is self-managing, meaning they internally decide who does what, when, and how. While some Scrum Teams may prefer that all team members participate in the refinement, other teams may organize so that only a few members meet the Product Owner to refine the items.

When it comes to Product Backlog refinement, there are two approaches:

All Scrum Team Members Meet: In this approach, all Scrum Team members, including the Product Owner, attend the Product Backlog refinement meeting. During this meeting, they review the Product Backlog and discuss potential changes to its content or order. This approach ensures that all team members have a shared understanding of the Product Backlog, which can help to reduce miscommunications and ensure that everyone is working towards the same goals.

Only a Few Members Meet: In this approach, only a subset of the Scrum Team members, usually the Product Owner and a few Developers, attend the Product Backlog refinement meeting. The goal is to ensure that the Product Owner has adequate time to refine the Product Backlog and that it is ready for the upcoming Sprint.

While both approaches have their advantages, the choice ultimately depends on the specific needs of the Scrum Team and the product development effort.

The advantage of having all Scrum Team members attend Product Backlog refinement meetings is that it promotes collaboration and shared understanding, which can improve the quality of the resulting work. However, this approach can be time-consuming and require additional coordination and planning.

On the other hand, having only a few Scrum Team members attend Product Backlog refinement meetings can be more efficient and may allow for more focused discussions. However, this approach risks siloed information and communication breakdowns between team members who did not attend the meeting.

In either approach, ensuring that the Product Owner has adequate time to refine the Product Backlog and that the Scrum Team members have a shared understanding of the product development effort is important.

15.9.2 *When there are no skills to build the items*

If, during a Product Backlog refinement session, the Developers identify that the upcoming Sprint requires skills unavailable within the team. Here are three possible approaches to deal with this issue:

- Explore if there are technical experts outside the team who can provide guidance or be invited to Sprint Planning to help the team learn the required skills.
- Discuss with the team the effort required to learn the new skills and how it might impact the expectations of the Product Owner.
- The team might find an alternative or temporary solution that does not require such skills.

- Ask the Product Owner if the goals can still be achieved without the features that require the skills that are unavailable within the team or by simplifying the requirements.
- Understand if there might be third-party solutions, components, or services that the team can buy to provide the expected functionality.

15.10 Not "ready" items during Sprint Planning

If an item is critical during Sprint Planning but was not properly refined, the Scrum Team may need to spend time refining the item during the Sprint Planning event or in a separate refinement session.

During Sprint Planning, the Scrum Team selects Product Backlog items to be worked on during the upcoming Sprint. The Scrum Team may realize that an item is critical, but they may not have enough information to estimate it or plan for its implementation.

In this case, the Scrum Team can take one of two approaches: either defer the item to a future Sprint or spend time refining it during the current Sprint Planning event. If they choose to refine the item during the current Sprint Planning event, they will need to break down and further define it into smaller, more precise items. This will help to ensure that the item is well-understood and transparent so that it can be estimated and included in the Sprint.

If the Scrum Team decides to defer the item to a future Sprint, they must add it to the Product Backlog and refine it during future refinement sessions. The Product Owner can then prioritize the item appropriately based on its criticality and impact on the product.

15.11 The Developers estimate

In Scrum, sizing is a process of estimating the effort required to complete a Product Backlog item according to the Definition of Done.

The size of a task or an item is typically measured in terms of story points, a relative measure of the complexity and effort required to complete it. However, no technique is mandatory, and Developers can choose any technique they want. However, they should be able to provide a reliable forecast.

The responsibility for sizing falls on the Developers, who will be doing the work. They have the technical expertise and knowledge required to understand the complexity of the work and make an accurate estimate.

However, the Product Owner also plays a role in the sizing process. They are responsible for setting priorities and deciding what work should be done. In addition, the Product Owner can help

It is important to note that while the Product Owner can influence the sizing process, they should not dictate the estimate to the Developers. Instead, the size of an item should be determined based on the Developers' understanding of the work involved and their experience with similar tasks.

The Scrum Master may help the Developers and the Product Owner understand the purpose and benefits of estimation and may facilitate the estimation process by ensuring that the team has the necessary information and resources to make an accurate estimate. They may also help the team identify any issues or challenges impacting the estimate's accuracy and help the team address these issues.

Additionally, the Scrum Master may help the team identify and adopt appropriate estimation techniques, such as Planning Poker or affinity mapping. They may also help the team to use estimation as a tool for continuous improvement by encouraging them to review and reflect on their estimates and identify areas where they can improve their estimation process.

In summary, the Developers are responsible for sizing in Scrum. Still, the Product Owner can guide and help the Developers understand the trade-offs in completing a particular task or item.

15.12 Anti-patterns with the Product Backlog

Product Backlog antipatterns are common mistakes or practices that can hinder the effectiveness of the Scrum framework. Here are a few examples:

1. Lack of prioritization: When the Product Backlog lacks clear priorities, the Scrum Team may struggle to focus on the most valuable work. This can lead to wasted time and resources and a product that does not meet the needs of the stakeholders.
2. Overloading the backlog: Too many items in the Product Backlog can make managing and prioritizing work difficult. It can also lead to confusion and a lack of focus, as the Scrum Team may not know which items are the most important.
3. Unclear or incomplete backlog items: Backlog items that are unclear or incomplete can lead to misunderstandings and delays. It is important to ensure that backlog items are well-defined and transparent so that the Scrum Team can estimate and plan for their implementation.
4. Lack of collaboration: If the Product Owner works in isolation from the rest of the Scrum Team, it can lead to a lack of collaboration and a misalignment of priorities. It is important to involve the entire Scrum Team in refining and prioritizing the Product Backlog.
5. Failure to refine the backlog: If the Product Backlog is not regularly refined, it can become outdated and irrelevant. It is important to regularly refine the backlog to ensure that it reflects the current state of the product and the needs of the stakeholders.

In summary, Product Backlog antipatterns can lead to a lack of focus, confusion, and delays. Therefore, it is important to prioritize, refine, and collaborate on the Product Backlog to ensure that the Scrum Team is working on the most valuable work and delivering a product that meets the needs of the stakeholders.

Part 16: Product Goal: Commitment to the Product Backlog

> *The Product Goal describes a future state of the product which can serve as a target for the Scrum Team to plan against. The Product Goal is in the Product Backlog. The rest of the Product Backlog emerges to define "what" will fulfill the Product Goal.*

The Product Goal is an overarching statement that describes the future state of the product that the Scrum Team is working towards. It serves as a target that the team can use to plan and prioritize the work that needs to be done. The Product Goal is a long-term focus that remains stable over several Sprints, and it should not change frequently.

The Product Goal is included in the Product Backlog, which is an ordered list of all the work needed to achieve the Product Goal. The Product Backlog is dynamic and evolves as the Scrum Team learns more about the product and the users' needs. As a result, the Product Backlog is a living artifact that is constantly refined, reordered, and reprioritized based on the feedback and insights gained from stakeholders and users.

The rest of the Product Backlog emerges to define "what" will fulfill the Product Goal. This means that the Scrum Team can add, remove, or modify items in the Product Backlog as needed to achieve the Product Goal. The Product Backlog is a powerful tool for the Scrum Team to manage and prioritize their work and ensure they are constantly working towards the Product Goal.

The Product Goal in Scrum is a long-term objective that describes the future state of the product.

16.1 The Product

Scrum defines the product as:

> *A product is a vehicle to deliver value. It has a clear boundary, known stakeholders, well-defined users or customers. A product could be a service, a physical product, or something more abstract.*

In Scrum, a product is viewed as a vehicle for delivering value to its stakeholders regardless of its form. It can take many forms, such as a physical product, a service, or an abstract concept. Regardless of the form, a product must have a clear boundary distinguishing it from other products or services.

Additionally, a product must have well-defined users or customers who will benefit from it. These users or customers have specific needs and expectations that the product must meet to deliver value. Finally, the stakeholders involved in the product, including users, customers, and investors, are also well-defined and known to the Scrum Team.

By defining a clear boundary and understanding the users and stakeholders, the Scrum Team can focus their efforts on delivering value and achieving the Product Goal. This enables the team to work efficiently and effectively, delivering a high-quality product that meets the needs of its users and customers.

In summary:

- A product is a vehicle to deliver value.
- It has a clear boundary, known stakeholders, well-defined users or customers.
- It could be a service, a physical product, or something more abstract.

The product is the main focus of Scrum, and satisfying the customer is the most important goal.

16.2 One Product Goal at a Time

The Product Goal is the long-term objective for the Scrum Team. They must fulfill (or abandon) one objective before taking on the next.

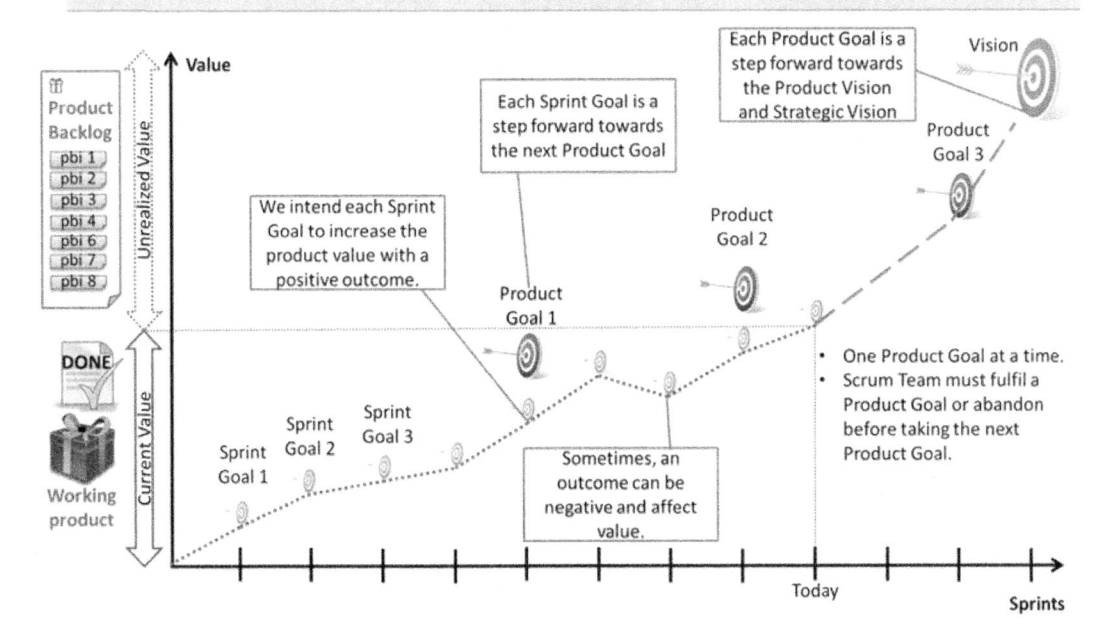

Figure 35 One Product Goal at a Time.

The Product Goal is the overarching objective that the Scrum Team works towards achieving over a longer period. It represents the ultimate outcome that the product is expected to deliver. A product may have many Product Goals during its lifetime. Therefore, the team needs to focus their efforts on achieving one Product goal before moving on to the next one, as this ensures that they stay aligned with the overall strategic direction of the product.

By fulfilling one objective before taking on the next, the team can clearly focus on what they are working towards and avoid getting sidetracked by competing priorities. In addition, this approach allows the team to work iteratively towards a larger objective, breaking it down into smaller pieces and addressing them in priority order while ensuring that each step aligns with the overall goal.

Suppose the team attempts to take on too many objectives simultaneously or switch between them frequently. In that case, it can lead to confusion, a lack of direction, and an inability to make meaningful progress toward one objective. Therefore, the team needs to have a clear understanding of the Product Goal and a plan in place to achieve it.

16.3 Why not work on two Product Goals?

Sometimes the Product Owner or stakeholders may push for multiple goals to be pursued simultaneously, leading to a lack of focus and confusion among the team. This can result in a diluted effort, a longer time to market for all goals, and reduced effectiveness in achieving any of the goals.

The idea of limiting work in progress (WIP) and short cycle times is to increase the speed of delivering value to customers. By focusing on one product goal at a time, the Scrum Team can prioritize their work and limit WIP, leading to shorter cycle times and faster time to market.

If the team tries to work on multiple product goals simultaneously, they risk spreading themselves too thin and not being able to deliver high-quality work on any of the goals. This can lead to longer cycle times and delayed time to market, which can negatively impact the product's success. By fulfilling one product goal before taking on the next, the Scrum Team can maintain focus and ensure they promptly deliver the most valuable work to their customers.

16.3.1 Context Switching

Working on two Sprint Goals or two Product Goals simultaneously can lead to context switching, which is the process of mentally shifting focus between different tasks or projects. Context switching can have both positive and negative effects on productivity and efficiency.

When working on two Sprint goals or product goals simultaneously, context switching may occur in the following ways:

- Task Interruptions: The need to frequently switch between tasks related to each goal can lead to interruptions, disrupting the flow of work and hindering progress. This can result in reduced efficiency, increased stress, and a longer time to completion for both goals.
- Cognitive Overhead: Context switching requires mental effort to adjust to new tasks, particularly if the goals differ or require different skill sets. This cognitive overhead can reduce focus and increase the likelihood of making mistakes.
- Time Cost: The time spent switching between tasks can accumulate, leading to a loss of productive time. This can slow down progress on both goals and negatively impact overall performance.
- Reduced Quality: Due to the constant shifting between tasks, it can be not easy to maintain a high level of quality and attention to detail. This may result in subpar outcomes for both goals.
- Burnout: Continuously working on multiple goals and context-switching can lead to increased stress and potential burnout, negatively affecting overall job satisfaction and performance.

16.3.2   *Return on investment (value maximization)*

Working on more than one Sprint Goal or more than one Product Goal simultaneously and experiencing context switching can impact time to market and return on investment (ROI). Here's how these factors relate:

- Time to Market: As discussed previously, context switching can slow progress on both goals. This may lead to product development or implementation delays, resulting in a long time to market. A longer time to market can have negative consequences, such as lost competitive advantage, missed opportunities, and reduced customer satisfaction. Being the first to market in highly competitive industries can be crucial, and delays may significantly impact a product's success.
- Return on Investment (ROI): The efficiency losses and potential reduction in quality associated with context switching can affect ROI in several ways:
    - Increased Development Costs: The time and resources spent on context switching can increase development costs. Higher costs can reduce the overall ROI for both goals, as it takes longer to recoup the investment.
    - Lower Quality: As mentioned earlier, context switching may result in lower quality outcomes. Lower-quality products may reduce customer satisfaction and loyalty, negatively impacting sales, revenue, and ROI.
    - Missed Opportunities: Delays in time to market due to context switching can lead to missed opportunities. For instance, if a competitor releases a similar product first, it may capture a significant portion of the market share, reducing the potential ROI for your product.

In the following example, imagine

- The Team costs $5.000 per week.
- After a goal is delivered, the company gets 15k, 10k, or 5k from the new features, respectively, in weekly profit.
- Each goal requires four weeks of work. Sometimes the team is blocked by shared resources.

The team is thinking of two approaches: working on three goals simultaneously or working on one at a time. The cash flow for both approaches will look something like the table below:

Longer cycle times   **Shorter cycle times**

Working on Multiple Goals   Vs.   **One Goal at a Time**

Week	Goal 1	Goal 2	Goal 3	Team Cost	Goal 1	Goal 2	Goal 3
1	Working	No work	No work		Working	No work	No work
2	No work	Working	No work		Working	No work	No work
3	No work	No work	Working		Working	No work	No work
4	Working	No work	No work	(20,000.00)	Done	No work	No work
5	No work	Working	No work		15000	Working	No work
6	No work	No work	Working		15000	Working	No work
7	Working	No work	No work		15000	Working	No work
8	No work	Working	No work	(20,000.00)	15000	Done	No work
9	No work	No work	Working		15000	10000	Working
10	Done	No work	No work		15000	10000	Working
11	15000	Done	No work		15000	10000	Working
12	15000	10000	Done	(20,000.00)	15000	10000	Done
	30,000.00	10,000.00		(60,000.00)	120,000.00	40,000.00	0.00
Profit	(20,000.00)				100,000.00		

The example is a simplification of the reality, but given the context switching the lead times for the first approach may look worse.

To mitigate the potential negative impact of context switching on time to market and ROI, it is essential to prioritize tasks and allocate resources effectively. This may involve focusing on one goal at a time, establishing clear milestones, and regularly reassessing priorities.

16.4 Product Goal, Product Vision, and Strategic Vision

The Scrum Guide 2020 does not mention the vision, but it was mentioned in previous versions. However, in addition to a Product Goal, there can typically be a Product Vision or Strategic vision by the organization. Additionally, frameworks such as Scrum@scale© or EBM™ that can be combined with Scrum include the concept of vision.

The Product Goal, Product Vision, and Strategic Vision of the organization are all important concepts in product development and strategic planning, and they are interconnected in various ways.

The Strategic Vision of the organization is a high-level statement that outlines the long-term goals and objectives, and aspirations of the organization. It helps to guide the direction and decision-making of the organization as a whole, including product development. Therefore, the Product Vision should be aligned with the Strategic Vision of the organization, reflecting how the product will contribute to achieving the organization's strategic goals.

The Product Vision is a high-level statement describing the product's long-term goal or purpose. It communicates the intended value of the product to stakeholders and helps the team to stay focused on the big picture and motivated to achieve the end goal. Therefore, the Product Vision should be established early in the product development process and guide decision-making throughout the project.

The Product Goal is a measurable objective the team wants to achieve within the various Sprints. It is a step toward achieving the Product Vision and should be achievable within one Sprint. Consider the Product Goal as the next milestone, version, or significant release for the market. It provides a clear direction and focus for the team during the Sprints and helps them to understand what they need to accomplish.

While an increment and Sprint Goal provide value through Sprints, the Product Goal is an important business achievement of value.

To sum up:

- A company typically has one Strategic Vision.
- A Product typically has one Product Vision aligned with the Strategic vision.
- A Scrum team will pursue many Product Goals during a Product's life, focusing on one at a time.
- The Product Goal is aligned with the Product Vision.

Example: Let's consider a software company that develops a project management tool for small businesses.

- Strategic vision: To become the leading provider of global project management tools for small businesses.

- Product vision: To create a project management tool that is easy to use, affordable, and specifically designed for small businesses.
- During the first two years, the Scrum Team fulfilled the following Product Goals, one at a time:
  1. MVP: To release a new version of the project management tool within the next three months that includes a mobile app, a new user interface, and enhanced reporting capabilities to help small businesses manage their projects more efficiently.
  2. Improve collaboration features: To improve team communication and productivity, develop a new version of the project management tool that includes enhanced collaboration features, such as a team chat and a task assignment tool.
  3. Expand integrations: Expand the integrations available with the project management tool to include popular software tools used by small businesses, such as Google Drive, Slack, and Trello, to provide users with a more seamless experience and increase adoption.
  4. Launch mobile app: Launch a mobile app for the project management tool to allow users to manage their projects on the go and increase accessibility to the tool. The mobile app will include all the features available in the desktop version and will be available for both iOS and Android platforms.
- Every Product Goal requires several Sprints.
- Every Sprint still has a Sprint Goal where valuable, potentially releasable increments are created.
- Each Sprint can be used to do experiments, validate the potential value of the Product Goal, and decide to continue, pivot, or abandon and set a new Product Goal.

Some Scrum Teams may not define a Product Vision and just use Product Goals. Some interpretations assume that the Product Goal and Product Vision are the same thing. However, that approach misses the opportunity of an overarching vision to move towards the achievement of every Product Goal.

In summary, the organization's Strategic Vision guides product development, while the Product Vision and Product Goal provide direction and focus for the product team at different levels of abstraction. All three are important for ensuring that the product development efforts are aligned with the organization's strategic goals and that progress is being made toward achieving them.

16.5 Progress towards the Product Goal

The Product Owner regularly assesses the total work remaining to reach the Product Goal and compares it to work remaining in previous Sprint Reviews. This assessment helps determine the progress toward completing the projected work by the desired time for the goal.

Various projective practices like Release burndowns, Release burn-ups, or cumulative flows can be used to forecast progress toward Product goals. However, Scrum recommends no practice, and it is important to note that these practices do not replace the importance of empiricism. In complex environments, predicting what will happen in the future is impossible, and only past events can be used for decision-making. Therefore, empiricism should be the primary means of assessing progress toward the Product Goal.

By regularly tracking the progress toward the Product Goal, the Scrum Team and stakeholders can make informed decisions on what to do next to achieve the desired outcome. In addition, transparency of this information to all stakeholders promotes collaboration and helps manage expectations.

16.6 Flexibility and variable scope

In Scrum, the product goal serves as a unifying objective for the team to work towards. This goal allows for flexibility in terms of scope, which should be variable and negotiated with stakeholders throughout the project. For example, if there is a deadline for the product goal, the team can negotiate with stakeholders on what is valuable and achievable by that date to reduce the scope of features to meet the deadline. This negotiation allows the team to prioritize work based on value, which can result in the delivery of a higher-value product within the given constraints. In contrast, if the team adheres to a hard list of features, they may miss the opportunity to make changes or adjust their approach as the project progresses. Overall, Scrum's Product Goal and flexible scope approach allow for greater adaptability and a focus on value delivery.

In some cases, the deadline cannot be extended, for example:

- Voting machines for an election: The deadline for developing and deploying voting machines cannot be extended as the election date is set and cannot be moved.
- A spacecraft for a space mission: The deadline for the development and launch of a spacecraft cannot be extended as the launch date is predetermined and cannot be changed.
- Tax preparation software for tax season: The deadline for developing and releasing tax preparation software cannot be extended as the tax season is set and cannot be delayed.
- Christmas toys: The deadline for the production and shipment of Christmas toys cannot be extended as they are expected to be available for sale during the holiday season.
- Seasonal products: The deadline for producing and releasing seasonal products like Halloween costumes or Easter chocolates cannot be extended as they are only in demand during a specific time of the year.
- Sports Events: Tournaments and games in sports have set schedules, and postponing them would affect players, fans, and sponsors, making it difficult to reschedule games or events.

- TV Live Shows: Some TV shows are broadcast live and have a specific time slot, such as talk shows, game shows, and news programs. The timing cannot be extended, as it would interfere with other programming or airtime.
- Conferences: Conferences are planned well in advance, and attendees travel far and wide to attend. Changing the dates or postponing the event would cause significant disruption to attendees, speakers, and organizers.
- Construction Projects: Construction projects have set deadlines due to contracts, permits, and weather conditions. Delays can result in additional costs, legal disputes, and loss of revenue.

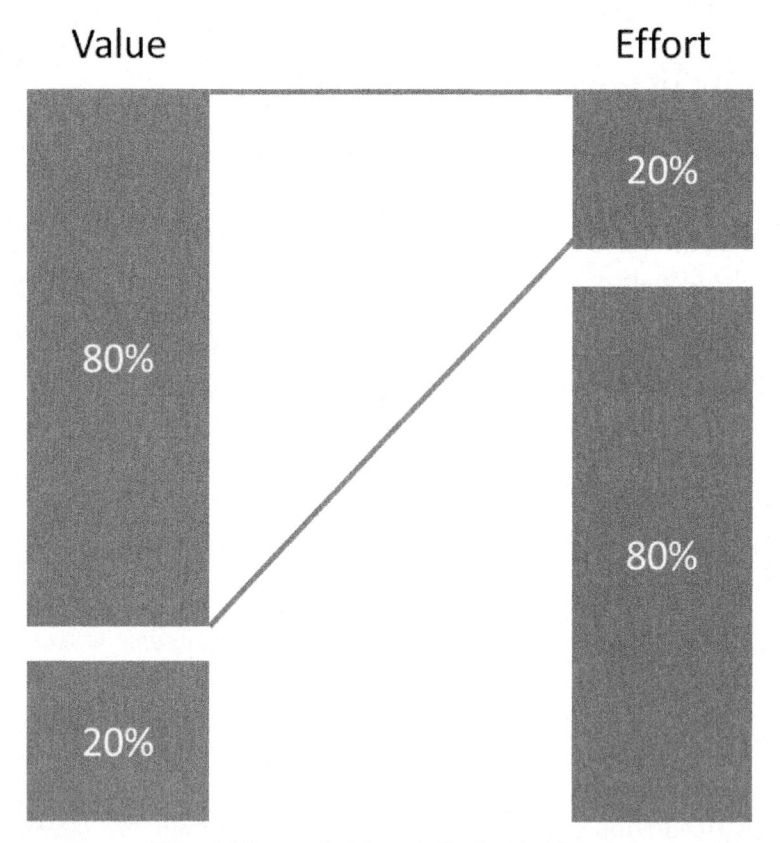

Figure 36 Pareto principle on the Product Backlog value.

The Pareto Principle, also known as the 80/20 rule, suggests that 80% of the effects come from 20% of the causes. This principle can be applied to Scrum in the context of the Product Backlog. The 80% of the value in the Product Backlog may be achieved with only 20% of the effort or features required to complete the entire backlog.

This means the Product Owner should prioritize the most valuable Product Backlog items contributing to achieving the product goal. The Scrum Team can deliver the most value with the least effort by focusing on the most important items. This also allows for flexibility in the scope of the product, as the team can negotiate the amount of work required to meet a certain deadline or achieve a specific goal.

In summary, the Pareto Principle can help the Scrum Team to be more efficient and effective in delivering value to the stakeholders.

16.7 Anti-patterns with the Product Goal

Antipatterns with the Product Goal include:

1. Lack of Clarity: The Product Goal is vague, unclear, or constantly changing, making it difficult for the Scrum Team to plan effectively.
2. Conflicting Goals: The Product Goal conflicts with other goals within the organization, leading to confusion and misalignment within the Scrum Team.
3. Unrealistic Goals: The Product Goal is unrealistic or unattainable, leading to frustration and demotivation within the Scrum Team.
4. Lack of Ownership: The Product Goal is owned by someone outside the Scrum Team, leading to a lack of buy-in and commitment from the team.
5. Lack of Focus: The Product Goal is too broad or unfocused, leading to a lack of direction and focus within the Scrum Team.
6. Ignoring Feedback: The Product Goal is not updated based on feedback from stakeholders, customers, or the Scrum Team, leading to missed opportunities for improvement.
7. Lack of Alignment: The Product Goal is not aligned with the overall strategy or vision of the organization, leading to wasted effort and resources.
8. Lack of Transparency: The Product Goal is not communicated clearly or transparently, leading to misunderstandings and misinterpretations within the Scrum Team.
9. Working on multiple product goals at the same time: Sometimes, the Product Owner or stakeholders may push for multiple goals to be pursued simultaneously, leading to a lack of focus and confusion among the team. This can result in a diluted effort and reduced effectiveness in achieving any of the goals.

Part 17: Sprint Backlog

17.1 Why, what, and how

> *The Sprint Backlog is composed of the Sprint Goal (why), the set of Product Backlog items selected for the Sprint (what), as well as an actionable plan for delivering the Increment (how).*

The Sprint Backlog is a plan of the Sprint created during the Sprint Planning event by the Developers to achieve the Sprint Goal. We commonly see it implemented as a "Scrum Board." It consists of three main elements:

1. The Sprint Goal: This is the objective or purpose of the Sprint, which provides the context for the Sprint Backlog and helps the Developers focus on what needs to be accomplished.

2. The set of Product Backlog items selected for the Sprint: These are the items from the Product Backlog that the Developers have committed to completing during the Sprint. These items are selected based on their priority and value to the product and should be refined and ready for the team to work on.

3. An actionable plan for delivering the Increment: This is the plan or strategy created by the Developers to complete the selected Product Backlog items and achieve the Sprint Goal. It includes the tasks, activities, and processes the team will use to deliver the Increment.

17.2 Owned by Developers

> *The Sprint Backlog is a plan by and for the Developers.*

The Sprint Backlog is a living document created by the Developers during Sprint Planning. The Sprint Backlog is owned by the Developers, who are responsible for organizing and updating it as necessary. In addition, the Scrum Master and Product Owner can offer guidance and support.

17.3 Transparent real-time picture

> *It is a highly visible, real-time picture of the work that the Developers plan to accomplish during the Sprint in order to achieve the Sprint Goal.*

The Sprint Backlog is highly visible, meaning that it should be accessible to all members of the Scrum Team and stakeholders interested in the Sprint's progress. his real-time representation of the work helps to keep the Scrum Team focused and accountable for delivering the Sprint Goal. The Sprint Backlog also helps to identify any obstacles or issues that may arise during the Sprint, allowing the team to adjust their plan accordingly.

Think of the Sprint Backlog as a photograph taken at any given time during the Sprint. Just like a photograph captures a moment in time and shows a snapshot of the scene, the Sprint Backlog captures the current status of the work that the Developers plan to accomplish during the Sprint. It provides a real-time picture of the progress toward the Sprint Goal and the remaining work to be done. As the Sprint progresses and more work is completed, the photograph (i.e., Sprint Backlog) is updated to reflect the new status and progress towards the Sprint Goal.

17.4 Developers update it during the Sprint

> *Consequently, the Sprint Backlog is updated throughout the Sprint as more is learned. It should have enough detail that they can inspect their progress in the Daily Scrum.*

Developers may add or remove items during the Sprint if it does not compromise the Sprint Goal. The Scrum Team may collaborate to identify the best way to complete each item on the Sprint Backlog.

The Sprint Backlog is a living document that Developers update throughout the Sprint as new information or requirements emerge. It provides transparency into the work that the Developers are doing and helps the Scrum Team and stakeholders understand the progress being made toward the Sprint Goal.

17.5 Anti-patterns with the Sprint Backlog

Here are some common antipatterns related to the Sprint Backlog:

1. Overcommitting: The Scrum Team may try to take on more work than they can realistically accomplish in the Sprint, leading to unfinished work and decreased morale.
2. Micromanaging: The Product Owner or Scrum Master act as a Project Manager and dictate how the Developers should accomplish the work in the Sprint Backlog rather than letting them self-organize.
3. Not ready items: Sprint Backlog contains items that are not ready and were not properly refined. If the Sprint Backlog contains items that are not ready and were not refined, the Developers will have a difficult time completing their work during the Sprint.
4. Lack of clarity: The Sprint Backlog may lack clarity or detail, leading to confusion or misunderstandings among the Developers about what needs to be accomplished.
5. Lack of transparency: The Sprint Backlog may not be updated in real-time or not made visible to all members of the Scrum Team, leading to misunderstandings or missed opportunities for collaboration.
6. Poorly defined Sprint Goal: If the Sprint Goal is not well-defined, the Sprint Backlog may lack focus or direction, leading to incomplete or ineffective work.
7. Not adapting: The Sprint Backlog may not be adjusted or refined throughout the Sprint as new information or feedback emerges, leading to wasted effort or missed opportunities for improvement.

Overall, the Scrum Team must work collaboratively, maintain transparency, and regularly inspect and adapt the Sprint Backlog to avoid these antipatterns and maximize the value delivered.

Part 18: Sprint Goal: Commitment of the Sprint Backlog

18.1 The objective of the Sprint

> *The Sprint Goal is the single objective for the Sprint.*

The Sprint Goal is a statement that describes the purpose of the Sprint and guides the Developers on why they are building the Increment. It is a clear, concise, and measurable objective that defines what the team intends to achieve by the end of the Sprint. The Sprint Goal is established during the Sprint Planning event based on the Product Goal and the selected Product Backlog items for the Sprint.

The Sprint Goal helps the team to stay focused on what is important, avoid distractions, and align their efforts towards a common objective. In addition, it provides a shared understanding of what needs to be done and why it is valuable, which fosters collaboration and commitment among team members.

Having a Sprint Goal is also important for transparency and inspection, as it allows the team and stakeholders to evaluate the progress made during the Sprint and whether the Sprint Goal has been met. The Sprint Goal is a powerful tool to promote empiricism, feedback, and continuous improvement.

18.2 Flexible scope

> *Although the Sprint Goal is a commitment by the Developers, it provides flexibility in terms of the exact work needed to achieve it.*

If the Sprint Goal depends on implementing all the Spring Backlog items, the Sprint Goal might be in danger from the first day of the Sprint, as it is based on a forecast with a non-flexible scope.

The Sprint Goal is the objective that the Scrum Team commits to achieving during the Sprint. It provides guidance and direction for the team regarding the work that needs to be done, but it is not prescriptive in terms of the specific tasks or activities the team needs to undertake to achieve the goal. This allows the team to be flexible and adaptive in their approach, as long as they work towards the Sprint Goal and produce a valuable Increment by the end of the Sprint. The Sprint Goal should be achievable, measurable, and communicated clearly to the team and stakeholders.

Let's say that the Sprint Goal for a particular Sprint is to improve the website's user registration process. The Product Owner has identified five items for the Sprint Backlog that will contribute to achieving this goal. However, during Sprint Planning, the Developers realize that the effort is bigger than they forecasted, but they can achieve the Sprint Goal with only three items.

In this case, the Developers can remove the remaining two items from the Sprint Backlog and focus their efforts on the three items that will achieve the Sprint Goal. Alternatively, they may decide to keep all five items in the Sprint Backlog but make some of them simpler to meet the Sprint Goal within the timebox. The Sprint Goal provides the guiding objective for the Sprint, while the specific work items in the Sprint Backlog can be adjusted as needed to achieve it.

In this scenario, the Scrum Team showed courage to do the right thing and commitment to meet the Sprint Goal.

In any of these scenarios, discussing the options with the Product Owner and agreeing on scope changes is always good to ensure it meets the expectations.

18.3 Coherence, focus, and collaboration

> *The Sprint Goal also creates coherence and focus, encouraging the Scrum Team to work together rather than on separate initiatives.*

The Sprint Goal serves as a guiding principle that helps the Scrum Team stay focused on the most important work that needs to be done during the Sprint. It creates coherence by ensuring that the work selected for the Sprint is aligned with the overall objective of the product. By having a shared Sprint Goal, the team is encouraged to work together and collaborate towards a common objective rather than focusing on separate initiatives that may not align with each other. This also helps minimize potential conflicts or competing priorities that may arise within the team.

In Scrum, the whole team is collectively responsible for delivering the Sprint Goal and the items in the Sprint Backlog. This means that even if one Developer works on an item, the entire team is responsible for completing it within the Sprint. The success or failure of the Sprint is a team effort and not the responsibility of any individual team member.

18.4 Discuss deviations

> *The Sprint Goal is created during the Sprint Planning event and then added to the Sprint Backlog. As the Developers work during the Sprint, they keep the Sprint Goal in mind. If the work turns out to be different than they expected, they collaborate with the Product Owner to negotiate the scope of the Sprint Backlog within the Sprint without affecting the Sprint Goal.*

During the Sprint Planning event, the Scrum Team collaborates to create a Sprint Goal that defines a clear and concise objective for the upcoming Sprint. The Sprint Goal provides direction and purpose for the entire Sprint and guides the work of the Developers.

Once the Sprint Goal is agreed upon, it is added to the Sprint Backlog along with the selected Product Backlog items. The Sprint Backlog represents the plan for the Developers to achieve the Sprint Goal.

As the Developers work on the Sprint Backlog, they constantly keep the Sprint Goal in mind to ensure that the work they are doing is aligned with the objective of the Sprint. If the work turns out to be different than expected or if new information arises, the Developers collaborate with the Product Owner to negotiate the scope of the Sprint Backlog. However, this negotiation cannot affect the Sprint Goal, which remains the single objective for the Sprint.

For example, the Sprint Goal for a two-week Sprint is to implement a new feature for an e-commerce website that allows customers to leave product reviews. The Sprint Backlog includes several user stories related to implementing this feature. However, during the Sprint, the Developers encountered technical issues that made it difficult to complete all of the items as planned. So, they collaborate with the Product Owner and decide to remove a lower-priority Sprint Backlog item related to adding social media sharing buttons to the review page from the Sprint Backlog. This reduces the scope of work but still allows the Sprint Goal to be achieved. By focusing on the Sprint Goal, the team can prioritize and negotiate the scope of work to ensure that the most important objectives are met within the Sprint.

In this way, the Sprint Goal creates coherence and focus for the Scrum Team, guiding their efforts towards a shared objective and encouraging collaboration and communication throughout the Sprint.

18.5 Bad Sprint Goals

Here are some examples of bad Sprint Goals:

1. "Complete all the tasks in the Sprint Backlog by the end of the Sprint." Unfortunately, this is a bad Sprint Goal because it only focuses on completing tasks and does not provide any direction or purpose for the work being done.
2. "Improve the user interface of the application." This is a bad Sprint Goal because it is too vague and does not provide a clear objective that the team can work towards.
3. "Add new features to the product." This is a bad Sprint Goal because it is too general and does not provide specific details about what features should be added or why they are important.
4. "Fix all the bugs in the system." Unfortunately, this is another bad Sprint Goal because it only focuses on fixing bugs and does not provide any direction for the team to work towards improving the product or providing value.

5. "Complete as many tasks as possible during the Sprint." This is a bad Sprint Goal because it encourages the team to focus on quantity over quality and does not provide any direction or purpose for the work being done.

18.6 Better Sprint Goals

Here are some examples of better goals with a SMART approach and how the Scrum Team will measure its success:

1. Increase user engagement on the website by 20% in the next month. Measurement: Measure website traffic and engagement metrics such as time spent on the site, page views, bounce rate, and click-through rate
2. Improve customer satisfaction ratings to 90% or higher by the end of the quarter. Measurement: Conduct customer surveys and measure the percentage of respondents who rate their satisfaction as 90% or higher
3. Reduce the time it takes to process customer support requests by 50% in the next two months. Measurement: Track the average response time and resolution time for support requests and compare it to the previous metrics
4. Increase revenue by 15% next quarter by launching a new product feature. Measurement: Track the revenue generated by the new product feature and compare it to the revenue generated by other existing product features
5. Improve website loading time by 30% in the next month. Measurement: Measure the website loading speed using tools such as Google PageSpeed Insights or Pingdom and compare it to the previous loading speed metrics.

Those examples could apply to Sprint Goals or Product Goals, depending on the impact and effort required. The Product Backlog items selected during the Sprint Planning should follow the Sprint Goal.

18.7 Anti-patterns with the Sprint Goal

Here are some antipatterns of the Sprint Goal:

1. Vague or undefined Sprint Goal: If the Sprint Goal is not clearly defined or is too vague, it can lead to confusion and lack of direction for the team.
2. Unrealistic or unachievable Sprint Goal: Setting a Sprint Goal that is unrealistic or unachievable can lead to demotivation and frustration among the team.
3. Multiple Sprint Goals: Having multiple Sprint Goals can lead to a lack of focus and coherence within the team. It is important to have a single objective for the Sprint.
4. Changing the Sprint Goal during the Sprint: Changing the Sprint Goal during the Sprint can lead to disruption and loss of focus. Therefore, it is important to stick to the original Sprint Goal unless there is a valid reason to change it.

5. Ignoring the Sprint Goal: If the team ignores the Sprint Goal and focuses on completing individual tasks instead, it can lead to a lack of coordination and coherence within the team.
6. Lack of collaboration with the Product Owner: If the team does not collaborate with the Product Owner to negotiate the scope of the Sprint Backlog within the Sprint, it can lead to confusion and lack of alignment.
7. Lack of transparency: If the Sprint Goal is not transparent and visible to all stakeholders, it can lead to a lack of understanding and misalignment of expectations.
8. Lack of commitment: If the team is not committed to the Sprint Goal, it can lead to a lack of motivation and focus. The team needs to take ownership of the Sprint Goal and work towards achieving it.

Part 19: Increment

19.1 A stepping stone toward the Product Goal

> *An Increment is a concrete stepping stone toward the Product Goal. Each Increment is additive to all prior Increments and thoroughly verified, ensuring that all Increments work together.*

An Increment is a part of the product that can be delivered to stakeholders and produced within a Sprint. Each Increment must be a concrete and functional addition to the overall product that fulfills the Product Goal. An Increment should also be thoroughly verified to ensure it is usable and works in conjunction with previous Increments. The concept of an Increment is based on the Agile principle of iterative development, where the product is built incrementally, adding more features and value with each iteration.

The Increment is a concrete stepping stone because it provides tangible progress toward the overall goal of the product. The Scrum Team works towards delivering an Increment in each Sprint, which helps to ensure that they are making continuous progress and moving closer to achieving the Product Goal. The Increment must be used to provide value to stakeholders, and it should be thoroughly tested to ensure that it works as expected.

Imagine each increment as the same product but with a few more features for the user. Those new features are part of the expectations of the Product Goal.

Let's say the Product Goal is to create a social media platform for photographers to showcase their work and connect with clients. Each Increment would represent a new version of the platform that includes additional features and improvements to existing ones.

For example, the first Increment may include the basic functionality of creating a profile, uploading photos, and searching for other photographers. The second Increment may add the ability to follow other photographers and receive notifications when they upload new photos. Finally, the third Increment may add a messaging system for photographers to communicate with clients and each other.

Each of these Increments builds on the previous ones, adding more value and usability to the platform. As a result, by the time the Product Goal is achieved, the platform will be fully functional and provide all the features and capabilities required to meet the needs of the target users.

19.2 Deliver vs. Release

In the context of Scrum, the terms "deliver" and "release" have different meanings.

"Deliver" refers to completing work on a Product Backlog item and making it potentially releasable. This means the item has met the Definition of Done and could be released to the customer or end user.

"Release" refers to making the potentially releasable product increment available to the customer or end user. This could involve various steps, such as testing, documentation, deployment, and marketing.

A potentially releasable increment is a concept in Scrum that refers to the state of the product at the end of each Sprint. It means that the Increment produced during the Sprint is in a condition to be released to the users, even if the Product Owner decides not to do so.

In summary, deliver means completing work on a Product Backlog item to make it potentially releasable, while release means making the product increment available to the customer or end user.

19.3 Usable Increment

> *In order to provide value, the Increment must be usable.*

In Scrum, the main objective is to deliver a potentially releasable product increment at the end of each Sprint. This means that the Increment must be usable, which implies that it must be functional and meet the user's needs. In addition, it should be able to provide some value to the end-users or customers and should be of high quality.

All untested work diminishes transparency and creates a risk, and this inspected Increment is not truly theoretically useable or releasable.

For example, suppose the Increment includes new features or changes. In that case, they must be thoroughly tested and verified to ensure that they work as expected and don't cause any negative impact on the existing functionality of the product. Moreover, the

Increment should also be usable in terms of its design, user interface, and user experience. They are crucial in ensuring the product is easy to use and provides a good end-user experience.

The Increment may or may not be released to the users at the end of a Sprint. The decision to release the Increment to the users depends on the Product Owner's discretion and the business needs. However, regardless of whether the Increment is released or not, it must be usable and thoroughly verified to ensure that it is a concrete stepping stone towards achieving the Product Goal. This is because each Increment is additive to all prior Increments and must work together to deliver value to the users.

While it is true that any increment is potentially usable and releasable, the decision to release or not may depend on various factors such as the business strategy, market conditions, customer feedback, and the potential impact of the release on the overall product.

19.4 Release or not, and when

Even if the increment is usable and according to the Definition of Done, it may not necessarily meet additional acceptance criteria or timing for release, or it may not provide enough value to the end-users. In addition, technical debt or other issues may need to be addressed in some cases before the increment can be released.

Furthermore, the decision to release or not may not be solely the responsibility of the Product Owner. The Scrum Team as a whole may need to be involved in the decision-making process, and in some cases, stakeholders outside the team may also have a say in when and how the increment is released.

The Product Owner is responsible for deciding when an Increment is released to customers or end-users based on the value it provides. The release decision is based on factors such as market conditions, customer feedback, the state of the competition, and the organization's overall strategy.

The Product Owner may choose to release an Increment as soon as it is usable and provides value to the stakeholders, or they may decide to wait and release a larger set of features that provide a bigger impact. This decision should be made based on maximizing the product's value to the stakeholders.

The release and its date can affect the product's value in a few different ways. For example, if the release is delayed, it may mean that the product does not meet the needs of the stakeholders as effectively as it could have, resulting in missed opportunities or even lost customers. On the other hand, releasing too early or with insufficient quality can also negatively impact the product's value, as it may lead to customer dissatisfaction or even harm the organization's reputation.

Therefore, the Product Owner should carefully balance the timing of the release with the value provided by the Increment, taking into account various factors that may influence the product's success in the market.

While the Product Owner ultimately decides when to release an Increment, they may delegate this decision-making to the Scrum Team or other stakeholders. For example, in organizations that use continuous delivery or continuous deployment, the decision to release may be automated or delegated to the Scrum Team. However, the Product Owner remains accountable for the positive or negative value each release provides.

In any case, it is still the responsibility of the Product Owner to ensure that the release decisions align with the overall Product Goal and maximize the value delivered to stakeholders. Any decision to delay or defer a release should be made with a clear understanding of the impact on the value delivered. The Product Owner should also work closely with the Scrum Team to ensure that the Increment is usable and potentially releasable at the end of each Sprint.

19.5 Multiple increments per Sprint

Multiple Increments may be created within a Sprint.

In Agile software development, a Sprint is a fixed period during which Developers work on a set of tasks to achieve specific goals or deliverables. These goals are usually represented as user stories or features that are prioritized and selected from the Product Backlog.

Multiple increments may be created within a Sprint, which refers to developing, integrating, and potentially delivering smaller, functional pieces of a product or feature throughout the Sprint rather than waiting until the end of the Sprint to deliver the entire product or feature. This approach has several advantages:

1. Continuous Integration: By developing and integrating smaller increments, the team can identify and fix integration issues early in the process, reducing the risk of larger problems down the line.
2. Early Feedback: Delivering smaller increments allows stakeholders and users to provide feedback quickly. This enables the Developers to make necessary adjustments and improvements, ensuring that the final product meets the needs and expectations of users.
3. Adaptability: Developing multiple increments within a Sprint allows the team to adapt more to changing requirements or priorities. If new information or requirements emerge during the Sprint, the team can adjust its focus and priorities without completely derailing the Sprint's progress.
4. Increased Transparency: By creating and demonstrating multiple increments during a Sprint, the team can provide stakeholders with a clearer view of progress. This transparency can help build trust and confidence in the development process.
5. Improved Quality: Developing and testing smaller increments can improve overall product quality, as issues can be detected and addressed more quickly.

6. Incremental Value Delivery: Multiple increments within a Sprint enable the Developers to deliver value to customers more frequently. This can result in higher customer satisfaction, as users can start benefiting from new features or improvements earlier than if they had to wait for the entire product or feature to be completed.
7. Enhanced Team Collaboration: Working on smaller increments encourages the Developers to collaborate more closely and frequently, as they need to integrate their work regularly. This can foster a stronger team dynamic and improve overall productivity.
8. Risk Management: By developing multiple increments, the team can better manage risks associated with large-scale changes. Smaller increments allow for easier identification of potential risks and issues, enabling the team to address them proactively.
9. Faster Learning: Developing and delivering multiple increments within a Sprint promotes a culture of continuous learning and improvement. The team can quickly learn from their experiences, adjusting their processes and practices to optimize their performance in future Sprints.
10. Higher Motivation: Delivering smaller increments and seeing the tangible progress made during a Sprint can boost the morale and motivation of the Developers. This positive reinforcement can lead to increased engagement and productivity.

In summary, creating multiple increments within a Sprint can offer several benefits, including improved integration, adaptability, transparency, and product quality. It allows for more frequent value delivery, fosters better team collaboration, and promotes continuous learning and improvement. By adopting this approach, Scrum Teams can better manage risks and optimize their performance throughout the Agile development process.

19.6 Increment during the Sprint Review

The sum of the Increments is presented at the Sprint Review thus supporting empiricism.

The Sprint Review is an event in Scrum that supports empiricism by allowing stakeholders to inspect the Increment and adapt the Product Backlog based on the feedback received.

When the Developers work on multiple increments within a Sprint, they create smaller, functional pieces of the product or feature. The sum of these increments represents the collective work completed during the Sprint. Presenting the sum of the increments at the Sprint Review supports empiricism in the following ways:

- Transparency: By demonstrating the work completed during the Sprint, the Scrum Team ensures that progress is visible to stakeholders. This transparency

allows stakeholders to understand the current state of the product and the development process, fostering trust and collaboration.
- Inspection: The Sprint Review allows stakeholders to inspect the increments and assess their quality, functionality, and alignment with the product vision and goals. This inspection allows for a thorough evaluation of the work completed and the identification of any issues or improvements that may be needed.
- Adaptation: Based on the feedback received during the Sprint Review, the Product Owner, Developers, and stakeholders can adapt the Product Backlog by refining, adding, or reprioritizing user stories or features. This adaptation helps ensure the product's development meets stakeholder needs and expectations.

Presenting the sum of the increments at the Sprint Review enables a regular cycle of transparency, inspection, and adaptation. This empowers the Scrum Team.

19.7 Release before Sprint Review

> *However, an Increment may be delivered to stakeholders prior to the end of the Sprint. The Sprint Review should never be considered a gate to releasing value.*

An Increment can be delivered to stakeholders before the end of a Sprint, but it's not required to be released at the Sprint Review. The Sprint Review aims to inspect the Increment and adapt the Product Backlog if necessary. Therefore, stakeholders may see the Increment at the Sprint Review and provide feedback, but the release decision is up to the Product Owner. It's important to note that the Sprint Review should never be seen as a gate to releasing value, as this can delay value delivery to the customers or end-users. Instead, the Scrum Team should focus on delivering value incrementally and iteratively, with each Increment building upon the previous one to move the product closer to the Product Goal.

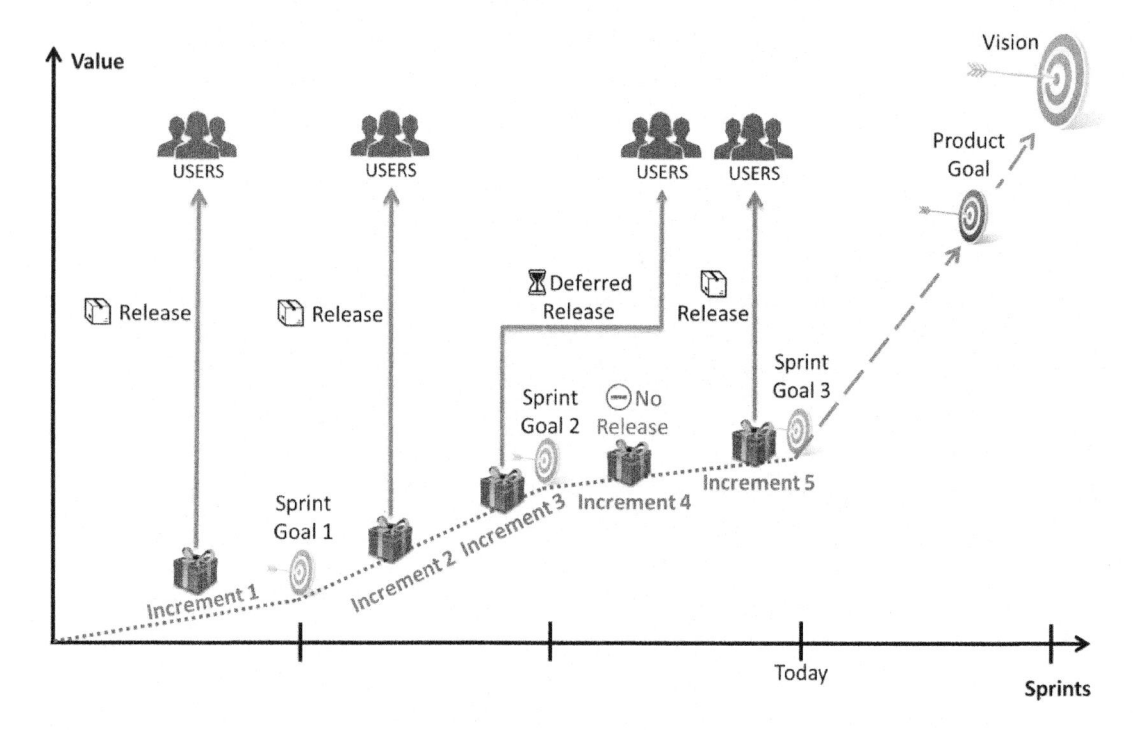

Figure 37 Increment Releases through Sprints.

Continuous deployment is a software development practice that allows Developers to automatically deploy code changes to production as soon as they are done and tested. This approach aims to reduce the time it takes to deliver value to users by eliminating manual deployment processes and reducing the feedback loop. In addition, by delivering value as soon as it is done, organizations can potentially improve their return on investment (ROI) by generating revenue or gaining a competitive advantage sooner.

In Scrum, delivering potentially releasable Increments throughout the Sprint supports this approach by enabling continuous deployment. It allows organizations to receive feedback from stakeholders early and often and adjust accordingly. The Sprint Review is not a gate to releasing value but an opportunity to gather feedback and improve further. By continuously delivering value, organizations can stay ahead of the competition and maximize their ROI.

19.8 All increments must be according to the Definition of Done

> *Work cannot be considered part of an Increment unless it meets the Definition of Done.*

The statement means that for any Product Backlog item, whether a task, feature, or functionality to be included in the final product increment, it must meet all the agreed-upon criteria specified in the Definition of Done. If a work item does not satisfy the

Definition of Done, it does not meet the quality standards, and therefore, it cannot be considered complete or part of the Increment.

In other words, the Developers commit that all the work added to an Increment is according to the Definition of Done.

19.9 Anti-patterns of the Increment

Anti-patterns are behaviors or practices that may appear beneficial but can have negative consequences or hinder the desired outcome of a project. Here are some common anti-patterns related to the Increment in Scrum:

1. Incomplete Definition of Done: An unclear or incomplete Definition of Done can lead to inconsistencies in quality, increased technical debt, and difficulty in integrating increments.
2. Ignoring the Definition of Done: When teams disregard the agreed-upon Definition of Done, it can result in inconsistent quality, integration issues, and reduced stakeholder confidence.
3. Partially done work: Teams may mark work as complete even though it does not fully meet the Definition of Done, leading to poor-quality increments and potential integration challenges.
4. Inconsistent increments across teams: When multiple teams work on the same product with different Definitions of Done or quality standards, it can lead to inconsistencies in the integrated product.
5. Overemphasis on new features: Focusing solely on adding new features without addressing technical debt, bugs, or other issues can result in a fragile product with poor overall quality.
6. Insufficient testing: Failing to conduct thorough testing, including unit tests, integration tests, and performance tests, may lead to undetected issues and a less stable product increment.
7. Delayed integration: Delaying the integration of increments from different teams or waiting until the end of a project can cause significant difficulties, including an increased effort to resolve integration issues and potential delays in product delivery.
8. "Big Bang" integration: Attempting to integrate all increments at once rather than iteratively can lead to a complex and error-prone integration process, making it difficult to identify and resolve issues.
9. Lack of transparency: Hiding or downplaying issues in the Increment can undermine trust among team members, stakeholders, and end-users, resulting in reduced collaboration and lower product quality.

To avoid these anti-patterns, it is essential to establish a clear Definition of Done, adhere to it consistently, and ensure effective collaboration and communication among team members and stakeholders. Regularly reviewing and refining practices and processes can also help identify and address potential issues and ensure continuous improvement.

Part 20: Definition of Done: Commitment of the Increment

20.1 Quality measures of the Increment

> *The Definition of Done is a formal description of the state of the Increment when it meets the quality measures required for the product.*

The Definition of Done is a set of criteria or guidelines that define the quality standards that must be met before an Increment can be considered "done." It is a formal description of the state of the Increment when it meets the quality measures required for the product. The Definition of Done is a shared understanding within the Scrum Team that ensures everyone understands what is expected of them when working on an Increment.

The Definition of Done typically includes a set of requirements that must be met for the work to be considered complete. These requirements may include factors such as functional requirements, performance requirements, security requirements, and usability requirements. The team must agree on these requirements and ensure that each item in the Product Backlog meets the Definition of Done before it is considered "done" and ready for release.

By having a well-defined Definition of Done, the Scrum Team ensures that each Increment meets the quality standards required for the product. This ensures the product is developed consistently, predictably, and of high quality.

20.2 Determines when an Increment is born

> *The moment a Product Backlog item meets the Definition of Done, an Increment is born.*

When a Product Backlog item, such as a new feature, meets the Definition of Done, it has been thoroughly tested, meets the required quality standards for the product, and is in usable condition. At this moment, an Increment is born, which is a concrete step toward the Product Goal. If needed, the Increment can be delivered to stakeholders or integrated with previous Increments, which makes the product more valuable and closer to fulfilling the overall Product Goal.

20.3 Shared understanding and transparency

> *The Definition of Done creates transparency by providing everyone a shared understanding of what work was completed as part of the Increment.*

The Definition of Done is a shared agreement within the Scrum Team on the quality standards that must be met for a Product Backlog item to be considered "done" and added to the Increment. It creates transparency by ensuring everyone understands what is expected and what has been completed.

The Definition of Done typically includes criteria for both technical and non-technical requirements, such as code review, testing, documentation, user acceptance testing, performance testing, and accessibility testing. By setting these quality standards up front, the Scrum Team can ensure that the Increment is of high quality and can be used by stakeholders.

The Definition of Done is reviewed and updated as needed during the Sprint Retrospective to ensure that it remains relevant and effective. In addition, it helps the team identify improvement areas and continuously refine their practices.

20.4 Unfinished items by the end of the Sprint

> *If a Product Backlog item does not meet the Definition of Done, it cannot be released or even presented at the Sprint Review. Instead, it returns to the Product Backlog for future consideration.*

This ensures that only completed work meets the required quality standards and is presented to stakeholders, which helps maintain trust and confidence in the Scrum Team's ability to deliver value.

If by the end of the Sprint, a Product Backlog item is incomplete or not finished according to the Definition of Done, it is removed from the Increment, and it is returned to the Product Backlog because the Scrum Team has not completed the work required to meet the quality measures and standards specified in the Definition of Done. This means that the work is not yet in a usable state or does not meet the necessary criteria for release. By returning it to the Product Backlog, the Scrum Team can decide when to revisit it in the future and how it can be improved to meet the Definition of Done. This ensures that only high-quality work is delivered to stakeholders and that the Increment is always in a releasable state. The Scrum Team may continue working on the item in the next Sprint, in some future Sprint, or remove the feature altogether. The decision depends on when comparing its value against the revised Product Backlog with new valuable Product Backlog items or changes in the market conditions and priorities.

When returning an unfinished item to the Product Backlog, the Developers can estimate the amount of work remaining to make it "Done." Then, the Product Owner will decide what to do with the item.

During the Sprint Retrospective, the Scrum Team should reflect on why the item did not meet the Definition of Done and identify any improvements they can make to their processes to ensure it is met in the future. This helps continually improve the Increment's quality and ensures that the product always delivers value to its stakeholders.

20.5 It follows organizational standards

> *If the Definition of Done for an increment is part of the standards of the organization, all Scrum Teams must follow it as a minimum.*

The Definition of Done is a formal description of the state of the Increment when it meets the quality measures required for the product. If the Definition of Done is part of the standards of the organization, it means that it's a non-negotiable standard that all Scrum Teams must adhere to as a minimum. This ensures consistency and quality across all products and services within the organization.

For example, if an organization has a software development standard requiring all code to pass automated testing, have user help documentation, and be code reviewed by a peer. The Definition of Done for all Scrum Teams working on software development must include these criteria as a minimum. However, any Scrum Team can create more stringent criteria for their Definition of Done, like Performance testing and UAT testing is required.

Having organizational standards for the Definition of Done can provide several benefits for an organization, including:

1. Consistency: By having a consistent Definition of Done across all Scrum teams within an organization, there is greater clarity and alignment on the quality standards and expectations for each increment. This can help ensure that all teams work towards the same goals and deliver high-quality products.
2. Efficiency: A consistent Definition of Done can also help streamline the product development process by reducing the need for teams to negotiate and agree on quality criteria for each increment. This can save time and effort and improve the organization's overall productivity.
3. Risk reduction: A clear and consistent Definition of Done can help mitigate risks associated with lower-quality products or incomplete work. By setting and adhering to a high-quality standard, the organization can reduce the risk of product defects, missed deadlines, and stakeholder dissatisfaction.
4. Quality standards among organization products: A consistent Definition of Done can help ensure that all products within the organization meet the same high-quality standards. This can help build trust and confidence among stakeholders who rely on the organization to deliver high-quality products consistently.
5. Continuous improvement: Having organizational standards for the Definition of Done can also provide a framework for continuous improvement. By

regularly reviewing and updating the Definition of Done, teams can identify areas for improvement and optimize their approach over time.

Taking everything into account, organizational standards for the Definition of Done can help promote consistency, efficiency, risk reduction, quality standards among organization products, and continuous improvement in the product development process. This can ultimately lead to higher-quality products, greater stakeholder satisfaction, and improved organizational business outcomes.

20.6 The Scrum Team creates the Definition of Done

> *If it is not an organizational standard, the Scrum Team must create a Definition of Done appropriate for the product.*

Suppose there is no existing organizational standard for the Definition of Done that applies to all Scrum Teams. In that case, the Scrum Team must create one that is appropriate for the product being developed. This might include criteria for coding standards, testing requirements, documentation, and other quality assurance measures that will ensure that the Increment meets the needs of the stakeholders. The Scrum Team should regularly review and update the Definition of Done to ensure it remains relevant and effective.

Ideally, the Definition of Done is updated as an agreement from the Sprint Retrospective. However, updating it during the Sprint may be confusing because it may affect the work in progress.

The Definition of Done can be updated during the Sprint, but the entire Scrum Team should agree upon any changes and evaluate the impact on achieving the Sprint Goal. The purpose of the Definition of Done is to provide a shared understanding of what work needs to be completed to ensure that the Increment is of high quality and meets the needs of the stakeholders. Therefore, if the Definition of Done needs to be updated, it is important to ensure that all team members are aware of the changes and that they are documented to ensure transparency.

20.7 Developers work according to the Definition of Done

> *The Developers are required to conform to the Definition of Done.*

The Developers are responsible for implementing the Product Backlog items and adhering to the Definition of Done for each increment.

By conforming to the Definition of Done, the Developers ensure that the increment meets the quality standards and is potentially releasable. This helps the Scrum Team to maintain transparency, gain feedback, and make better-informed decisions. Therefore, the Scrum Team should review and refine the Definition of Done regularly to ensure that it continues to reflect the standards and expectations for the product.

20.8 Multiple Scrum Teams, one Definition of Done

> *If there are multiple Scrum Teams working together on a product, they must mutually define and comply with the same Definition of Done.*

When multiple Scrum Teams are working on a single product, they must work together in a coordinated manner to achieve a common goal. One aspect of this coordination is ensuring that they are all working towards a shared understanding of the Definition of Done. This means that the various teams must come together to define and agree upon a common set of standards that will be used to determine when a piece of work is "done." In addition, according to the shared Definition of Done, they must also integrate their work into one integrated Increment at least once per Sprint.

Each team may have its own more stringent Definition of Done, but they all need to comply with the minimum Definition of Done agreed upon by all teams. This ensures that each team's work is of high quality and can be integrated with the work of other teams to create a shippable product increment.

Multiple Scrum Teams – One Product

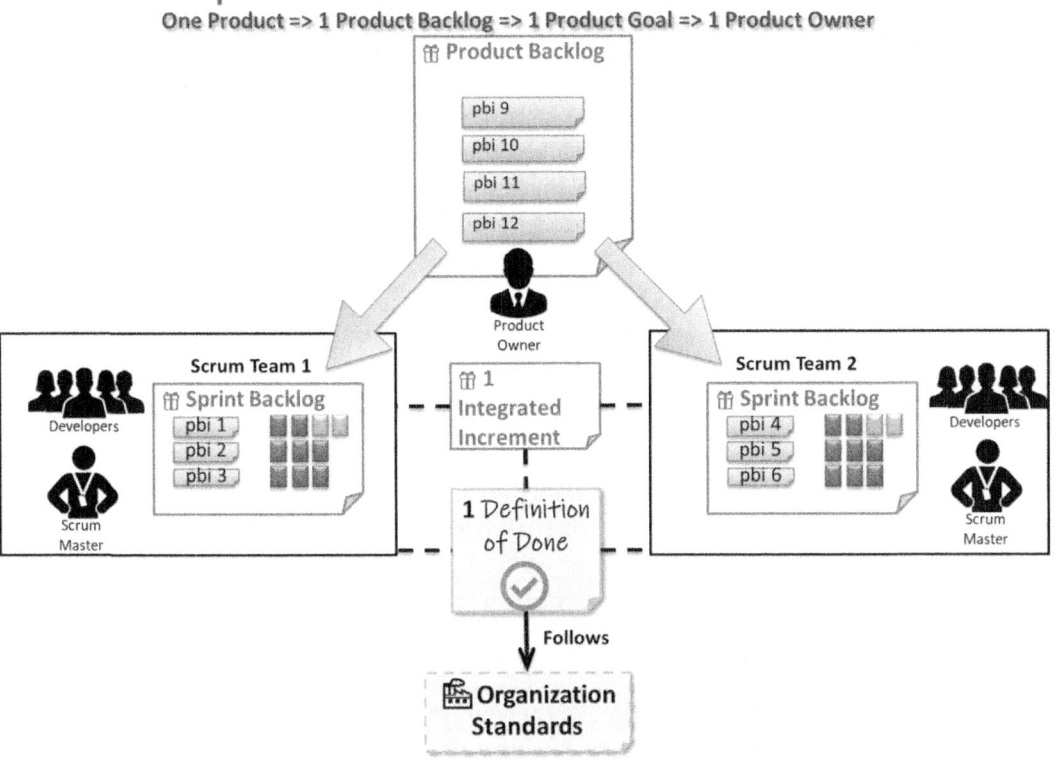

One Product => 1 Product Backlog => 1 Product Goal => 1 Product Owner

Figure 38 Multiple Scrum Teams.

20.8.1 Example of two teams with different criteria

Suppose two Scrum teams are working on the same product but have different criteria when work is done regarding code coverage and performance tests. Team A includes a 90% code coverage requirement and performance tests in their DoD, while Team B considers these optional.

When integrating the increments from both teams with differing Definitions of Done, several potential impacts may arise that can affect the product's overall quality, consistency, and maintainability. These impacts include:

1. Inconsistent quality: With Team A following stricter quality measures, such as a 90% code coverage and mandatory performance tests, their increments will likely be more robust and reliable. In contrast, Team B's increments may have varying quality levels due to the optional nature of code coverage and performance testing. This inconsistency in quality can lead to a less stable and unreliable product.
2. Increased technical debt: The lack of consistent quality measures between the two teams might result in technical debt, which refers to the long-term cost of cutting corners or not addressing issues during development. This debt can

accumulate over time, leading to higher maintenance costs and a more challenging codebase to work with in the future.
3. Difficulty in diagnosing and fixing issues: Inconsistency in code quality and testing standards may make identifying and fixing the issues' root cause challenging. Team members may struggle to pinpoint whether a problem is due to a specific increment, differing quality standards, or an integration issue.
4. Reduced team efficiency: The discrepancies in quality measures may result in extra work when integrating the increments from both teams, as additional time and effort might be needed to identify, diagnose, and address inconsistencies or issues. This can reduce overall team efficiency and prolong the development cycle.
5. Lower stakeholder confidence: The inconsistent quality of the integrated product might lead to reduced confidence from stakeholders, such as customers, end-users, or management, in the Scrum Teams' ability to deliver a stable and reliable product.

To mitigate these potential impacts, aligning the Definition of Done across teams working on the same product is essential. A shared and consistent DoD ensures that all teams adhere to the same quality standards and deliver product increments that meet desired quality benchmarks. In addition, this alignment fosters better collaboration, reduces integration issues, and helps maintain a high-quality and consistent product.

20.9 Definition of Done Template

The following template is only an example of what a Definition of Done may include.

Instructions: You can use this template to start discussions with your Scrum Team about the quality standards of every Product Backlog item before it is considered done. The items below are not required. The Scrum Team can collaboratively pick some of these items for its Definition of Done or use them for inspiration.

Team: _____

Product: _____

As a team, before saying that an item of the Sprint Backlog is Done, we agree that it will meet the following:

- ☐ The code is complete and according to Developers' standards.
- ☐ The code is refactored.
- ☐ Technical Debt is removed.
- ☐ Meet the acceptance criteria.
- ☐ Code checked into the repository.
- ☐ Unit tests are written and green.
- ☐ Test coverage: __ %.

- ☐ Pair programming.
- ☐ Peer review.
- ☐ Code merge and tagged.
- ☐ Deployed to the development environment.
- ☐ Integration tests are written and green.
- ☐ Deployed to the QA environment.
- ☐ Bugs, improvements, and changes are done.
- ☐ Changes were communicated and updated in the ticket description.
- ☐ Regression tests.
- ☐ Performance tests.
- ☐ Approved by QA.
- ☐ Deployed to UAT.
- ☐ Reviewed and accepted by the Product Owner.
- ☐ Reviewed and accepted by the customer or user(s).
- ☐ Final approval in the Sprint Review or demo by the Product Owner and customer.
- ☐ Deployed to production.
- ☐ Production tests are successful.
- ☐ Other:

_____

_____

_____

_____

20.10 Anti-patterns with the Definition of Done

Here are some examples of anti-patterns related to the Definition of Done in Scrum:

- Incomplete or vague Definition of Done: If the Definition of Done is not clearly defined or lacks specific criteria, it can lead to ambiguity and inconsistency in the team's work. This can result in misunderstandings, delays, and lower-quality deliverables.
- Applying the Definition of Done only every other Sprint: This approach undermines the effectiveness of the Definition of Done, which is designed to ensure that every increment of work meets the same high standards of quality and completeness. By delaying the application of the Definition of Done, the team increases the risk of missing critical elements, which can lead to issues and rework down the line. It also hinders the team's ability to achieve transparency and deliver value consistently. The feedback loop will be too long, and the Scrum Team will miss opportunities to properly inspect and adapt the Increment.

- Ignoring the Definition of Done during Sprint Planning: If the team does not consider the Definition of Done during Sprint Planning, they may underestimate the effort or complexity of the work and fail to deliver a potentially releasable increment. This can lead to missed deadlines, incomplete work, lower transparency of the Increment, and lower stakeholder satisfaction.
- Ignoring the Definition of Done during the Sprint: If the team does not consistently apply the Definition of Done during the Sprint, or it decides to ignore part of it, it may produce work that is not up to the required standard or quality. This can result in rework, delays, and increased technical debt.
- Allowing incomplete or defective work to pass through the Definition of Done: If the team allows incomplete or defective work to pass through the Definition of Done, it can lead to lower-quality products and potentially harm the team's reputation and credibility. This can result in lower stakeholder satisfaction and negatively impact the organization's bottom line.
- Treating the Definition of Done as a checklist: If the team treats the Definition of Done as a simple checklist of tasks to complete rather than a set of quality criteria, they may fail to understand or appreciate its importance fully. This can result in lower-quality work, missed opportunities for improvement, and lower stakeholder satisfaction.
- Multiple Scrum Teams have different Definition of Done: If different Scrum teams working on the same Product have different Definitions of Done, it can lead to confusion, misalignment, and inconsistency in the product development and integrating the Increment. In addition, this can result in missed deadlines, incomplete work, and lower stakeholder satisfaction.
- Not following standards of the organization: If the Definition of Done for an increment is part of the standards of the organization, but the Scrum Team does not follow it consistently, it can lead to lower-quality products and potentially harm the team's reputation and credibility of quality among products. This can result in lower stakeholder satisfaction and negatively impact the organization's bottom line.

To avoid these anti-patterns, the team needs to define a clear and specific Definition of Done, consistently apply it during Sprint Planning and execution, and treat it as a key element of the team's quality assurance and continuous improvement process.

Part 21: Scrum is immutable

Scrum is free and offered in this Guide. The Scrum framework, as outlined herein, is immutable. While implementing only parts of Scrum is possible, the result is not Scrum.

The statement means that Scrum is a framework with defined accountabilities, events, artifacts, and rules that interact to provide a structured way of working on complex problems. These elements are interdependent and work together to deliver value. Each element of Scrum is designed to complement and reinforce the other, and the absence of one element can affect the effectiveness of the entire framework. As a result, teams are encouraged to implement Scrum as a whole rather than just specific parts of it.

If a team does implement partially or does not implement some of the accountabilities, events, artifacts, or rules, even if the team claims the changes work fine for them, they are not using Scrum.

The framework is also described as "immutable" because Scrum's core principles and values are fixed and should not be changed.

> *Scrum exists only in its entirety and functions well as a container for other techniques, methodologies, and practices.*

However, Scrum allows flexibility and adaptation within the framework to fit the organization's and its team's unique needs. This means that while the core principles remain the same, the specific practices and tools used can vary to adapt to the specific context.

Scrum can also be used with other techniques, methodologies, and practices to enhance its effectiveness. For example:

- A Scrum Team might incorporate agile practices like test-driven development or pair programming alongside Scrum to improve their development process.
- A Scrum Team may use the Kanban method to visualize and manage their work in progress, but they still adhere to Scrum's core principles and events, such as the Sprint Review and Sprint Retrospective.
- A Scrum Team uses user stories to capture requirements but still follows the framework of Scrum to plan and execute the work.

Overall, Scrum provides a solid foundation for managing complex projects, but it can also be customized to fit specific team needs and work in conjunction with other practices.

21.1 Scrum But

"Scrum but" is a term used to describe when a team or organization is using the Scrum framework but not fully implementing all of its principles and practices. This can result in a situation where the team or organization is not realizing the full benefits of Scrum and may be experiencing issues with productivity, quality, or team morale.

Some examples of "Scrum but" include:

- The team is not doing daily stand-up meetings, or they are not following the recommended format.
- The Product Owner is not fully empowered to decide about the product backlog.

- The team is not doing regular Sprint Retrospectives to reflect on their performance and identify areas for improvement.
- The team is not using a physical Scrum board to visualize their work.

While it is possible to succeed with Scrum but not fully implement all of its principles and practices, it is generally recommended to try to follow Scrum as closely as possible to reap the full benefits of the framework. Teams and organizations should regularly assess their use of Scrum and look for opportunities to improve and fully embrace its principles.

"Scrum But" is not Scrum. Because a "Scrum But" implementation omits one or more components of the frameworks, the result is not Scrum.

Part 22: Scaling Scrum

The Scrum Framework mostly covers the rules of working with one Scrum Team. However, it is important to remark on a few rules that apply to Scrum when multiple Scrum Teams work together on the same Product.

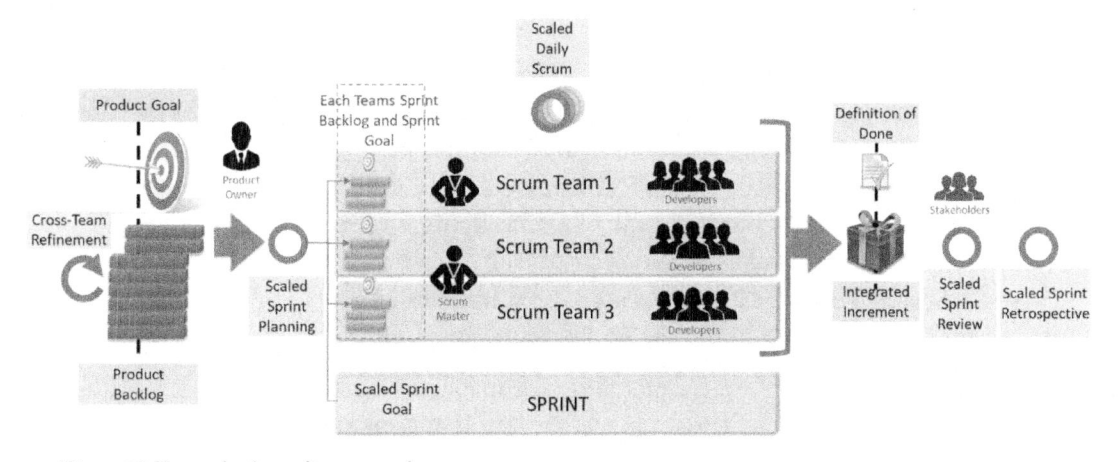

Figure 39 Example of a scaling approach.

22.1 Scaling frameworks

Scrum is a framework designed for small, cross-functional teams, but applying it to large, complex projects can be challenging. To address this issue, several frameworks have been developed for scaling Scrum. Some of the most popular frameworks include:

- Large-Scale Scrum (LeSS): This framework is designed to help organizations scale Scrum by applying the same principles and practices as in traditional Scrum but with a larger group of people. It emphasizes the importance of creating a shared understanding of the product and encourages team communication and collaboration.
- Nexus: This framework is designed to help organizations scale Scrum by providing a framework for coordinating and integrating work across multiple

Scrum Teams. It provides a set of rules and guidelines for managing dependencies, conducting planning and review meetings, and ensuring alignment with the Product Owner.
- Scrum@Scale: This framework is designed to help organizations scale Scrum by applying the principles and practices of Scrum to the entire organization. It provides a framework for managing work across multiple teams and departments and emphasizes the importance of continuous improvement and adaptability.
- Unfix: "Unfix" refers to an approach in scaling frameworks that emphasizes adaptability and flexibility over strict adherence to a fixed framework or process. This approach allows organizations to tailor their scaling practices to their unique context and needs rather than blindly following predefined rules. In addition, Unfix encourages continuous improvement and experimentation, enabling organizations to evolve and optimize their scaling practices over time.
- Scaled Agile Framework (SAFe): This framework is designed to help organizations apply Agile and Scrum principles to large-scale software development. It provides a structured approach for organizing teams and managing work across multiple levels of the organization, from teams to portfolios.

Each framework provides a structured approach for scaling Scrum to larger, more complex projects. However, they all share the same basic principles and practices of Scrum, such as focusing on cross-functional teams, iterative development, and continuous improvement. The key is to choose the framework that best fits the needs of your organization and your specific project.

22.2 Scrum team size is a guideline, not a rule

In a scaled environment, the ideal Scrum team size may vary depending on the organization's context, product complexity, and available resources. While Scrum recommends a team size of 10 or fewer members, this is only a guideline, not a hard rule. It is crucial to consider the unique needs and constraints of the organization and adapt the team size accordingly.

Factors that can influence the ideal Scrum team size in a scaled environment include:

- Product complexity: Complex products may require larger teams with diverse skill sets to address the various challenges involved.
- Available resources: Smaller organizations may have limited resources, requiring more extensive teams to handle the workload effectively.
- Geographic distribution: Teams may need to account for differences in time zones, language, or culture, affecting team size and composition.

As self-managing teams, the Scrum Teams should decide the best approach for organizing into multiple teams.

By adapting the Scrum team size to meet the organization's specific context, organizations can better support their product development goals and promote effective collaboration, communication, and continuous improvement.

22.3 Rules of multiple teams working together on the same product

Multiple Scrum Teams – One Product
One Product => 1 Product Backlog => 1 Product Goal => 1 Product Owner

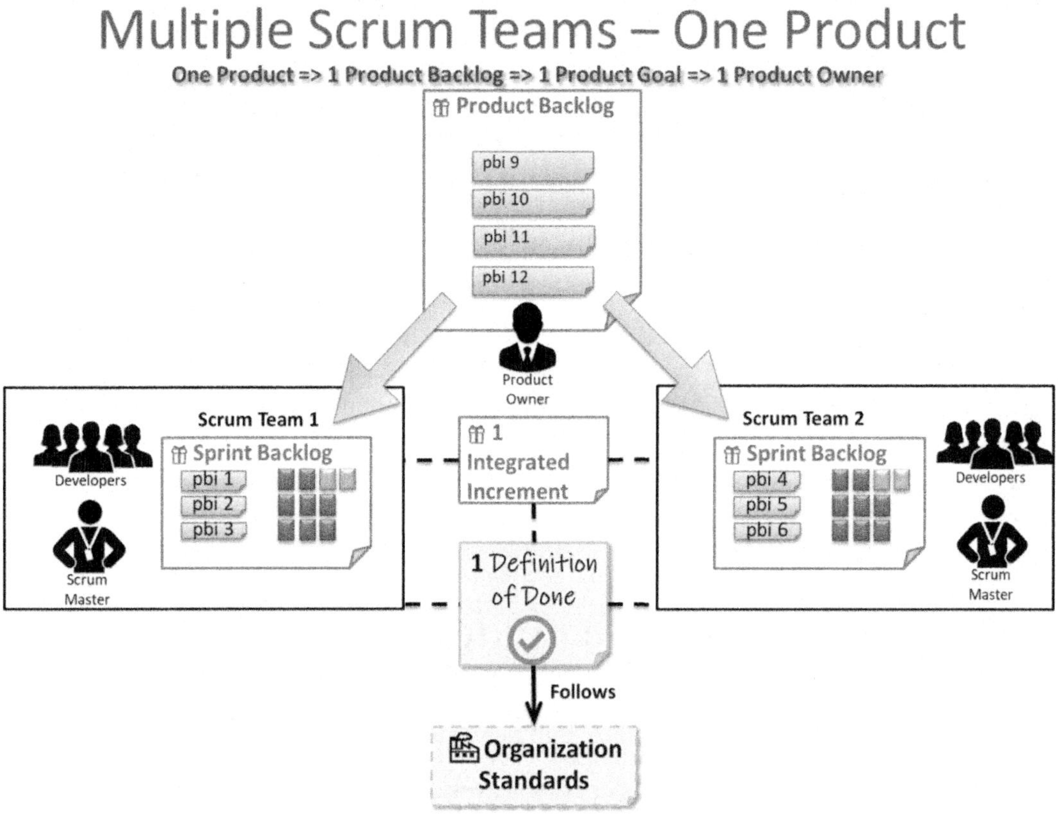

Figure 40 Multiple Scrum Teams.

When multiple teams work together on the same product, following certain rules can help ensure efficient collaboration, consistent quality, and successful product delivery.

22.3.1 All Scrum rules apply when scaling Scrum

Scrum Teams must follow the rules and guidelines of the Scrum Guide for effective collaboration, communication, and product development. When scaling Scrum to multiple teams or a larger organization, it is important to remember that the rules from the Scrum Guide still apply.

All Scrum rules, including the accountabilities, events, artifacts, and values, should be upheld and adapted to meet the organization's unique needs and context. For example, while each Scrum team may have its own Sprint Backlog and daily standup, they must still align with the overall product goal and the Sprint timeline.

A Scaling framework may enhance these rules and add new accountabilities, events, and artifacts but cannot modify or skip the Scrum rules for each Scrum Team.

22.3.2 Definition of Done

1. Align Definition of Done: Ensure all teams have a shared understanding of the quality standards and criteria required for a task to be considered complete.
2. Mutually defined Definition of Done: Developers from all Scrum Teams must work together to establish a mutually agreed-upon Definition of Done, ensuring a shared understanding of quality standards and expectations across all teams. This collaboration helps maintain consistency and facilitates smoother integration of work increments.
3. Organization-wide Definition of Done: If the Definition of Done for an increment is part of the organization's standards, the Scrum Teams' Definition of Done must follow it as a minimum requirement. This ensures consistency in quality and adherence to the organization's expectations, while individual teams may still choose to adopt additional criteria specific to their project or domain.

22.3.3 Clear communication

Establish open communication channels between teams to share updates, issues, and progress between Scrum Teams. The scaled scrum events and transparency of artifacts typically help to collaborate, but the Scrum Teams should communicate and collaborate as needed. The Scrum Masters help to encourage cross-team collaboration and communication.

22.3.4 Scaling the Sprint

Scrum Team 1 (4-week Sprint)			
Scrum Team 2 (4-week Sprint)			
Scrum Team 3 (2-week Sprint)		Scrum Team 3 (2-week Sprint)	
Scrum Team 4 (1-week Sprint)	Scrum Team 4 (1-week Sprint)	Scrum Team 4 (1-week Sprint)	Scrum Team 4 (1-week Sprint)
4 WEEK SPRINT			

Figure 41 Teams with different Sprint lengths in a scaling approach.

Coordinate Sprint schedules and major milestones to facilitate better collaboration and planning.

1. Scaled Sprint length for coordination: At the scaling level, there is a single Sprint length for all teams to coordinate work, which includes scaled Sprint, scaled Daily Scrum, scaled Sprint Review, and scaled Sprint Retrospective. This unified Sprint length ensures effective cross-team collaboration, synchronization, and alignment of activities, enabling the teams to work together efficiently and achieve shared goals.
2. Flexibility in Sprint length for each team: Each Scrum Team may have different Sprint lengths and start or end dates, allowing them to adapt their working process to their specific project needs, team dynamics, and other factors. However, it is crucial to maintain alignment with the scaling Sprint dates and length requirements for effective cross-team collaboration and coordination.
3. Alignment of Sprints at the scaling level: While each Scrum Team may have its own Sprint length with different start and end dates, they must align with the scaling Sprint dates and length. This ensures coordination at the organizational level and facilitates synchronization of cross-team activities, dependencies, and product integration efforts.

22.3.5 Cross-team coordination

Hold regular cross-team meetings to discuss progress, challenges, and dependencies. For instance: Scaled Sprint Planning, Scaled Daily Scrum, Cross-team refinement, Scaled Sprint Review, and Scaled Sprint Retrospective.

Dependencies and coordination between teams are the major concerns when scaling Scrum. As self-managing teams, the Scrum Teams are responsible for coordinating and cross-team collaboration to collaborate and remove dependencies.

The Scrum Master can coach them that it is their responsibility to organize the teams so that each team will have the necessary skills to remove dependencies, create an Integrated Increment at the end of every Sprint, and collaborate with other Developers needed.

22.3.6 Consistent processes and alignment of tools

While each team is self-managing and can decide on the tools and processes they use, aligning certain practices across all teams is beneficial to ensure smooth collaboration and reduce friction. This alignment helps maintain consistency in working methods and facilitates effective communication and coordination among teams, enabling them to work together efficiently towards shared goals.

22.3.7 All teams are cross-functional

In a scaled environment, each team must be cross-functional, possessing the skills and expertise required to work on all layers of the product. This allows each Scrum Team to deliver complete functionality with little or no dependencies on other teams. Having cross-functional teams promotes self-sufficiency and reduces bottlenecks, as teams can independently design, build, test, and deliver features. This setup contributes to more efficient collaboration, shorter feedback loops, and faster value delivery to the end users. For instance, all Scrum Teams are feature teams.

22.3.8 Integrated Increment

- One integrated Increment for all teams: At the scaling level, all teams must consistently integrate their work into a single, cohesive increment. This unified increment should meet the agreed-upon Definition of Done and reflect the combined efforts of all teams, ensuring a high-quality, consistent, and valuable product for the end users.
- Integrate often: Regularly or daily integrating increments help to identify and address any integration issues early, improving overall product stability and reducing the risk of delays or complications later in the development process.
- Jointly address integration issues: Collaboratively and regularly tackle integration challenges to minimize the impact on the overall product quality and schedule.

22.3.9 One integrated increment for the Sprint Review

In a scaled environment, all teams must present a single, unified increment during the Sprint Review. This integrated increment should represent the combined efforts of all teams, showcasing the value delivered to the end users during the Sprint. Each team mustn't present its isolated increment, as doing so may not accurately reflect the overall progress and value added to the product.

Presenting one integrated increment during the Sprint Review helps to:
1. Demonstrate cohesive progress: By integrating the work of all teams into a single increment, stakeholders can better understand the overall progress made during the Sprint and the value delivered to the end users.
2. Promote collaboration: Teams are encouraged to collaborate, coordinating their efforts to ensure seamless integration and alignment with the shared product goal.
3. Identify and address integration issues: Regularly integrating work from different teams allows for early detection of integration issues, making it easier to address potential problems and improve the overall stability and quality of the product.
4. Enhance transparency: Presenting a unified increment during the Sprint Review offers stakeholders a clear and accurate understanding of the product's current state and the work completed by all teams.

By focusing on one integrated increment for the Sprint Review, organizations can foster better collaboration, transparency, and alignment among teams, ensuring a cohesive, high-quality product for end users.

22.3.10   Regularly review and adjust

Periodically review and refine team practices, processes, and DoD to ensure continuous improvement and alignment.

22.3.11   Foster a collaborative culture

Encourage a supportive environment that promotes teamwork, knowledge sharing, and mutual understanding.

When working on complex problems in complex environments, the tools can help avoid many mistakes and issues provoked by manual work. Still, they cannot guarantee communications and other human issues. While there is value in "processes and tools," we value "Individuals and interactions" more. Although multiple teams will work as independently as possible, they must integrate the increment and coordinate to remove dependencies or common impediments.

22.3.12   One Product Goal

Keep all teams aligned and working towards the same product vision and objectives, ensuring cohesive product development. In a scaled environment, it is crucial to have a single product goal that guides the work of all teams. This unified goal ensures that everyone is working towards the same vision and objectives, fostering cohesive product development and effective collaboration across teams.

22.3.13 One Product Backlog

Maintain a single Product Backlog for the Product for all teams to provide a unified view of priorities, dependencies, and progress.

22.3.14 Each Scrum team has its Sprint Backlog

In a scaled environment, each Scrum team maintains its own Sprint Backlog, which contains the tasks and user stories the team has committed to completing during the Sprint. This enables each team to focus on their specific responsibilities and priorities while contributing to the overall product goal. In addition, maintaining separate Sprint Backlogs for each team helps ensure that work is efficiently distributed and clearly defined, promoting accountability and effective collaboration within and between teams.

22.3.15 One Product Owner

When multiple teams work on the same product, having a single Product Owner who oversees the entire project is essential. The Product Owner is responsible for aligning priorities, managing the shared Product Backlog, and ensuring that all teams work towards the same vision. This unified approach helps maintain consistent product direction and facilitates effective team collaboration and communication.

However, this means one decision-maker has the last say on the Product. In large-scale projects or organizations with multiple teams working on the same product, it might become challenging for a single person to manage all aspects effectively. The Product Owner role can be scaled using various approaches to address this challenge.

22.4 Dedicated or shared team members

The Scrum Master or Developers can work for one team or multiple teams depending on the organization's structure, size, and needs. Each arrangement has its own benefits and challenges:

Here are the pros and cons of each approach, along with the values affected, when the Scrum Master or Developers work with one team versus multiple teams:

Dedicated to one team:

- Pros:
    - Focused attention: Scrum Master or Developers can concentrate on their team's specific needs, challenges, and dynamics, leading to more effective problem-solving and support.
    - Enhanced collaboration and communication: Close involvement with the team fosters better communication, collaboration, and understanding among team members.

- o Deeper connection: A dedicated Scrum Master or Developers can build trust and strong relationships within the team, resulting in increased motivation and commitment.
- Cons:
  - o Limited resource utilization: Having dedicated Scrum Masters or Developers for each team may not be efficient or feasible for organizations with limited resources or many teams.
  - o Potential isolation: Teams may become isolated from other teams' best practices or ideas, potentially missing valuable insights and learning opportunities.
- Positively affected values:
  - o Focus: Increased focus on the specific team and its unique context enhances the Scrum Master's or Developers' ability to support and address challenges effectively.
  - o Commitment: Stronger relationships and trust within the team lead to higher commitment levels and motivation among team members.
- Negatively affected values:
  - o Openness (potentially): Teams may become isolated from other teams' best practices or ideas, limiting opportunities for learning and collaboration.

Working with multiple teams:

- Pros:
  - o Knowledge sharing: Scrum Master or Developers can share their expertise and experiences across different teams, leading to the exchange of ideas and best practices.
  - o Cost-effectiveness: This arrangement can be more resource-efficient for organizations with limited resources or many teams.
- Cons:
  - o Diluted focus: Balancing multiple teams might reduce the Scrum Master's or Developers' ability to address each team's specific needs and challenges effectively.
  - o Time management challenges: Scrum Masters or Developers may struggle to allocate time and prioritize work across multiple teams, potentially reducing engagement with individual teams.
  - o Weaker team connections: With less time spent with each team, the Scrum Master or Developers may not develop as deep relationships, impacting trust and collaboration.
- Positively affected values:
  - o Openness: Scrum Masters or Developers working with multiple teams can promote openness by sharing best practices, ideas, and experiences across different teams, leading to a cross-pollination of knowledge.
- Negatively affected values:

- Focus: Balancing multiple teams might dilute the Scrum Master's or Developers' focus, making it harder to address each team's specific needs and challenges effectively.
- Respect: Juggling the needs and priorities of multiple teams may impact the Scrum Master or Developers' ability to fully respect each team's unique context and challenges.
- Commitment (potentially): With less time spent with each team, the Scrum Master or Developers may not develop deep relationships, which can affect trust, collaboration, and commitment levels within the team.

Ideally, the Scrum Teams should decide whether the Scrum Masters or Developers should work with one team or multiple teams depending on the organization's specific context, resources, and goals. Ensuring that the chosen arrangement aligns with Scrum values and promotes effective collaboration, communication, and continuous improvement is essential.

22.5 Anti-patterns of scaling Scrum

Lack of coordination and communication: When scaling Scrum, it's important to ensure that all Scrum Teams are aligned and working towards a common goal. Lack of coordination and communication can lead to duplication of efforts, conflicting priorities, and inefficient use of resources.

1. Over-reliance on hierarchy and command-and-control management: Scrum is designed to be a collaborative and self-organizing framework. Over-reliance on hierarchy and command-and-control management can undermine the effectiveness of Scrum and lead to a lack of innovation and engagement among team members.
2. Lack of cross-functional teams: Scrum emphasizes the importance of cross-functional teams that can work on all aspects of the product. A lack of cross-functional teams or teams split by architectural layer can lead to siloed information and dependencies between teams.
3. Lack of focus on value delivery: Scrum is designed to maximize value delivery to customers and stakeholders. A lack of focus on value delivery can lead to a lack of alignment between the Scrum Teams and the overall product vision and goals.
4. Lack of shared standards and practices: When scaling Scrum, it's important to ensure that all Scrum Teams follow shared standards, Definition of Done, and practices to ensure consistency and quality across the product development effort.
5. Lack of training and support: Scrum is a complex framework requiring effective implementation and support. Lack of training and support can lead to confusion and frustration among team members and a lack of understanding of Scrum's principles and practices.

6. Every Scrum Team shows its own increment: When scaling Scrum. It's important to ensure that each Scrum Team contributes to a single, integrated increment that reflects progress towards the overall product goal. However, allowing each Scrum Team to show its own increment or from different branches can lead to misalignment and confusion among stakeholders and undermine the Scrum framework's effectiveness.
7. Multiple Product Owners: When scaling Scrum, having multiple Product Owners can lead to conflicting priorities, decisions, and a lack of alignment between the Scrum Teams. Having a single Product Owner responsible for defining and prioritizing the Product Backlog is important.
8. One Product Backlog for each team: When scaling Scrum, having separate Product Backlogs for each Scrum Team may be tempting. However, this can lead to duplication of effort and a lack of alignment between the Scrum Teams. Therefore, having a single Product Backlog that reflects the overall product vision and goals is important.

Part 23: Related Topics

23.1 Velocity

Velocity is commonly mentioned in Scrum implementations to track past performance, but it is not part of Scrum and is not mandatory.

Velocity only measures the team's average speed. Therefore, it reflects the amount of work delivered but not how much value is being received by the customers.

Velocity is a metric used in Scrum to measure how a team delivers completed work during a Sprint. It represents the amount of work the team can complete in a given Sprint based on its historical performance and capacity.

Velocity is typically calculated by adding up the total number of points or tasks completed during a Sprint and dividing it by the length of the Sprint in days. For example, if a team completes 30 story points in a 2-week Sprint, their velocity would be 15 story points per week.

Velocity is a useful tool for teams to plan their work and estimate how much work they can complete in future Sprints. It can also help teams identify potential roadblocks or inefficiencies hindering productivity and inform continuous improvement efforts.

It is important to note that velocity is not a measure of a team's performance or productivity but rather a tool for estimating and planning. In addition, it is influenced by various factors, such as the complexity of the work, team composition, and external dependencies, and can fluctuate from Sprint to Sprint. As such, it should be used with other metrics and qualitative assessments to ensure an accurate and comprehensive analysis of a team's performance.

23.1.1 *Velocity does not measure value*

Here's an example of a team with high velocity but not providing value:

Imagine a team that has a velocity of 40 story points per Sprint. They consistently deliver many features each Sprint, and their velocity is the envy of other teams in the organization. However, upon closer examination, it becomes apparent that the team focuses on low-priority or unnecessary features that do not align with the organization's overall product goals.

Despite their high velocity and impressive output, the team is not providing value to the organization or its stakeholders. The features they deliver may not be useful, usable, or desirable to the end users, and they may not contribute to the organization's bottom line.

This example highlights the importance of recognizing that velocity alone does not measure value. Instead, teams must prioritize and focus on delivering high-quality, valuable features that align with the product goals and meet the needs of the end users. It is not enough to simply deliver many features without considering their quality, relevance, or impact on the organization's overall success.

23.1.2 *Velocity chart*

Although Velocity chart is popular in Scrum implementations, it is not part of Scrum Framework and is not mandatory by Scrum.

The velocity chart is a Scrum artifact showing the amount of work the team completes in each Sprint. It is a graphical representation of the number of story points completed over several Sprints, allowing the team to track its progress over time.

The vertical axis of the velocity chart represents the total number of story points completed, while the horizontal axis represents the Sprints. Each Sprint is represented by a column that shows the total number of story points completed during that Sprint.

The velocity chart helps the team plan future Sprints based on past performance. It provides insight into the team's capacity and allows them to estimate how much work they can realistically complete in future Sprints. It also helps the Product Owner to forecast when the Product Backlog will be completed.

It is important to note that the velocity chart should not be used to measure individual performance or compare teams. The velocity of a team can vary due to various factors, including changes in team composition, changes in technology, or changes in the Product Backlog.

The velocity chart can also track progress toward the product goal. By comparing the total number of story points completed to the estimated total size of the Product Backlog, the team can track its progress toward completing the product goal.

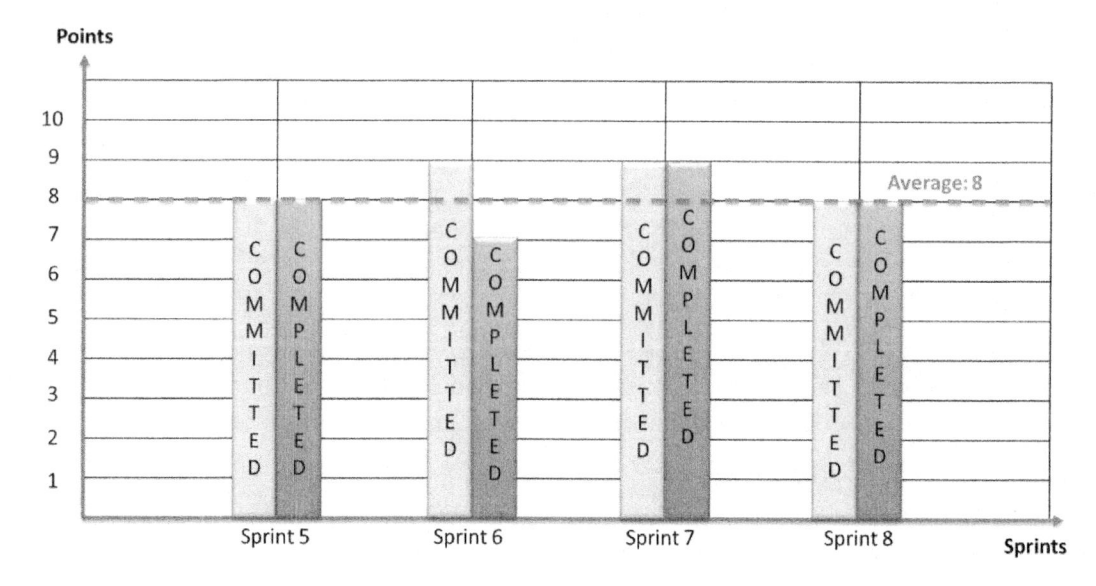

Figure 42 Example of a Velocity chart.

23.1.3 Velocity must not be standardized across teams

It is important to note that velocity should not be standardized across teams.

Each Scrum Team is unique, and the factors that affect their velocity can vary greatly. For example, one team may have more experienced members, better tools, or fewer dependencies than another team, which can impact their ability to complete work. As a result, it is not appropriate to compare one team's velocity to another or to use velocity as a standardized metric for all teams. In addition, the way, measures, and techniques each team sizes and the Product Backlog items differ.

Standardizing velocity across teams can harm the accuracy of Sprint Planning and lead to unrealistic expectations for delivery. For example, if a team has a lower velocity than another team but is expected to deliver the same amount of work, it may lead to burnout, missed deadlines, and decreased morale.

When velocity is standardized across teams, it can lead to gaming the system by teams focusing on inflating their velocity numbers instead of delivering actual value to customers. This can happen when managers or stakeholders use velocity as a performance metric. Teams feel pressured to deliver high numbers, even if it means sacrificing quality or working on low-priority tasks. When teams inflate their velocity by padding estimates or completing low-value tasks, it can create a false sense of progress and hide underlying problems, such as technical debt or ineffective processes. Ultimately, the focus on velocity over value can decrease overall productivity and jeopardize the product's success. Therefore, it's important to remember that each team sizes items differently, and velocity should not be used as a performance metric or compared across teams. The focus should always be on delivering value to the customer and continuously improving the process.

Attempting to standardize velocity across teams ignores these differences and can lead to inaccurate comparisons, misaligned expectations, and inappropriate resource allocation. Instead, each team should focus on improving their velocity relative to their own past performance rather than trying to match or outdo other teams. This approach allows teams to focus on delivering value, improving their own processes, and avoiding the negative impacts of comparing apples to oranges.

Instead of standardizing velocity across teams, it is important to focus on each team's individual performance and work towards continuous improvement. Each team should have its own unique velocity that reflects its capacity and ability to deliver value. By allowing each team to work at their own pace and focusing on their strengths and weaknesses, the Scrum framework can lead to more efficient and effective development processes.

23.2 Burn down charts

Although Burn-down charts are popular in Scrum implementations, Burn-down charts are not part of the Scrum Framework and are not mandatory by Scrum. Scrum is based on empiricism and does not include any tool.

A burn-down chart is an effective tool for monitoring the team's progress and identifying any issues that may arise during the Sprint, release, or goal. It can help the Scrum Master, and team members identify when they are falling behind schedule or over-committing and adjust their approach accordingly. It also provides stakeholders with a clear understanding of the team's progress and helps them to identify any potential risks or issues that may need to be addressed.

23.2.1 Sprint Burndown chart

The Sprint Burn-Down Chart visually represents the team's progress during the Sprint. It shows how much work the team can complete in the Sprint and how quickly they complete it.

The chart has two axes: the horizontal axis shows the Sprint's time frame, divided into days, while the vertical axis represents the remaining amount of work in the Sprint. The chart begins with the full amount of work remaining at the top of the vertical axis, and as the team completes work, the line on the chart descends the axis. Ideally, the line should be trending downward toward zero by the end of the Sprint. The remaining work is typically represented in Story Points, the number of Product Backlog items, or another effort unit.

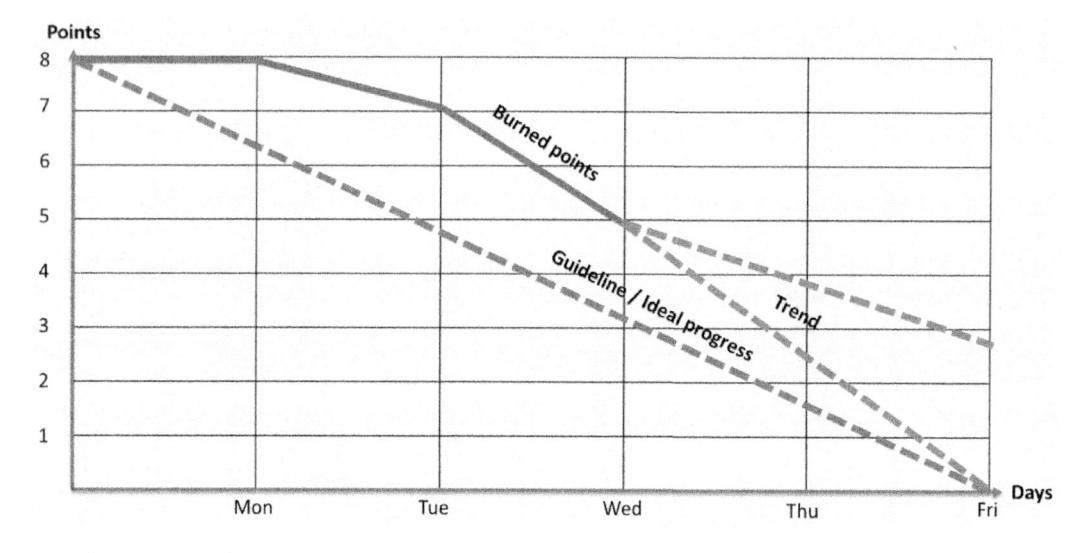

Figure 43 Example of Sprint Burn-Down chart

23.2.2 Release Burn-Down chart

A Release Burn-Down chart is a visual representation that shows the Scrum team's progress toward achieving the product goal for a release. It shows the amount of work remaining in the Product Backlog compared to the time available for the release. The chart is updated at the end of each Sprint and is used to track the team's progress toward the product goal.

The chart's vertical axis represents the total amount of work remaining in the Product Backlog, while the horizontal axis represents the time available for the release. The chart begins with the total amount of work in the Product Backlog at the beginning of the release, and the goal is to have the chart reach zero by the end of the release, indicating that all work has been completed. The remaining work is typically represented in Story Points, the number of Product Backlog items, or another effort unit.

The Release Burn-Down chart can be used to track progress toward the product goal and ensure that the team is on track to deliver the required value by the end of the release. It can also be used to identify any potential risks or issues that may impact the release, allowing the team to take corrective action to address them.

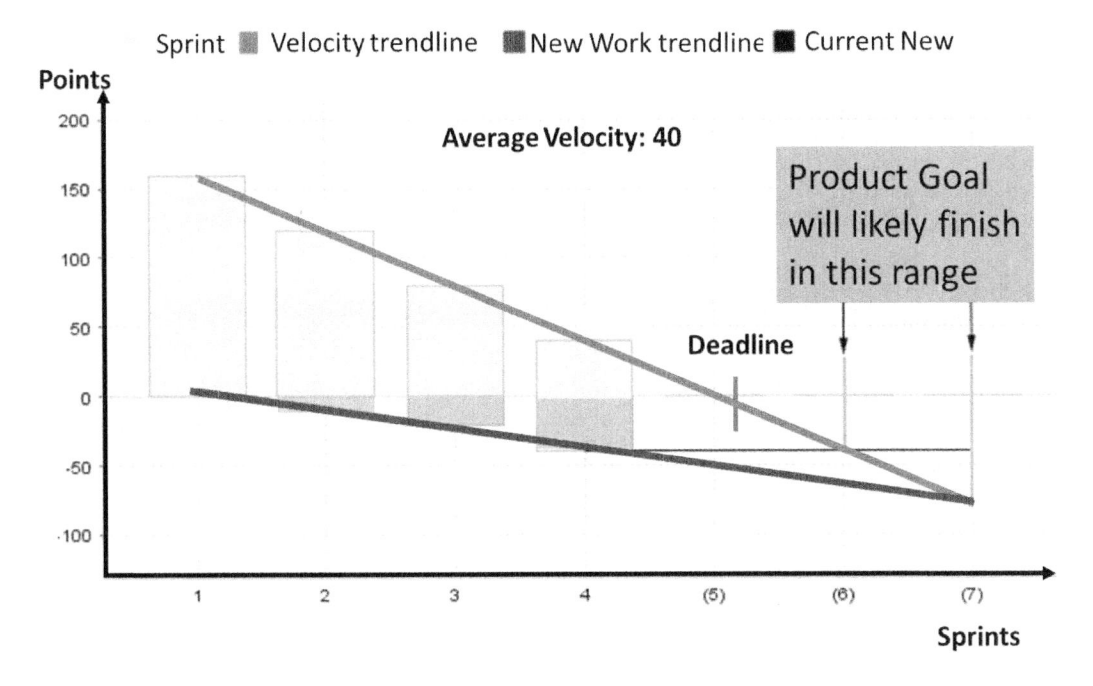

Figure 44 Example of Release Burn-Down chart for a Product Goal.

The example above shows the total points at the beginning of each Sprint. The team started with 160 story points to complete all the features desired for a Product Goal; the team completed 40 story points per Sprint. The Developers originally forecasted to complete the work in 4 Sprints. However, after receiving feedback from the stakeholders, the Scrum Team also added 10 story points per Sprint of new ideas to the Product Backlog. Therefore, by the Sprint Planning of the 4th Sprint, they have 70 remaining points, composed of 40 from the original Product Backlog and 30 points from new ideas that were added to the Product Backlog during the Sprints. Therefore, Developers are unlikely to complete 70 points in one Sprint. When projecting the performance to the future, the Developers forecast that with the current velocity, they will need 2 Sprints to finish all the work. However, if the Product Owner continues to add 10 points per Sprint of new ideas to the Product Backlog, the Developers will need 3 Sprints to complete all the work. Therefore, the Scrum Team has some options:

1. Reduce the scope to deliver the most important items and still meet the Product Goal by the deadline in one Sprint. Sometimes, a deadline cannot be extended, for instance, elections, Christmas toys, seasonal products, a TV live show, etc.
2. Negotiate with the Stakeholders if the new ideas are important or optional to meet the Product Goal and if they are willing to extend the deadline to include them.
3. Meet the Product Goal with the must-have features now and create a new Product Goal to complete all the ideas as enhancements or nice to have.

In all cases, it is important to involve the Scrum Team and stakeholders, bring transparency to the situation, and maximize to deliver the most value on time.

In summary, the Release Burn-Down chart is useful for tracking progress toward the product goal and ensuring that the team delivers value to the customers. It helps the team to focus on completing the most important work items and allows the stakeholders to have visibility into the progress of the release.

23.3 Mechanical Scrum vs. Professional Scrum

Mechanical Scrum is when a Scrum team and its organization follow Scrum by the book, but they do not actively seek ways to inspect, adapt, and improve in the next Sprint. Instead, they do Scrum mechanically or aesthetically. In contrast, Professional Scrum may have started as a Mechanical Scrum and led the team and organization to discover the values and principles of Scrum. A Professional Scrum Team improves its product and process to continuously serve its users and customers, creating a more positive and innovative workplace better and faster. The Professional Scrum Team truly lives the values, as seen by their conduct and attitudes. They organically and actively seek to inspect and adapt to provide additional value. Showing values and improving is just part of the team's habits. In Mechanical Scrum, the team and organization go through the motions of Scrum without embracing the values and do not use the transparency that Scrum gives for their own work and context to improve it by addressing the most significant concerns. This part of Scrum may be difficult, requiring courage, tenacity, and discipline that not many teams and companies possess. In Mechanical Scrum, the team may be concerned with following Scrum without paying too much attention to satisfying the customers. In Professional Scrum, the team understands Scrum is useful, but the main goal is to satisfy the customers and create a successful product.

23.4 The Cone of uncertainty

The cone of uncertainty is a concept in project management that describes how the level of uncertainty is high at the beginning of a product's development lifecycle and decreases over time as a project progresses. It is represented as a cone because there is a wide range of uncertainty and risk at the beginning of a project. As the project progresses, the uncertainty and risk level decreases and narrows.

The cone of uncertainty shows the relationship between the estimation uncertainty and time spent researching, analyzing, prototyping, designing, and building a feature or project.

The Cone of Uncertainty affects the work of a Scrum Team during a product's development life cycle in several ways, including:

- Helping the team understand how investing time in estimations increases accuracy over time.

- Determining the appropriate amount of time to spend on estimation while balancing acceptable variability.
- Guiding the team in selecting estimation techniques that provide useful estimates without requiring excessive time investment.

Estimates (e.g., on duration, costs, or quality) are inherently very vague at the beginning of a project

At the beginning of product development, the uncertainty is high, and the intent of estimation will be highly inaccurate and with a high error margin or estimation variability. Therefore, making a promise with an estimate at the beginning of the cone would not be a good idea.

Suppose the team invests more time in research, prototype, analysis, and design. So on, the team will reduce this cone of uncertainty and will be able to provide more accurate estimates with less variability.

However, suppose the team researches too much to reduce the cone. In that case, the estimation will take too much effort compared to the total effort required for its actual implementation, and the estimate will be too late for practical purposes. Furthermore, estimating in such a way would be too expensive if, finally, the Product Owner decides not to implement the feature.

If the Developers estimate with very little knowledge too early in the cone, the estimate will be useless because of the high error margin and inaccuracy.

The team needs a point where an estimate is usable and does not require much effort to obtain it.

The team members can use the cone of uncertainty to find the right spot of the minimal possible time invested in estimation with an error rate that they feel comfortable understanding the size of the problem compared to other problems without being too precise. For instance, at a point, the team can compare a feature's expected value against the estimated effort required to be implemented. Then, the Product Owner can use this information to order the Product Backlog to maximize the value.

There are estimation techniques based on Delphi, like Planning Poker, which help find the right spot on what is needed to know and understand collectively by a group to size an item and quickly find a consensus of the relative size of an item compared to other items.

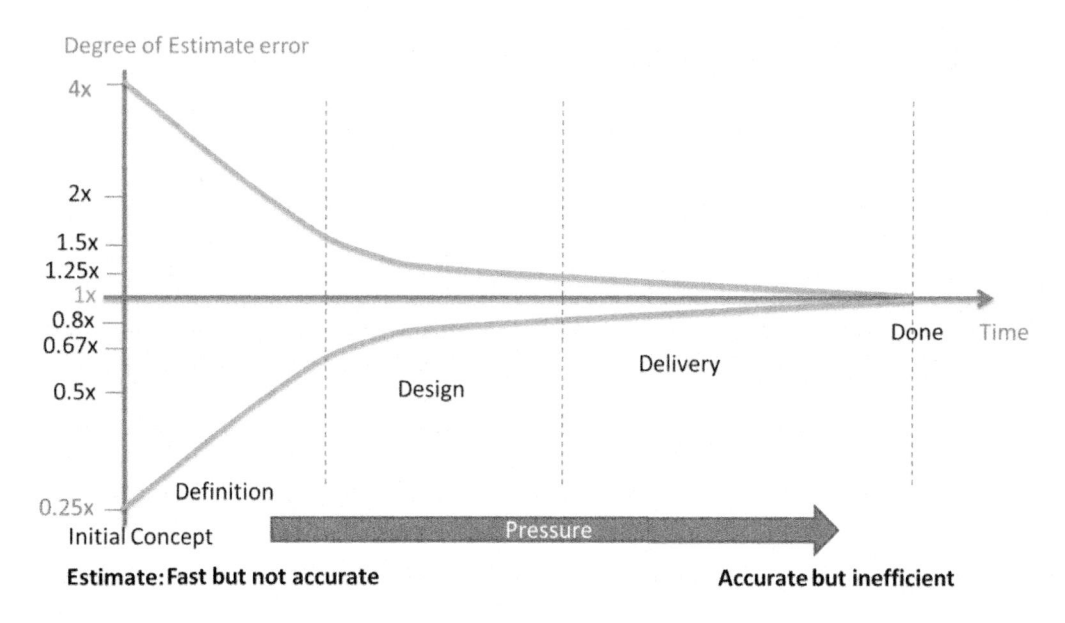

Figure 45 Cone of uncertainty. Based on: Software Estimation – Steve McConnel.

The cone of uncertainty also highlights the importance of regular inspection and adaptation in Scrum. Because there is always some level of uncertainty and risk involved in a project, it is important to continuously evaluate and adjust plans and processes to stay on track and meet the product goals.

23.5 Technical Debt

Technical debt is a metaphorical term used in software development to describe the consequences of choosing a suitable, short-term solution over a more comprehensive long-term solution. It results from compromising quality for speed or other factors, such as cost or deadlines.

Technical debt accumulates over time as changes are made to the software, and the cost of maintaining and evolving the software increases. As a result, it can lead to various problems, such as increased bugs, decreased performance, and decreased productivity. If technical debt is not managed properly, it can eventually become so significant that it becomes difficult or even impossible to maintain or update the software.

Several types of technical debt exist, such as design debt, code debt, and infrastructure debt. Design debt refers to compromises made in the software's design, such as using a less-than-ideal architecture. Code debt refers to compromises made in the software's code, such as using shortcuts or avoiding code refactoring. Finally, infrastructure debt refers to compromises made in the software's supporting infrastructure, such as using outdated servers or not updating third-party libraries.

To manage technical debt, the team must recognize it and prioritize its reduction as part of the Product Backlog. This can involve refactoring code, improving the architecture, updating infrastructure, and implementing better testing and quality control practices. The Product Owner and the Developers should work together to identify and prioritize technical debt reduction tasks to ensure the long-term sustainability and maintainability of the software.

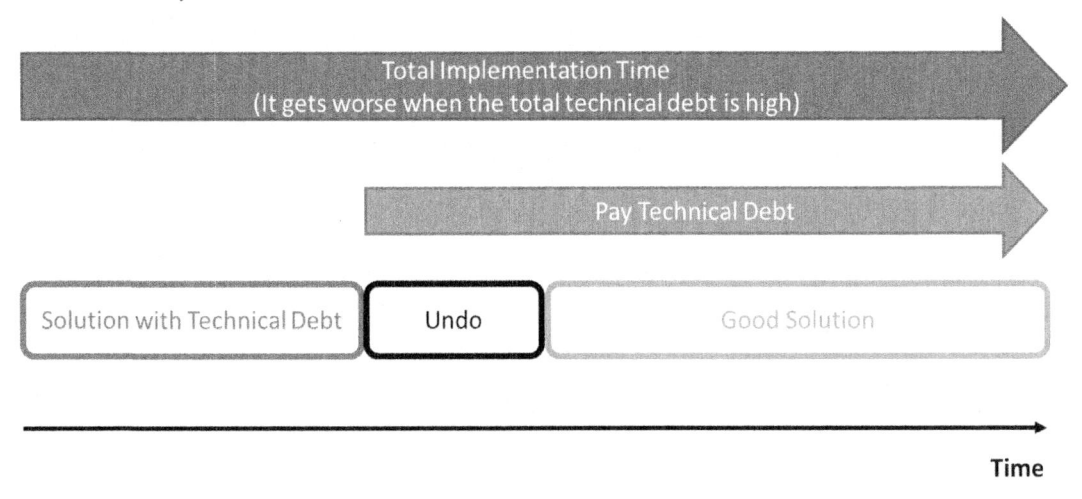

Figure 46 Implementing and paying a solution with Technical Debt.

Some of the effects of technical debt are:

- Paying off technical debt is like paying off unpaid monetary debt; it takes time and resources to address the problem.
- Technical debt can harm the stability and safety of the product, as it may lead to bugs and defects that can compromise the security of the software.
- New solutions take longer to implement because of the technical complexity of updating the code or product.
- False assumptions about the present status of the Product and the Increment being examined at Sprint Review might be made.
- Technical debt can have a short-term positive effect on velocity, allowing for quick delivery of features. However, in the long term, technical debt can slow down velocity as it becomes more difficult to maintain and update the software.
- Technical debt can lead to the addiction of stakeholders to fast results, as it allows for quick implementation of features without considering the long-term consequences.
- Technical debt can lead to a decrease in morale among the Developers, as they may feel overwhelmed and unable to keep up with the demands of maintaining the software.
- Technical debt can increase the cost of maintaining and updating the software over time, as adding new features or making changes to existing ones becomes more difficult and time-consuming.
- To avoid the negative effects of technical debt, the team must prioritize technical debt reduction and incorporate it into the Product Backlog.

Sprint Burn down vs Tech Debt

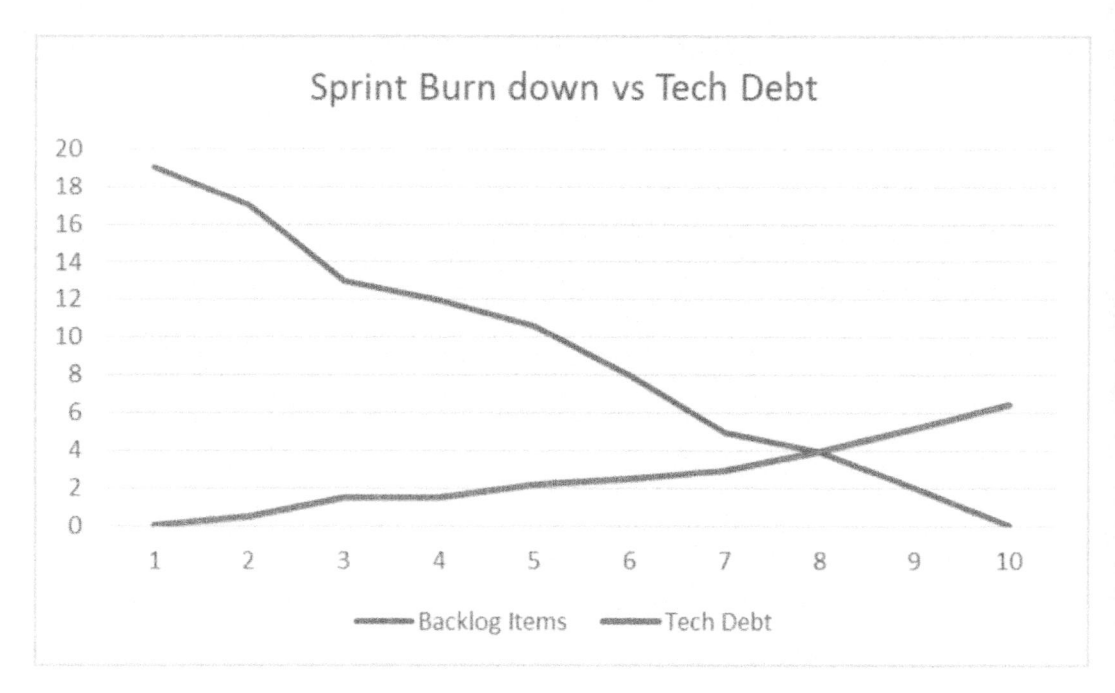

―――― Backlog Items ―――― Tech Debt

In the short term, technical debt can positively affect velocity, as it allows the Developers to implement features quickly and deliver working software faster. However, technical debt can slow down velocity over time as the software becomes more difficult to maintain and update.

23.5.1 *Typical excuses for incurring technical debt*

Here are some typical excuses that may lead to incurring technical debt:

- Weak Definition of Done: If the Definition of Done is not well-defined or not enforced, Developers may not prioritize quality, leading to technical debt. For example, suppose the Definition of Done only requires a feature to be "functional" without specifying quality requirements such as code reviews or automated testing. In that case, Developers may not prioritize these tasks, leading to technical debt. It's important to have a strong and well-defined Definition of Done to prevent this from happening.
- Rushing to meet a deadline: When there is pressure to deliver a feature or product quickly, Developers may cut corners and sacrifice quality to meet the deadline. This can lead to technical debt.
- Lack of resources: When there are not enough resources or time to do things properly, Developers may take shortcuts or leave issues unresolved, leading to technical debt.
- Lack of experience: Developers who lack experience or knowledge may create technical debt by not using best practices, writing poor-quality code, or making poor design choices.

- Poor communication: When there is poor communication between stakeholders and Scrum Teams, requirements may be unclear or change too frequently, leading to technical debt as Developers struggle to keep up with changes.
- Legacy code: When working with legacy code, Developers may need to make compromises to maintain compatibility, leading to technical debt.
- Unforeseen complexity: Sometimes, Developers may encounter unforeseen complexity when implementing a feature or fixing a bug, leading to technical debt as they rush to find a solution.

It's important to remember that technical debt is not always avoidable but should be managed and minimized to the greatest extent possible. When technical debt is incurred, it's important to have a plan in place to pay it off in a timely manner.

23.6 Forming, storming, norming, performing

23.6.1 How a team evolves, and how can you help?

Many people don't understand how a team evolves and grows through different phases. This is key to coaching a team or being part of one. So why do some teams suck and others outperform? Teams with problems may not have been appropriately coached throughout their growth.

Through its existence, a team goes through the phases of Forming, storming, norming, and performing.

Bruce Tuckman developed this model of group development in 1965, claiming that these phases are natural and unavoidable for a team to grow, face difficulties, solve issues, plan work, and achieve outcomes. These inevitable stages are crucial to team growth and development, but it is also possible to help a team navigate through them properly to construct an effective group dynamic.

Let's take a look at each phase, and as a bonus, at the end of each phase, you will get tips on how to help your team.

A Team Coach or Scrum Master should be aware of these phases to help and assist the team with its growth without rushing a team through these natural phases. In addition, the Coach will notice when the team is moving to a new phase because of the nature of the team's discussions.

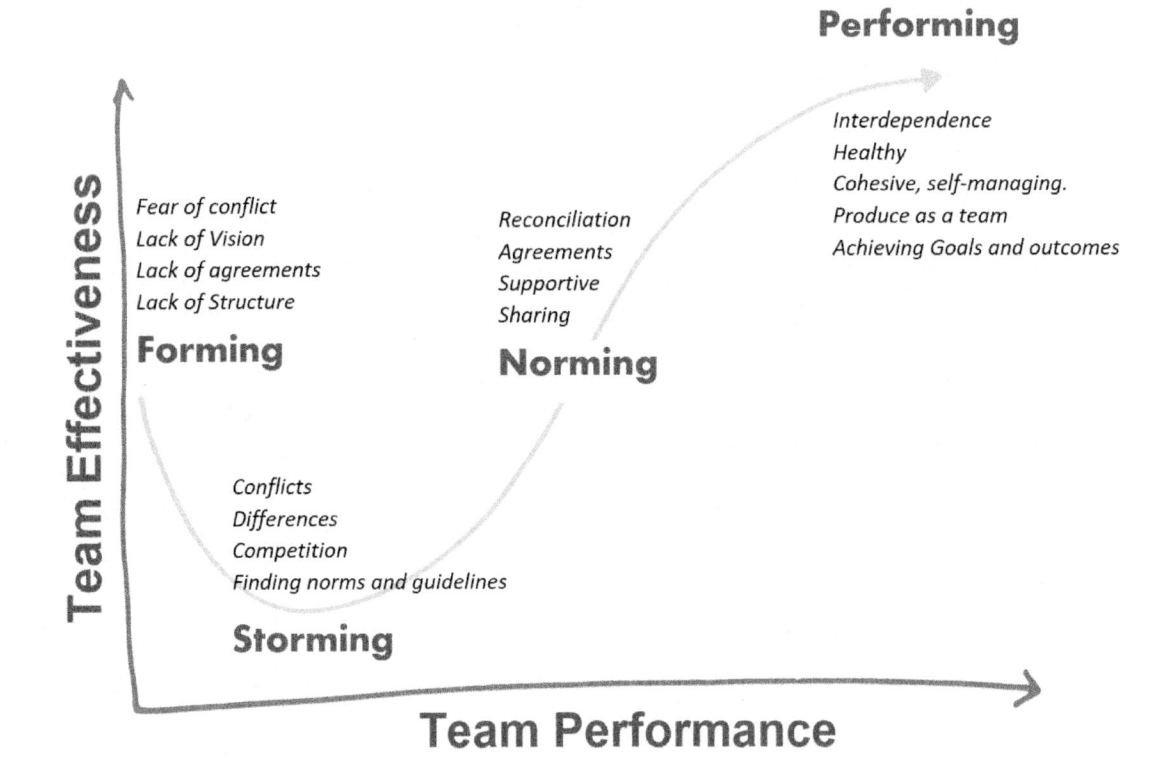

Figure 47 Phases of group development.

23.6.2 Forming Phase: A new team was born.

The team meets to learn about the opportunities and challenges, then sets goals and works on the tasks. Team members tend to act autonomously. They may be motivated but frequently misinformed about the team's difficulties and goals. Team members are generally on their best behavior yet quite self-centered. Even at this early stage, experienced team members begin to model exemplary conduct. The team is primarily concerned with their reason for existing throughout this first phase, thinking but perhaps not communicating questions like Why are we together? What is our vision? What duties should we take on? People are typically unfamiliar with each other at this stage. The sense of security that comes with familiarity is still lacking, which means that criticism, irritations, doubts, and uncertainties are not openly expressed. Instead, people prefer to concentrate on the work and what is expected. People don't feel like they're part of a team now.

23.6.2.1 What can you do during the Forming phase?

The Team Coach or Scrum Master can help as a teacher and ensure that everyone knows and understands what to do, the Product Goal, accountabilities, the initial structure of the team, and the initial process. The Coach can also facilitate kick-off meetings, futurespectives, future searches, get-to-know activities, team genesis activities, team formation workshops, a review of the selected framework like Scrum, a review of the roles and expectations, and define working agreements standards, a Definition of Done, vision, and so on.

23.6.3 Storming phase: This is scary, but do not push!

This is the second stage of team growth, in which the group begins to sort itself out and acquire the trust of one another. They frequently initiate this stage by expressing their ideas; disagreement may emerge amongst team members when authority and status are assigned. People grow more comfortable with one another as a sense of familiarity and safety develops inside the team. The willingness to express doubts, concerns, and displeasure rises. The initial disputes appear. Conflicts will focus on tasks ('Who will do what?', 'How will we accomplish this?'), not on each other. However, little irritants amongst members (including you) will emerge as familiarity grows. This is a natural byproduct of individuals' differing expectations of themselves, each other, and the team. Keep in mind that disagreements can be active (people express them) or passive (no one expresses them) (resistance or withdrawal). Although it is not always a pleasurable phase, it is a crucial stage in team development. If enough opportunities for constructive conflict resolution are provided, the team will learn to trust one another. Trying to avoid this period by burying or dismissing problems is the worst thing you can do.

23.6.3.1 What can you do during the Storming phase?

The Team Coach or Scrum Master can be a "coach." Don't handle problems for the team; instead, assist them in identifying and resolving issues independently. In other words, help the team to feel empowered and encourage self-managing. The Scrum Master as a facilitator, can create the environment and space to discuss conflicts and allow trust to emerge positively. In addition, the Scrum Master can teach or reinforce the idea of a cohesive team and that there are no hierarchies within the Scrum Team.

23.6.4 Norming phase: It feels normal, but there is much to improve!

The team enters the norming phase when disagreements are resolved productively and safely. This phase aims to balance what team members anticipate from one another and the team. This has to deal with features of the job (such as quality, speed, and thoroughness) and how individuals behave (social norms). In other words, the team decides on the norms, values, and standards governing their collaborative work. Discussions become more task-oriented during the norming phase. This is similar to what happened in the previous phase, but more aware of the team's established standards. This is the stage at which people begin to feel a member of and loyal to the team.

23.6.4.1 What can you do during the Norming phase?

A Team coach or Scrum Master may help as a mentor. You may assist the team in determining a productive mode of operation by utilizing the Scrum Framework and providing examples of other cases of your experience when useful. Humbly share your experiences, suggestions, and examples, and let the team decides what to do. The Scrum Master helps to consolidate empowerment in the organization.

23.6.5 Performing phase: Now, that's high performance.

Now that there is safety in the team and a clear understanding of what is and is not important, the team can work effectively together and focus on achieving goals. People become more adaptable in their responsibilities and activities at this stage. The team self-organizes and makes decisions without supervision. A team member may fill the gap for an unavailable Scrum Master or Developers to take on tough work beyond their comfort zone. The anxiety of failing and making errors has mostly subsided. Even though task-oriented debates are regular, the overall tone within the team is cheerful and productive.

23.6.5.1 What can you do during the Performing phase?

The Team Coach or Scrum Master can help as an advisor. The team can solve most problems independently, but help them by suggesting or finding the best solutions or techniques for the team to try or consider.

23.6.6 Adjourning phase: Time to say goodbye.

Every team ultimately disbands. Perhaps the team's goal has been met, or the team has been disbanded for other reasons. This may be upsetting and difficult, especially for long-running teams or teams that have worked together extensively for even a short time. Therefore, it is critical to employ rituals and ceremonies to say farewell to the team at this time and celebrate achievements and learnings.

23.6.6.1 What can you do during the Adjourning phase?

The Team Coach or Scrum Master should always be a good facilitator, but, at this stage, facilitating a close-out workshop would be very appreciated. Allow individuals to express their feelings linked with departures, assist them in making sense of it, and retrospect the journey.

Part 24: Putting concepts together

24.1 How is Scrum aligned with Agile Manifesto?

Here we will explore how the Scrum Guide relates to the Agile mindset according to the Agile Manifesto. https://agilemanifesto.org/

24.1.1 Scrum and the Agile Values

Here's a table with the Agile Manifesto's four values and related quotes from the Scrum Guide 2020.

Agile Manifesto Value	Related Scrum Guide 2020 Quote
1. Individuals and interactions	"Scrum is a lightweight framework that helps people, teams and organizations generate value through adaptive solutions for complex problems."
over processes and tools	"Scrum is not a process, technique, or definitive method."
	"Scrum Teams are self-managing and cross-functional."
2. Working software	"The Product Goal describes a future state of the product which can serve as a target for the Scrum Team to plan against."
over comprehensive documentation	"An Increment is a concrete stepping stone toward the Product Goal."
	"The Increment is the sum of all the Product Backlog items completed during a Sprint and the value of the increments of all previous Sprints."
3. Customer collaboration	"The Product Owner is accountable for maximizing the value of the product resulting from the work of the Scrum Team."
over contract negotiation	"The Product Owner is accountable for developing and explicitly communicating the Product Goal."
	"The Product Owner works with stakeholders to define the Product Goal."
4. Responding to change over following a plan	"Scrum Teams must frequently inspect their work and progress toward the Product Goal to detect undesirable variances, and adapt the process or the materials being worked on to minimize further deviations."
	"Sprint Review is an event at the end of the Sprint where the Scrum Team and stakeholders inspect the outcome of the Sprint and figure out what to do next."
	"A Sprint could be cancelled if the Sprint Goal becomes obsolete."

These quotes demonstrate how the Scrum framework aligns with the Agile Manifesto values by emphasizing people, working products, collaboration, and adaptability.

24.1.2 Scrum and the Agile Principles

Here's a table with the 12 principles of the Agile Manifesto along with related quotes from the Scrum Guide 2020.

Agile Manifesto Principle	Related Scrum Guide 2020 Quote
1. Our highest priority is to satisfy the customer through early and continuous delivery of valuable software.	"The Product Owner is accountable for maximizing the value of the product resulting from the work of the Scrum Team."
	"The Product Goal describes a future state of the product which can serve as a target for the Scrum Team to plan against."
	"The Product Owner may represent the needs of many stakeholders in the Product Backlog."
	"A product is a vehicle to deliver value. It has a clear boundary, known stakeholders, well-defined users or customers."
	"The whole Scrum Team then collaborates to define a Sprint Goal that communicates why the Sprint is valuable to stakeholders."
2. Welcome changing requirements, even late in development. Agile processes harness change for the customer's competitive advantage.	"Scrum Teams must frequently inspect their work and progress toward the Product Goal to detect undesirable variances, and adapt the process or the materials being worked on to minimize further deviations."
3. Deliver working software frequently, from a couple of weeks to a couple of months, with a preference to the shorter timescale.	"A Sprint is a short, time-boxed event of one month or less, during which the Scrum Team creates a potentially releasable, "Done" Increment."
4. Business people and Developers must work together daily throughout the project.	"The Product Owner works with stakeholders to define the Product Goal."

	"The entire Scrum Team is collectively responsible for creating a valuable, useful Increment every Sprint."
	"The Scrum Team is responsible for all product-related activities from stakeholder collaboration."
5. Build projects around motivated individuals. Give them the environment and support they need, and trust them	"Scrum Teams are self-managing and cross-functional."
to get the job done.	"Scrum's roles, events, artifacts, and rules are immutable and although implementing only parts of Scrum is possible, the result is not Scrum."
6. The most efficient and effective method of conveying information to and within a development team is	"The Daily Scrum is a 15-minute event for the Developers of the Scrum Team."
face-to-face conversation.	"To maximize transparency and alignment, the Product Owner and Scrum Master should attend the Daily Scrum."
7. Working software is the primary measure of progress.	"An Increment is a concrete stepping stone toward the Product Goal."
	"The Increment is the sum of all the Product Backlog items completed during a Sprint and the value of the increments of all previous Sprints."
8. Agile processes promote sustainable development. The sponsors, Developers, and users should be able	"The Sprint Retrospective is an opportunity for the Scrum Team to inspect itself and create a plan for improvements to be enacted during the next Sprint."
to maintain a constant pace indefinitely.	"They are structured and empowered by the organization to manage their own work. Working in Sprints at a sustainable pace improves the Scrum Team's focus and consistency."
9. Continuous attention to technical excellence and good design enhances agility.	"Scrum is founded on empiricism and lean thinking."
	"Scrum Teams must frequently inspect their work and progress toward the Product Goal to detect

	undesirable variances, and adapt the process or the materials being worked on to
	minimize further deviations."
10. Simplicity--the art of maximizing the amount of work not done--is essential.	"The Scrum Master is accountable for the Scrum Team's effectiveness."
	"The Developers are accountable for creating a plan for the Sprint, the Sprint Backlog."
11. The best architectures, requirements, and designs emerge from self-organizing teams.	"Scrum Teams are self-managing and cross-functional."
	"The Scrum Master is accountable for the Scrum Team's effectiveness and serves the Scrum Team in several ways, including coaching the team members in self-management and cross-functionality."
12. At regular intervals, the team reflects on how to become more effective, then tunes	"The Sprint Retrospective is an opportunity for the Scrum Team to inspect itself and create a plan for improvements to be enacted during the next Sprint."
and adjusts its behavior accordingly.	"The purpose of the Sprint Retrospective is to plan ways to increase quality and effectiveness."

24.1.3   Scrum values and the Agile principles

Here is an example of how the Scrum values are related to the Agile principles of the Agile manifesto:

Scrum Value	Related Agile Principles (from Agile Manifesto)
Commitment	1. Our highest priority is to satisfy the customer through early and continuous delivery of valuable software. 5. Build projects around motivated individuals. Give them the environment and support they need, and trust them to get the job done.
Courage	9. Continuous attention to technical excellence and good design enhances agility.

	11. The best architectures, requirements, and designs emerge from self-organizing teams.
Focus	2. Welcome changing requirements, even late in development. Agile processes harness change for the customer's competitive advantage.
	3. Deliver working software frequently, from a couple of weeks to a couple of months, with a preference for the shorter timescale.
	8. Agile processes promote sustainable development. The sponsors, Developers, and users should be able to maintain a constant pace indefinitely.
	10. Simplicity--the art of maximizing the amount of work not done--is essential.
Openness	4. Business people and Developers must work together daily throughout the project.
	6. The most efficient and effective method of conveying information to and within a development team is face-to-face conversation.
	12. At regular intervals, the team reflects on how to become more effective, then tunes and adjusts its behavior accordingly.
Respect	4. Business people and Developers must work together daily throughout the project.
	5. Build projects around motivated individuals. Give them the environment and support they need, and trust them to get the job done.

24.2 Scrum Guide Cheat Sheet

This document is based on the Scrum Guide™ 2020, but it is not intended to be used to skip the reading of the Scrum Guide. Instead, please go to https://www.scrumguides.org/ and read the original scrum guide carefully.

Scrum: **Framework**, not methodology. From **Complex adaptive problems** -> people, teams, and organizations -> Deliver Adaptive Products of the highest value.

Empirical process control: Knowledge comes from experience - Scrum Pillars: **Transparency**, **Inspection**, **Adaptation**.

Lean Thinking: reduce waste and focus on the essentials.

5 Values: **Commitment**, **Courage**, **Focus**, **Openness**, and **Respect**.

Scrum Pillars + Scrum Values => Trust.

Scrum contains no tools, no methods, and no practices.

Accountabilities	Scrum Team (ST): PO+DT+SM	Product Owner (PO)	Developers (DT)	Scrum Master (SM)
Main Goal / Accountability	Deliver **valuable and usable increment** every Sprint.	**Maximize Value** of the Product obtained from DT's work.	**Build** the usable increment.	Promote **Scrum** as it is in the Scrum guide.
Size	Typically 10 or fewer.	1 per Product. Can work as Dev too.		1 per Scrum Team. Can work as Dev too.
Also accountable for	All product-related activities. Creating a valuable, useful Increment every Sprint.	Product Backlog Management	Create Sprint Backlog. Commit to Sprint Goal. Quality and adherence to DoD. Adapt their plan every day. Holding each other.	Scrum Team's **effectiveness.**
Owns	Increment.	PB.	SB.	Scrum adoption in ST and Org.
Multiple Teams working on a Product	Integrate increments often. Coordinate, minimize dependencies. In Nexus: 3-9 STs.	1 PO for all Scrum Teams.	Frequently integrate.	Up to 1 per ST or shared by many STs.
Responsibilities	**Improve** every Sprint. Optimize **flexibility,**	Manages the **PB**. Decides how to manage it.	**Estimate**. Meet in **Daily Scrum**.	Ensures **time-boxes**. Teaches to keep **events** within time boxes.

	creativity, and **productivity**. Receive **feedback**. Work iteratively and incrementally. Definition of "Done" (DoD) <ul><li>ST defines DoD.</li><li>DoD must follow organizational standards.</li><li>Multiple teams have one DoD.</li><li>Includes testing.</li></ul>	Assess the **Value** of PBIs. **Order** PBIs. **Clarify** PBIs. Make PB **visible**, **transparent**, and **clear**. **Progress** of product goals. Interacts with **Stakeholders**.	Decide **how** to build. Manage/Monitor **progress** of Sprint. Membership changes -> short term reduction in productivity. Decides on how to organize new teams and team members. Solve internal conflicts.	**Facilitates** Scrum Events as needed or requested. Teach outsiders how to **interact** with the Scrum Team. Brings Artifacts **Transparency** Serves **PO**: goals, PB management, clear PBIs, empirical, maximize value. Serves **ST**: Self-managing, cross-functionality, protect, empower, high-value products, remove impediments, adopt scrum. Serves **Organization**: Scrum adoption/implementation, avoid vocabulary change, ST productivity, work with other SMs.
Characteristics / Skills	Self-managing. Cross-functional. Mixed skills, No dependencies. Creative and productive. No sub-teams, no titles, No hierarchies.	Not a committee. Represents stakeholders. Stances: Visionary, Collaborator, Customer Representative, Decision Maker, Experimenter, and Influencer.	Accountability as a team. Self-organizing. Cross-functional, multi-skills. Work on all layers. No titles. No sub-teams.	Stances: Servant Leader, Facilitator, Coach, Manager, Mentor, Teacher, Impediment Remover, and Change Agent.
Role of the Organization or management	The Organization or management supports and respects the roles	Respects PO decisions. Supports PO with insights	Empowers the DT.	Support SM.

255

	and empowers them to decide who does what, when, and how.	into high value.		

EVENTS	Sprint	Sprint Planning	Daily Scrum	Sprint Review	Sprint Retrospective
Goal	Build one or many PI.	Plan why, what, and how to build in the Sprint.	Inspect and adapt the progress toward the Sprint Goal.	Inspect Increment and adapt PB.	Inspect ST and create a plan for improvements for the next Sprint.
Max Time-box	1 month.	8 hours.	15 min.	4 hours.	3 hours.
Participants	PO, DT, SM	PO, DT, SM, (invitees).	DT	PO, DT, SM, Stakeholders	PO, DT, SM
Optional attendees		Experts invited by ST (only for advice).	SM to facilitate, keep time-box, avoid other attendees to participate/disrupt		
Input	Last increment.	PB, PI, Capacity, Past Performance, DoD.	SB, Sprint Goal.	PB, PI, SB.	Current Sprint.
Required Outputs	Increment.	Sprint Goal, SB.	Revised SB.	Revised PB.	Improvement(s).

| Characteristics | Constant Length. **Length** cannot be changed once started. **No changes** that endanger Sprint Goal. **Quality goals** do not decrease. **Scope** may be clarified and re-negotiated. No special Sprints. Sprint cancellation: Only by **PO**. When **Sprint goal** becomes **obsolete**. Done items are typically accepted. Not done items re- | **Topic 1: Why** Set Sprint Goal. **Topic 2: What can be done.** ST adds PBIs to Sprint Backlog **Topic 3: How will be done.** DT Decompose PBIs for the first days of Sprint. PO clarifies PBIs. DT can explain to SM and PO how they will deliver. Sprint goal provides guidance to DT. | DT decides **structure**. Optional format: Yesterday, Today, Impediments. Eliminates the need for other meetings. Actions for the day to meet the Sprint goal. Work plan for 24hs. | ST presents results to SH. Review progress to PG. Receive feedback. Ideas, changes in market and potential uses. What to do next. | Review: people, relationships, process, tools. Detect What went well and opportunities. **Plan** for **Improvements.** Review **DoD**. |

		estimated and added to PB. ST regroups in a Panning. Length: Short enough for PO's risks and DT's work						

ARTIFACTS (Transparents)	Product Backlog (PB)	Sprint Backlog (SB)	Product Increment (PI)
Description	List of Product Backlog items (PBIs) known that are needed for the product.	Sprint Goal + Set of PBIs selected for the Sprint + Plan for delivering. Why + what + how.	PBIs completed in Sprint + value of previous increments.
Multiple Scrum Teams	One PB per Product.	One SB per DT.	At least one Integrated Increment by Sprint Review.
Commitment	Product Goal: One at a time. Progress Towards Product Goals: Remaining work to reach a goal can be summed from PB and monitored.	Sprint Goal: single objective. Progress Towards Sprint Goal: Remaining work of Sprint can be summed from SB and monitored.	Definition of Done (DoD): ST understands what done means. Defined by ST. DoD is a standard of the Organization -> ST must follow at a minimum. Many STs working on the same Product =>

			one DoD defined mutually by all STs.
Characteristics	Maintained by PO. Belongs to PO. Single source of requirements. Never complete. Dynamic. PBIs have description, Value, estimate, order. Optional: Tests to validate when they are done. Higher ordered PBIs are clearer. PB Refinement: Ongoing process DT+PO. As needed. SG2017 "suggests" < 10% capacity DT. Add detail, estimates, and order PBIs. Make PBIs ready for SB. Ready PBI: it can be done within 1 Sprint.	Maintained by DT. Belongs to DT. Forecast by DT of what may be in the increment. May include 1+ improvement from Retrospective. Details and new work emerge during the Sprint. Progress managed by DT.	Potentially releasable. Usable. PO decides whether to release it. Can be released before Sprint Review. Only DT can build it. Meets DoD. A step towards the Product Goal. One or more increments/releases per Sprint. A PBI meets DoD -> new Increment.

24.2.1 Scrum Values Summary

1. Openness: Honesty about the work of the Sprint. I.e., ask for help, offer help, raise mistakes/issues.
2. Commitment: People/teams commit to goals. I.e., PG, SG, DoD

3. Courage: Do the right thing, question the status quo. I.e., Say no to SH. Discover features of high value.
4. Focus: Focus on work and goals. I.e., Limit WIP.
5. Respect: To each other. i.e., Respect accountabilities, contribution, capabilities, accomplishments.

24.2.2 Additional concepts

1. Technical debt: Technical debt is incurred by quick and dirty solutions that will need some rework in the future. This might artificially increase velocity in the short term, but it will make changes and maintenance harder in the future.
2. Changes vs. performance: Changing the members of the Scrum Team is allowed as needed, but a short term reduction in performance or velocity might be considered. Adding or removing members will require coordination, onboarding, and productivity will drop.
3. No special Sprints: There is no such thing as a hardening Sprint, special Sprint, or Sprint 0. The rules of a Sprint apply to all Sprints from the very first one.
4. Scaling Teams vs. performance: Adding a new Scrum Team to work on the same product will cause a drop in productivity or velocity for the original team because they need to coordinate with the new Scrum Team and integrate the increment.
5. Scrum Team or Developers Organization: When changing the membership or adding a new Scrum Team to work on the same product, the Scrum Team decides how to re-organize the team members.
6. Integrated Increment: Multiple teams must produce one integrated increment at the end of the Sprint.
7. Scaling vs. Sprint lengths: Multiple Scrum Teams working on the same product are neither required to have the same Sprint lengths nor the same Sprint start or end dates. The only requirement is that they must integrate the increment by the Sprint Review.
8. Start the first Sprint: To get started in terms of what to Develop, Scrum requires no more than a Product Owner with enough ideas for a first Sprint, a Developer to implement those ideas, and a Scrum Master to help guide the process.

24.3 Scrum Guide 2020 vs. Scrum Guide 2017

Disclaimer: This comparison chart is based on the Scrum Guide 2020 and Scrum Guide 2017, but it is not intended to be used to skip the reading of the Scrum Guide. Please go to https://www.scrumguides.org/ and read the original Scrum Guides carefully.

The table below provided in the digital version of this book contains links to video lessons of the online course **Agile & Scrum in Depth: Guide, Simulation and Best Practices** for simplicity and to foster further learning. The course is not included in this book and must be purchased separately.

Main differences between Scrum Guide 2017 and Scrum Guide 2020:

Component / Concept	Scrum Guide 2017	Scrum Guide 2020	Explanation
Empiricism and Lean	Scrum is founded on **empiricism**.	Scrum is founded on **empiricism** and **lean thinking**.	Banish waste and create wealth.
Development Team -> Developers	Scrum Team consists of Development Team, Scrum Master, Product Owner.	Scrum Team consists of: **Developers**, Scrum Master, Product Owner.	Reduce the potential for dysfunctions between the Product Owner and the Development Team.
Roles -> Accountabilities	The term "Roles" was used.	Replaced by "Accountabilities."	See ST more as a cohesive unit. ST as a product team.
Self-Managing	The term "Self-Organizing" was used	Replaced by "Self-managing."	Scrum Team decides who does what, when, and how.
Recommended Team Size	Development Team size: 3-9.	Scrum Team: 10 or fewer.	See ST more as a cohesive unit. Reduce the potential for dysfunctions between accountabilities.
Team Skills	Scrum Team: Cross-functional, self-organizing. Development Team: Cross-functional, self-organizing, no titles, no sub-teams.	Scrum Team: Cross-functional, self-managing, no sub-teams, no hierarchies.	The fundamental unit of Scrum is the Scrum Team.
Scrum Team responsibilities	Incremental deliveries of "Done" product.	Cohesive unit. All product-related activities Creating a valuable, useful Increment every Sprint.	ST full accountable for results as a whole.
PO responsibilities	May delegate to the Development Team.	May delegate to others.	Flexibility.

SM accountable for	Establishing Scrum.	Establishing Scrum and Scrum Team's effectiveness.	Reinforce the goals of the SM.
SM serves to	PO, DT, Organization.	PO, ST, Organization.	See ST more as a cohesive unit. ST as a product team.
Events that are held at the same time and place	Daily Scrum.	All events.	Unified criteria.
Sprint Planning invitees	Invited by DT.	Invited by ST.	See ST more as a cohesive unit.
Sprint Planning Topics	2 Topics: What, How.	3 Topics: Why, What, How.	Discuss the value and make it transparent.
Meet after Daily Scrum	Unspecified.	Developers often meet throughout the day.	Clarification.
Sprint Review Stakeholders	Invited by PO.	It is not prescribed who invite them.	Scrum Team decides who does what, when, and how.
Sprint Review Demo and Steps	PO explains items that were Done Demonstration by DT. Prescribed steps about who does what.	ST presents Attendees collaborate on what to do next.	Scrum Team decides who does what, when, and how.
Improvements from Retro	SB contains at least one process improvement.	SB may contain process improvements.	A Suggestion that allows other methods for follow-up impediments.
Sprint Backlog	Set of Product Backlog items selected for the Sprint (what), as well as an actionable plan for delivering the Increment (how).	Sprint Goal (why), the set of Product Backlog items selected for the Sprint (what), as well as an actionable plan for delivering the Increment (how).	Discuss the value and make it transparent.
Refinement	Usually consumes no more than 10%	As needed.	As needed, as long as the capacity used

		of the capacity of DT.		does not endanger the Sprint Goal.
Product Goal (PG)	Not required.		Commitment of PB.	Discuss the value and unify ST as a Product Team.
Artifacts commitments	Monitoring progress toward goals. Monitoring Sprint Progress. DoD as artifact transparency.		Replaced by Commitments: PB->PG. SB->SG. PI->DoD.	Unify ST as a Product Team with clear goals.
1+ Increments per Sprint	Not clear.		One or multiple increments per Sprint.	Clarification. Kanban Guide for Scrum Teams: "It's a common misconception that teams can only deliver value once per Sprint."
Born of Increment	Not specified.		A PBI meets DoD.	
Release before the Sprint Review	Not clear.		Explicitly allowed.	Clarification. Kanban Guide for Scrum Teams: "It's a common misconception that teams can only deliver value once per Sprint."
Potentially releasable -> valuable, Usable	The term "Potentially releasable Increment" was used.		Replaced by "Valuable, usable Increment."	Focus on value. Implicit: Still not required to release the Increment, but it can be.
Definition of Done	Defined by Development Team.		Defined by **Scrum Team**.	See ST more as a cohesive unit.

References:

DT: Developers   PO: Product Owner   SB: Sprint Backlog

ST: Scrum Team   SM: Scrum Master   PB: Product Backlog

PG: Product Goal   PI: Increment

SG: Sprint Goal   DoD: Definition of Done

24.4 Scrum concepts challenges

The following challenges are exercises to validate your knowledge of Scrum.

24.4.1 Scrum Components challenge

This is a challenge to validate your knowledge of the Scrum components. Difficulty: Low.

24.4.1.1 Problem statement

- Match or assign the text box labels with each component of the drawing. The Product Goal is provided as an example.
- Compare your solution with the solution below.

Developers   Product Backlog Refinement

Definition of Done   Increment   Sprint Planning

Sprint Backlog   Sprint   Daily Scrum   Product Owner

PBIs   Product Backlog   Sprint Goal   Improvements

Sprint PBIs + Work Plan   Sprint Review   Sprint Retrospective

Scrum Master

The Scrum Framework

Product Goal

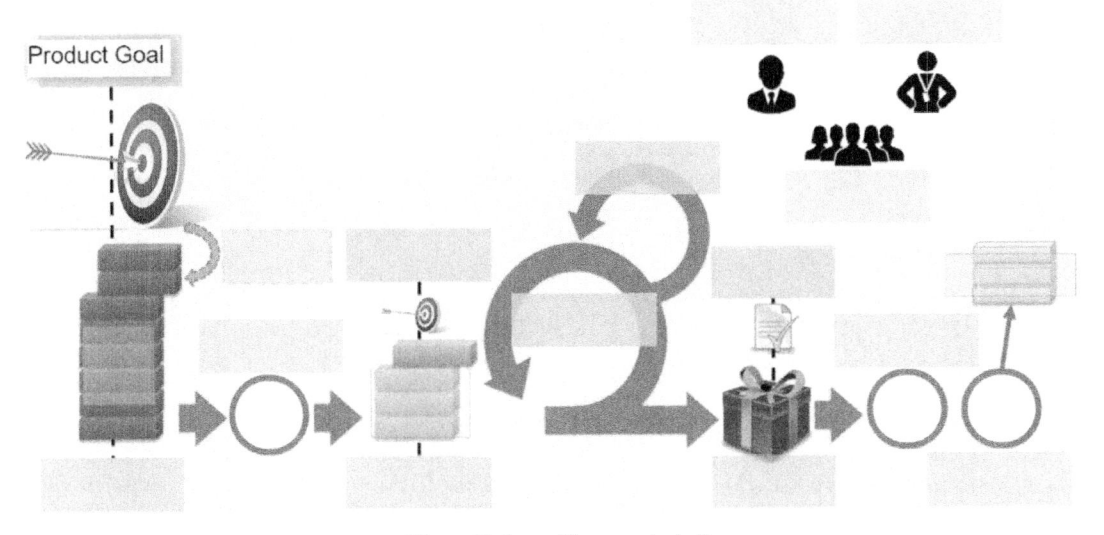

Figure 48 Scrum Framework challenge

24.4.1.2 Solution

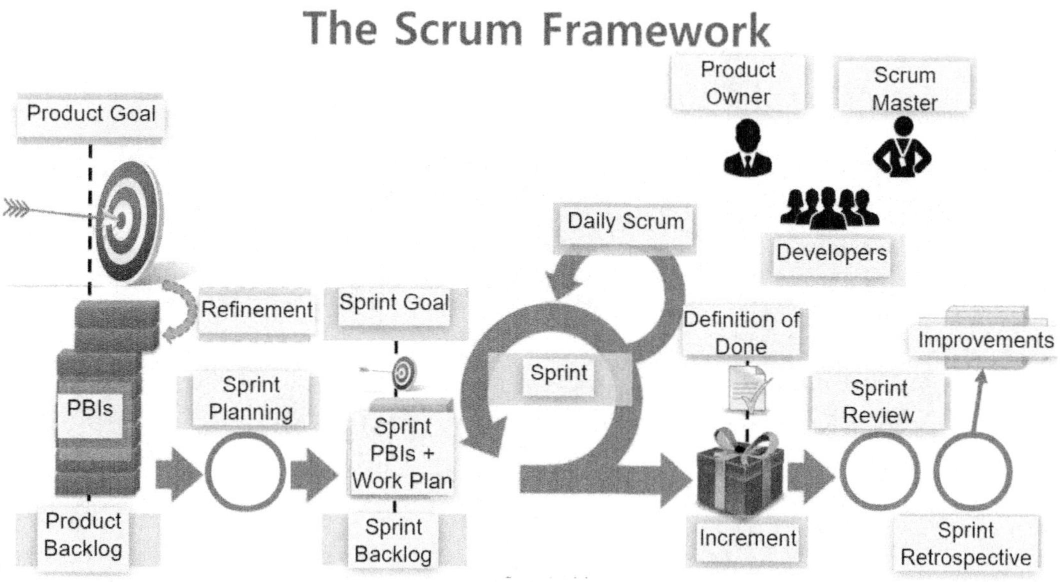

Figure 49 Scrum Framework Challenge - Solution

24.4.2 Scrum Accountabilities challenge

This is a challenge to validate your knowledge about Scrum Accountabilities. Difficulty: Medium.

24.4.2.1 Problem statement

- Match the responsibilities in the textboxes with each accountability or role. A few items are provided as an example.
- Compare your solution with the solution below.

Receive value	Affected by outcome	Interested in Product Goal	1 for one or more STs
Serves Devs	Establishes Scrum	ST Effectiveness	Collaborate in Sprint Review
Maximizes Value	Serves Org	Can delegate to others	Serves ST
Manages PB	Clarify PBIs	1 per Product	Create Sprint Work Plan	10 or fewer
Provides Support to ST	Create usable Increment	Define DoD	Self-Managing	
			Cross-functional	
Estimate	Adhere to DoD	Accountable for Increment	May advise in Sprint Planning
Manage Sprint progress	Develop Product Goal	Invited to Sprint Review and collaborate	
Participate in Sprint Planning			

Scrum Accountabilities

| Can cancel the Sprint | Orders PB |

Stakeholders

Product Owner   Scrum Master

Organization and Management

Developers   **Scrum Team**

Invitees

| Update Sprint Backlog | Attend Daily Scrum |

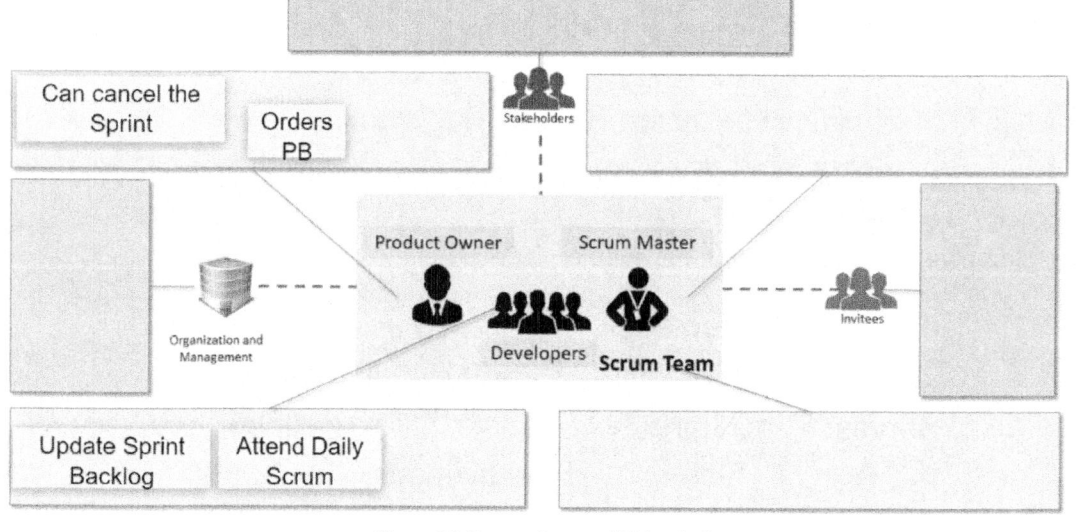

Figure 50 Scrum Accountabilities challenge

24.4.2.2 Solution

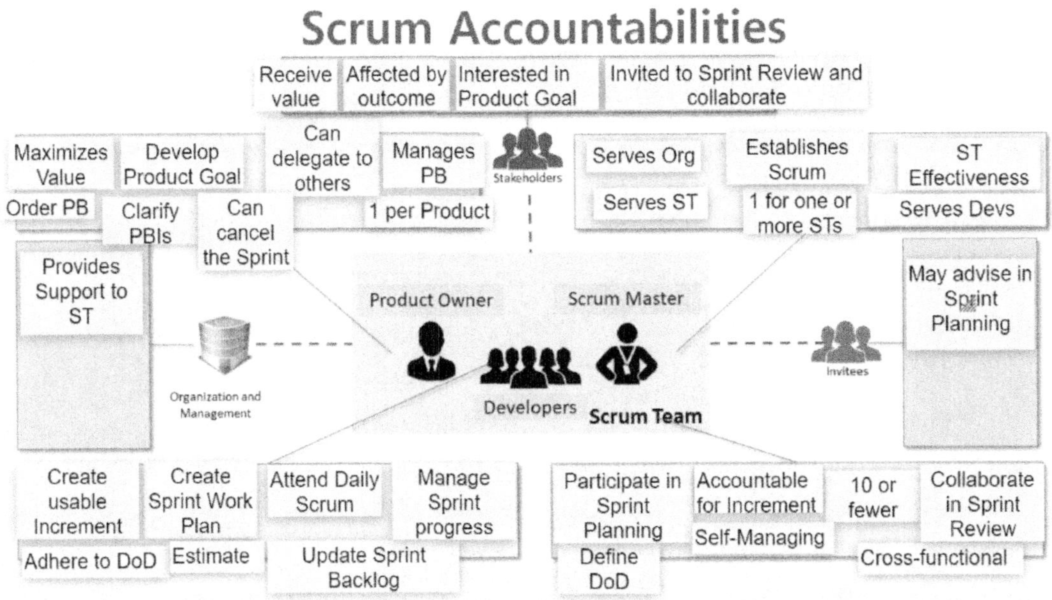

Figure 51 Scrum Accountabilities Challenge - Solution

24.4.3 Scrum Rules challenge

This is a challenge to validate your knowledge of the rules of Scrum. Difficulty: high.

24.4.3.1 Problem statement

- Match the responsibilities with each accountability or role. A few solutions are provided as an example.
- Compare your solution with the solution below.

- One at a time
- May include improvements
- Gets refined
- Future state of the product
- Scope can be negotiated
- Meeting format by Devs
- PO and SM don't need to attend
- Objective of the Sprint
- Define Product next steps
- Composed of why, what, how
- Quality goals do not decrease
- Topics: why, what, how
- Meets the DoD
- Guidance on why creating an Increment
- ST and Stakeholders collaborate
- Plan by and for the Developers
- Updated by Developers
- Devs participate
- 8 hours or less
- Multiple STs must agree
- Sum of all previous of it
- Defined by ST
- PB is refined as needed
- ST attend
- ST is accountable for it
- 4 hours or less
- Its items can be Done in 1 Sprint
- Usable
- PB is revised
- 1 per Product
- 1 month or less
- Allows invitees
- 3 hours or less
- Changes can't endanger SG
- A step toward PG
- At least 1 created per Sprint

Scrum Rules

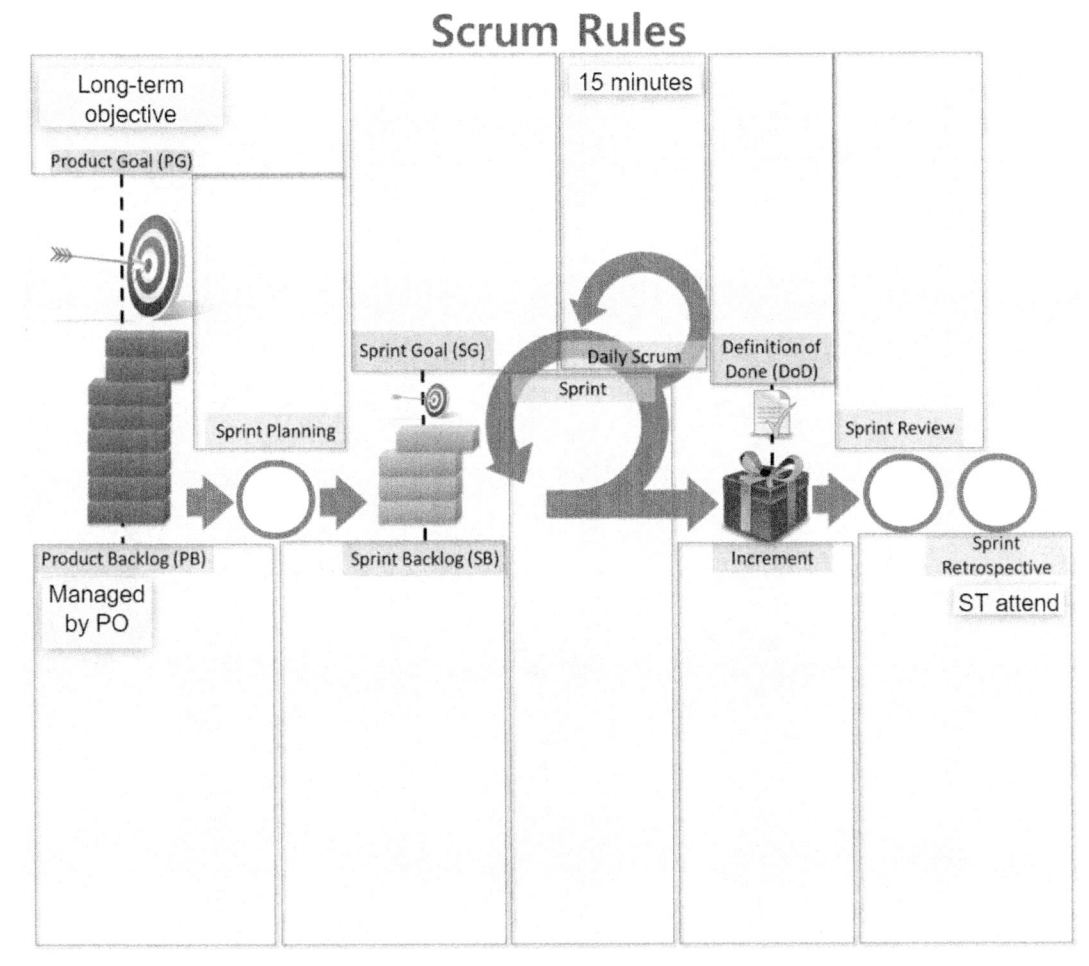

Long-term objective		15 minutes		
Product Goal (PG)	Sprint Planning	Sprint Goal (SG) / Daily Scrum / Sprint	Definition of Done (DoD)	Sprint Review
Product Backlog (PB)		Sprint Backlog (SB)	Increment	Sprint Retrospective
Managed by PO				ST attend

Figure 52 Scrum Rules challenge

24.4.3.2 Solution

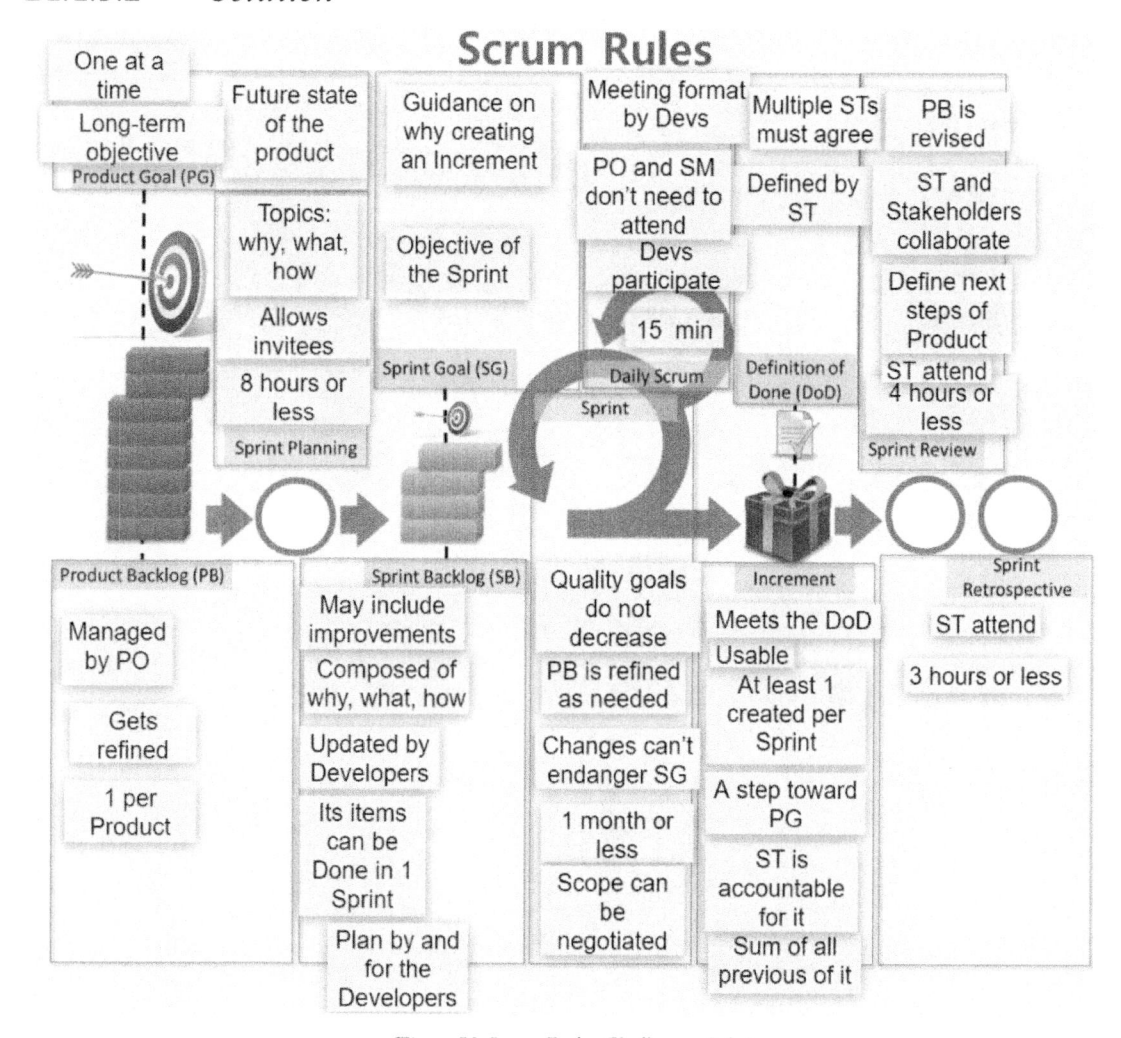

Figure 53 Scrum Rules Challenge - Solution

Part 25: Scrum in Practice

Scrum does not encourage or suggest any technique, method, or concrete approach to implement the framework. All the content in the section are suggestions and ideas on how different Scrum Teams usually implement Scrum, but Scrum does not require them, and they are not part of Scrum.

25.1 Product Vision

A product vision is a high-level description of the future state or end goal that a product or service aims to achieve. It outlines the desired outcome of the product or service. It serves as a guiding principle for the development team to ensure that the product stays focused on its core purpose and value proposition.

A well-defined product vision can motivate team members by providing them with a sense of purpose and a shared goal to work toward. When team members understand the vision, they are more likely to feel connected to the product and invested in its success. A strong product vision can also help align team members' efforts and priorities, ensuring everyone is working toward the same goal.

When defining a product vision with a multidisciplinary group, including representatives from different departments or areas of expertise is important. This can include designers, developers, product managers, marketing specialists, and other stakeholders. You can create a more comprehensive and well-rounded product vision by bringing together a diverse group of perspectives.

To define a product vision with a multidisciplinary group, it can be helpful to start by brainstorming and gathering input from all participants. This can involve asking questions such as:

- What problem is this product solving?
- Who is the target audience?
- What are the key features and benefits of the product?
- What are the core values or principles that guide the product development process?

Once you have collected input from all participants, you can work together to distill these ideas into a clear and concise product vision statement. This statement should be simple and inspiring and communicate the core purpose and value of the product. With a well-defined product vision, your multidisciplinary team can work together more effectively and achieve greater success.

25.1.1 *Techniques to Achieve Product Vision*

Here are some techniques that can help companies achieve their product vision:

1. Define a clear product vision: The first step in achieving a product vision is to define a clear and compelling vision for the product. This vision should clearly articulate the product's value to customers and how it will differentiate from competitors.
2. Conduct customer research: To ensure that the product vision aligns with customer needs and preferences, it is important to conduct extensive customer research. This research can include surveys, focus groups, and user testing to gather feedback on product features, user experience, and overall satisfaction.
3. Use agile methodologies: Agile methodologies and frameworks, such as Scrum or Kanban, can help companies achieve their product vision by providing a structured approach to product development. These methodologies emphasize continuous improvement, frequent feedback, and iterative development, which can help companies rapidly iterate and refine their product vision.

4. Create a product roadmap: A product roadmap can help companies align their product vision with business goals and development priorities. The roadmap should outline key milestones, timelines, and deliverables and be updated regularly to reflect market conditions and customer needs changes.
5. Foster a culture of innovation: To achieve a product vision, companies need to foster a culture of innovation and creativity. This can include encouraging experimentation, empowering employees to take risks, and providing professional development and growth opportunities.
6. Measure progress: To ensure progress toward the product vision, it is important to establish key performance indicators (KPIs) and regularly track progress. These KPIs can include metrics such as customer satisfaction, revenue growth, and market share.

By using these techniques, companies can align their product vision with customer needs and business goals and achieve success in the marketplace.

25.1.2 Product Vision Canvas

The Product Vision Canvas is a tool product teams use to develop and communicate a shared vision of their product. It helps to align team members around a common goal and ensure everyone works toward the same objectives. Here are the key elements that can be included in a Product Vision Canvas:

1. Target Customer: This element defines the ideal customer for the product, including their demographics, behavior, and pain points.
2. Needs: This element outlines the key needs and problems the product will address for the target customer.
3. Value Proposition: This element defines the product's unique value to the target customer, including how it differentiates from competitors.
4. Benefits: This element outlines the specific benefits the target customer will receive from using the product, such as time savings, cost savings, or improved performance.
5. Features: This element defines the specific features and functionality that the product will offer to deliver on the value proposition and benefits.
6. Business Goals: This element outlines the specific business goals that the product is intended to achieve, such as revenue targets, market share, or customer retention.
7. Metrics: This element defines the specific metrics that will be used to measure the success of the product, such as user engagement, conversion rates, or customer satisfaction.

By using the Product Vision Canvas, product teams can develop a clear and shared understanding of their product's goals and objectives. This can help to align team members, prioritize development efforts, and ultimately create a product that delivers value to the target customer while achieving business goals.

A simplified version of a Product vision canvas may look like this:

Product Vision Template			
VISION What is the purpose of this product? Which positive changes will it bring?			
TARGET GROUP What are the market and specific segments of the product? Who are the customers of this product?	**NEEDS / PROBLEMS** Which problems are they having? Are there people that have those problems? Do they need a solution? Which benefits will they get? Would they pay for a solution?	**PRODUCT** The product should solve the identified problems. What is this product? What makes it unique? Is it viable to build it? What makes it different from its competitors?	**BUSINESS GOALS** What is the benefit of the company for building this product? What are the business goals?

25.1.3 Template for Product Vision

Here is a template for a product vision:

[Product Name] will [describe the specific and measurable outcome the product will deliver] for [describe the target customer or user] by [describe the key features and benefits of the product], providing [describe the value or impact the product will have on the customer or user]. Unlike our competitors, [describe the key differentiator of the product].

Example of a product vision using this template:

XYZ Fitness Tracker will revolutionize how people monitor their health and fitness by providing an easy-to-use device that tracks activity levels, heart rate, and sleep quality. Our product will be tailored to meet the needs of busy professionals and fitness enthusiasts, offering personalized coaching and customized workout plans based on real-time data. We will give our customers the tools they need to achieve their fitness goals and live healthier, more active lives. Unlike our competitors, our product will use advanced AI technology to analyze data and provide personalized recommendations for optimizing fitness performance.

25.2 Product Backlog Management

25.2.1 *Techniques to maximize the value*

No technique or approach is required from the Product Owner. However, there are several techniques that Product Owners can choose to maximize the value of the product resulting from the work of the Scrum Team. Some examples of these techniques include:

- User Story Mapping: This technique involves creating a visual map of the user stories in the Product Backlog, which helps the Product Owner to understand how the product features fit together and prioritize them based on their importance to the customer.
- Value-based Prioritization: This technique involves prioritizing the items in the Product Backlog based on their potential value to the customer. The Product Owner considers factors such as customer needs, market trends, and business goals to determine which items will provide the greatest value to the customer.
- Kano Model Analysis: This technique involves analyzing the features in the Product Backlog to determine which ones are basic requirements, performance requirements, or delighters. The Product Owner can then prioritize the delighters, the features that exceed customer expectations and provide the greatest value.
- Cost of Delay: This technique involves estimating the cost of delaying the delivery of a Product Backlog item, which helps the Product Owner prioritize items based on their potential impact on the product's overall value.
- MoSCoW Prioritization: This technique categorizes the Product Backlog items into Must-have, Should-have, Could-have, and Won't-have categories. The Product Owner can then prioritize the Must-have items first, followed by the Should-have and Could-have items, and leave the Won't-have items for later or remove them from the backlog altogether.

These techniques can help Product Owners maximize the product's value by prioritizing the most important features and ensuring that they are delivering the greatest possible value to the customer. In addition, by using these techniques, Product Owners can collaborate effectively with the Scrum Team and other stakeholders to ensure that the product meets the customer's needs and achieves its overall goals.

25.2.2 *Techniques for gathering requirements*

As the custodian of the Product Backlog, the Product Owner is responsible for documenting requirements for the product. There is no mandatory or forbidden technique in Scrum. However, here are some techniques that the Product Owner can use to document requirements:

1. User Stories: User stories are a popular technique used by Product Owners to document requirements. They are brief descriptions of a feature or functionality

written from the user's perspective. User stories typically follow the format "As a [user], I want [feature/functionality], so that [benefit]." They are concise, easy to understand, and help to keep the focus on the customer.
2. Acceptance Criteria: Acceptance criteria are a set of conditions that must be met for a user story to be considered complete. They define the specific requirements and expectations for a feature or functionality. Acceptance criteria should be measurable and testable and help ensure that the product meets the customer's needs.
3. Use Cases: Use cases are a technique used to document the various ways the customer can use the product. They provide a detailed description of the interactions between the user and the product and can help to ensure that all possible scenarios are accounted for. However, Use Cases are not very popular in the Agile community.
4. Prototypes: Prototyping is a technique used to represent a product or a particular feature visually. Prototypes can be used to document requirements and to get feedback from stakeholders and users. In addition, they can help to identify potential issues early on and to refine the requirements as needed.
5. Requirements Workshops: Requirements workshops are a collaborative technique to gather requirements from stakeholders and team members. The Scrum Master or Product Owner can facilitate them and help ensure that all stakeholders are aligned on the requirements for the product.

There is no preferred technique for documenting requirements as different techniques have strengths and weaknesses, and what works best depends on the specific project and team. Therefore, the Product Owner should choose the technique(s) that work best for their team and their project.

That being said, user stories are a popular and effective technique for gathering requirements in Scrum. User stories are concise, customer-focused, and easy to understand, which makes them a good fit for agile development. They also help to keep the focus on the customer and their needs, which is a core principle of Scrum.

Acceptance criteria are another commonly used technique for agreeing on requirements. They provide a clear and measurable Definition of Done for each user story, which helps to ensure that the team is aligned on the requirements and that they can be tested and verified.

Gathering requirements aims to ensure that the product meets the customer's needs and that the organization is aligned with the Product Goal. The Product Owner should choose the technique(s) that best help them achieve this goal.

25.3 Retrospectives

25.3.1 5-Step Retrospective

The 5-step retrospective is a simple and effective technique for conducting retrospectives. Here are the five steps:

1. Set the stage: This step involves setting the tone and expectations for the retrospective. It can include activities such as a brief overview of the agenda and ground rules for participation.
2. Gather data: This step involves collecting information about the Sprint. It can include asking team members to share their observations, reviewing metrics or data, or creating a timeline of key events.
3. Generate insights: This step involves identifying patterns or themes in the data that has been collected. It can include activities such as clustering similar ideas or identifying common issues or challenges.
4. Decide what to do: This step involves prioritizing the insights and deciding what actions to take. It can include voting on ideas, ranking issues by importance or urgency, or creating action plans.
5. Close the retrospective: This step involves summarizing the key insights and actions and ensuring everyone is clear on what needs to be done. It can include activities such as assigning tasks, setting goals for the next Sprint, or reviewing the retrospective process itself.

The 5-step retrospective is a flexible and adaptable technique that can be customized to meet the needs of different teams and contexts. By following these steps, teams can reflect on their work, identify opportunities for improvement, and take action to improve their processes and practices continuously.

25.3.2 Ideas for Retrospectives

Retrospectives are an important part of the Scrum framework, as they allow the Scrum Team to reflect on their work and identify opportunities for improvement. Here are some popular techniques that can be used during retrospectives:

- Start, Stop, Continue: This technique involves asking team members to identify things that the team should start doing, stop doing, and continue doing. This can help to identify areas where the team is doing well and areas where there is room for improvement.
- Mad, Sad, Glad: This technique involves asking team members to identify things that made them mad, things that made them sad, and things that made them glad during the Sprint. This can help to identify areas of frustration and areas where the team is doing well.
- Liked, Learned, Lacked, Longed For (4Ls): This technique involves asking team members to identify things that they liked about the Sprint, things that they

learned, things that they lacked, and things that they longed for. This can help to identify areas where the team needs more support or resources.
- Starfish: This technique involves drawing a starfish shape and labeling the five points as Keep, Less of, More of, Stop, and Start. This can help identify specific actions the team should take to improve their work.
- Timeline: This technique involves creating a timeline of the Sprint and identifying key events and milestones. This can help the team to identify areas where they did well and areas where they struggled.
- Appreciative Inquiry: This technique involves asking team members to identify the Sprint's positive aspects and explore how those aspects can be amplified or extended. This can help to build on the team's strengths and identify growth opportunities.

Here are some websites that offer material, templates, and activities for retrospectives:

- Retromat (https://retromat.org): Retromat is a popular website that offers a variety of activities, games, and exercises for retrospectives. It allows teams to customize their retrospectives based on their needs and preferences.
- Fun Retrospectives (https://www.funretrospectives.com): Fun Retrospectives offers activities, games, and templates for conducting retrospectives. It includes various activities that can be used for virtual and in-person meetings.
- Liberating Structures (https://liberatingstructures.com): Liberating Structures is a collection of simple yet powerful activities and techniques for fostering collaboration and creativity. It offers a variety of activities that can be used for retrospectives.
- Retrospective Wiki (http://retrospectivewiki.org): Retrospective Wiki offers a range of activities, techniques, and templates for conducting retrospectives. It includes various activities that can be used for different team sizes and contexts.

In summary, many different techniques can be used during retrospectives, and the key is choosing a technique appropriate for the team and the context. Using these techniques, the Scrum Team can reflect on their work, identify opportunities for improvement, and continuously improve their processes and practices.

25.4 Best wishes

Thank you for taking the time to read this book on Scrum. I hope that the concepts and principles discussed have been helpful in your journey toward applying Scrum and becoming a more effective Scrum practitioner.

Remember that Scrum is a framework that requires continuous learning and improvement, and we encourage you to apply what you have learned to your projects and teams.

If you have any questions or would like to share your feedback and stories using Scrum, please do not hesitate to contact me. I am always happy to hear from readers and provide support where possible.

Finally, if you found this book useful, we would greatly appreciate it if you could take a few moments to leave a review on Amazon. Your feedback will help others discover this book and benefit from its insights.

Best wishes on your Scrum journey!

Part 26: Bibliography and references

The following sources were used as references to support the content of this book. I highly recommend reading them.

26.1 Books

26.1.1 Scrum books

- Succeeding with Agile: Software Development Using Scrum, Addison-Wesley Professional, 2009, Mike Cohn.
- Essential Scrum: A Practical Guide to the Most Popular Agile Process, Kenneth Rubin, Addison-Wesley Professional, 2012, Kenneth Rubin.
- Scrum: The Art of Doing Twice the Work in Half the Time, Currency, 2014, Jeff Sutherland and J.J. Sutherland.

26.1.2 Lean

- Lean Software Development: An Agile Toolkit, Addison Wesley, 2003, Mary Poppendieck and Tom Poppendieck.

26.1.3 Practices and Techniques books

- Agile Estimating and Planning, Pearson, Mike Cohn, 2005.
- The Lean Startup: How Today's Entrepreneurs Use Continuous Innovation to Create Radically Successful Businesses, Currency, Eric Ries, 2011.
- User Stories Applied: For Agile Software Development, Addison-Wesley Professional, Mike Cohn, 2004.
- Agile Retrospectives: Making Good Teams Great, Pragmatic Bookshelf, Esther Derby and Diana Larsen, 2006.
- User Story Mapping: Discover the Whole Story, Build the Right Product, O'Reilly Media, Jeff Patton, 2014.

- Software Estimation: Demystifying the Black Art (Developer Best Practices), Microsoft Press, Steve McConnell, 2006.

26.1.4 Teams and coaching books

- Coaching Agile Teams: A Companion for Scrum Masters, Agile Coaches, and Project Managers in Transition, Addison-Wesley Professional, Lyssa Adkins, 2010.
- The Five Dysfunctions of a Team Patrick Lencioni, Jossey-Bass, 2002.
- EMPOWERED: Ordinary People, Extraordinary Products (Silicon Valley Product Group), Wiley, Marty Cagan, 2020.

26.1.5 Product books

- Lean UX: Creating Great Products with Agile Teams, O'Reilly UK Ltd, by Jeff Gothelf and Josh Seiden, 2021.
- The Lean Product Playbook: How to Innovate with Minimum Viable Products and Rapid Customer Feedback, Wiley, Dan Olsen, 2015.
- INSPIRED: How to Create Tech Products Customers Love (Silicon Valley Product Group), Wiley, Marty Cagan, 2018.
- Hooked: How to Build Habit-Forming Products, Portfolio Penguin, Nir Eyal, 2014.
- Continuous Discovery Habits: Discover Products that Create Customer Value and Business Value, Product Talk LLC, Teresa Torres, 2021.
- Sprint: How to Solve Big Problems and Test New Ideas in Just Five Days, Simon & Schuster, Jake Knapp, John Zeratsky, and Braden Kowitz, 2016.
- Testing Business Ideas: A Field Guide for Rapid Experimentation (Strategyzer), Wiley, David J. Bland, Alexander Osterwalder, 2019.
- Value Proposition Design: How to Create Products and Services Customers Want (Strategyzer), Wiley, Alexander Osterwalder, Yves Pigneur, Gregory Bernarda, Alan Smith, Trish Papadakos, 2014.

26.2 Guides

- The Scrum Guide, Ken Schwaber and Jeff Sutherland, 2020 https://scrumguides.org/
- The Scrum Guide, Ken Schwaber and Jeff Sutherland, 2017 https://scrumguides.org/
- The Nexus Guide, Ken Schwaber and Scrum dot org, 2021. https://www.scrum.org/resources/online-nexus-guide
- Evidence-Based Management (TM), Scrum .org (TM), the Professional Scrum Trainer community, Ken Schwaber, and Christina Schwaber, 2020 https://www.scrum.org/resources/evidence-based-management-guide
- The Kanban Guide for Scrum Teams (TM), Scrum .org, Daniel Vacanti, and Yuval Yeret, 2021. https://www.scrum.org/resources/kanban-guide-scrum-teams

- Kanban Guide, Orderly Disruption Limited, Daniel S. Vacanti, Inc, 2020. https://kanbanguides.org/html-kanban-guide/

26.3 Articles, papers, blogs, and websites

- Agile Manifesto https://agilemanifesto.org/
- SCRUM Development Process, 1995, Ken Schwaber https://scrumorg-website-prod.s3.amazonaws.com/drupal/2016-09/Scrum%20OOPSLA%201995.pdf
- The New Product Development Game, Harvard Business Review, 1986, Takeuchi, Hirotaka and Nonaka, Ikujiro. https://hbr.org/1986/01/the-new-new-product-development-game
- Scrum: A Brief History of a Long-Lived Hype, 2020, Gunther Verheyen https://www.scrum.org/resources/blog/scrum-brief-history-long-lived-hype
- Scrum Glossary, Scrum.org. https://www.scrum.org/resources/scrum-glossary
- Scrum Values Poster https://www.scrum.org/resources/scrum-values-poster
- What is Scrum https://www.scrum.org/resources/what-is-scrum
- The 8 Stances of a Scrum Master, Barry Overeem, https://www.scrum.org/resources/8-stances-scrum-master
- Stances of a Product Owner, Robbin Schuurman, https://www.scrum.org/resources/blog/stances-product-owner
- ScrumBut https://www.scrum.org/resources/what-scrumbut
- Scrum.org blog https://www.scrum.org/resources/blog
- Scrum.org resources https://www.scrum.org/resources
- About Scrum, Scrum Alliance. https://www.scrumalliance.org/about-scrum
- 2020 Scrum Guide Changes Updates Explained https://www.scruminc.com/2020-scrum-guide-changes-updates-explained/
- Tuckman's stages of group development https://www.wcupa.edu/coral/tuckmanStagesGroupDelvelopment.aspx
- Forming, Storming, Norming, and Performing https://www.mindtools.com/pages/article/newLDR_86.htm
- The Five Stages of Team Development https://courses.lumenlearning.com/suny-principlesmanagement/chapter/reading-the-five-stages-of-team-development/
- Tuckman's stages of group development https://en.wikipedia.org/wiki/Tuckman%27s_stages_of_group_development
- Product vs. Project Teams https://svpg.com/product-vs-project-teams/
- Are feature teams or component teams right for your product? https://www.romanpichler.com/blog/feature-teams-vs-component-teams/
- Feature Teams vs. Component Teams https://www.knowledgehut.com/tutorials/scrum-tutorial/feature-teams-vs-component-teams

- Keys To Successful Transformation https://svpg.com/keys-to-successful-transformation/
- Technical Debt https://www.productplan.com/glossary/technical-debt/
- Technical Debt https://en.wikipedia.org/wiki/Technical_debt

26.4 Index of Figures

Figure 1 The Scrum Framework..15
Figure 2 Defined process control...27
Figure 3 Empirical process control...27
Figure 4 Linear approach..30
Figure 5 Iterative Approach..31
Figure 6 Modular vs. Incremental approach..33
Figure 7 Scrum pillars...38
Figure 8 Transparency enables inspection; inspection enables adaptation...................43
Figure 9 Scrum values...44
Figure 10 The five dysfunctions of a team (Patrick M. Lencioni)..................................50
Figure 11 When the Scrum Team embodies the Scrum values, the pillars come to life and build trust...51
Figure 12 Scrum accountabilities...55
Figure 13 Cross-functional teams have the skills to work on all architectural layers and deliver features every Sprint..57
Figure 14 Communication between a team with 4 members..60
Figure 15 Communication between a team with 8 members..61
Figure 16 Feature teams vs. Component Teams..71
Figure 17 Creating value through Sprints..84
Figure 18 The Scrum Master serves the Scrum Team, Product Owner, and the organization...99
Figure 19 Coaching a team...100
Figure 20 Scrum events...118
Figure 21 Parkinson's law and timebox..120
Figure 22 Example of a schedule of a two-week Sprint...124
Figure 23 The Sprint...124
Figure 24 Adding value to each Sprint towards goals..134
Figure 25 Canceling a Sprint..137
Figure 26 Sprint Planning..142
Figure 27 Daily Scrum..150
Figure 28 Sprint Review...160
Figure 29 Adding value to each Sprint towards goals..161
Figure 30 Sprint Retrospective...167
Figure 31 Scrum artifacts..175
Figure 32 Scrum artifacts and commitments...178

Figure 33 Example of how a Product Backlog can be ordered. 179
Figure 34 Product Backlog Refinement. 186
Figure 35 One Product Goal at a Time. 191
Figure 36 Pareto principle on the Product Backlog value. 198
Figure 37 Increment Releases through Sprints. 212
Figure 38 Multiple Scrum Teams. 219
Figure 39 Example of a scaling approach. 224
Figure 40 Multiple Scrum Teams. 226
Figure 41 Teams with different Sprint lengths in a scaling approach. 228
Figure 42 Example of a Velocity chart. 236
Figure 43 Example of Sprint Burn-Down chart 238
Figure 44 Example of Release Burn-Down chart for a Product Goal. 239
Figure 45 Cone of uncertainty. Based on: Software Estimation – Steve McConnel.... 242
Figure 46 Implementing and paying a solution with Technical Debt 243
Figure 47 Phases of group development 246
Figure 48 Scrum Framework challenge 265
Figure 49 Scrum Framework Challenge - Solution 266
Figure 50 Scrum Accountabilities challenge 268
Figure 51 Scrum Accountabilities Challenge - Solution 269
Figure 52 Scrum Rules challenge 271
Figure 53 Scrum Rules Challenge - Solution 272

Printed in Great Britain
by Amazon